Krishnamurti to Himself: His Last Journal

克里希那穆提的独白：最后的日记

[印度] 克里希那穆提 ——— 著　Sue ——— 译

九州出版社 JIUZHOUPRESS｜全国百佳图书出版单位

图书在版编目（CIP）数据

克里希那穆提的独白：最后的日记／（印）克里希
那穆提著；Sue译. -- 北京：九州出版社，2023.9
ISBN 978-7-5225-2190-9

Ⅰ.①克… Ⅱ.①克… ②S… Ⅲ.①克里希那穆提（
Jiddu Krishnamurti 1895-1986）－哲学思想 Ⅳ.
①B351.5

中国国家版本馆CIP数据核字（2023）第179493号

版权合同登记号：图字01-2022-6522
Copyright © 1995 Krishnamurti Foundation Trust, Ltd. and Krishnamurti Foundation of America
Krishnamurti Foundation Trust Ltd.,
Brockwood Park, Bramdean, Hampshire, SO24 0LQ, England.
E-mail: info@kfoundation.org
Website: www.kfoundation.org And Krishnamurti Foundation of America
P.O. Box 1560, Ojai, California 93024 USA
E-mail: kfa@kfa.org. Website: www.kfa.org
想要了解克里希那穆提的更多信息，请访问：www.jkrishnamurti.org。

克里希那穆提的独白：最后的日记

作　　者	[印]克里希那穆提 著 Sue 译
责任编辑	李文君
出版发行	九州出版社
地　　址	北京市西城区阜外大街甲35号（100037）
发行电话	（010）68992190/3/5/6
网　　址	www.jiuzhoupress.com
印　　刷	鑫艺佳利（天津）印刷有限公司
开　　本	880毫米×1230毫米　32开
印　　张	9.125
字　　数	250千字
版　　次	2025年3月第1版
印　　次	2025年3月第1次印刷
书　　号	ISBN 978-7-5225-2190-9
定　　价	58.00元

出版前言

克里希那穆提 1895 年生于印度，十三岁时被"通神学会"带到英国训导培养。"通神学会"由西方人士发起，以印度教和佛教经典为基础，逐步发展为一个宣扬神灵救世的世界性组织，它相信"世界导师"将再度降临，并认为克里希那穆提就是这个"世界导师"。而克里希那穆提在自己三十岁时，内心得以觉悟，否定了"通神学会"的种种谬误。1929 年，为了排除"救世主"的形象，他毅然解散专门为他设立的组织——世界明星社，宣布任何一种约束心灵解放的形式化的宗教、哲学和主张都无法带领人进入真理的国度。

克里希那穆提一生在世界各地传播他的智慧，他的思想魅力吸引了世界各地的人们，但是他坚持宣称自己不是宗教权威，拒绝别人给他加上"上师"的称号。他教导人们进行自我觉察，了解自我的局限以及宗教、民族主义狭隘性的制约。他指出打破意识束缚，进入"开放"极为重要，因为"大脑里广大的空间有着无可想象的能量"，而这个广大的空间，正是人的生命创造力的源泉所在。他提出："我只教一件事，那就是观察你自己，深入探索你自己，然后加以超越。你不是去听从我的教诲，你只是在了解自己罢了。"他的思想，为世人指明了东西方一切伟大智慧的精髓——认识自我。

本书是克里希那穆提生前最后的口述日记，和克氏其他的谈话相比，这本书的语言充满诗意，他用优美的自然景色描写将读者带入他的心灵世界。为了更好地传达克氏语言的美感，本书以双语对照的形式呈现。

克里希那穆提一生到处演讲，直到 1986 年过世，享年九十岁。他的言论、日记等被集结成六十余册著作。克里希那穆提系列作品得到了台湾著名作家胡因梦女士的倾情推荐，在此谨表谢忱。

九州出版社

序　言

这本书是独一无二的，因为这是唯一一部记载了克里希那穆提孑然独处时的口述录音内容的出版物。

《克里希那穆提日记》在 1982 年成功出版之后，他热切地希望继续把日记写下去。然而，由于当时他双手的颤抖已然相当剧烈（时年他已八十七岁高龄），于是有人建议，与其劳累地书写，不如改由他自己来口述。克里希那穆提觉得这个想法很不错，但是他无法马上就着手开始，因为当时他正要飞往印度，到了印度他就无暇顾及了。1983 年 2 月 1 日，一回到加利福尼亚，他就立刻在一台新的索尼录音机上录制了本书的第一篇。

除其中一篇外，所有的口述录音都是在他自己的家——松舍中完成的，松舍位于洛杉矶北方约八十英里的欧亥山谷之中。早餐后的上午他会坐在床上，在丝毫不受打扰的情况下进行口述。

克里希那穆提起初是在 1922 年和他弟弟一起住在松舍的，当时松舍是由一个朋友借给他暂住的。而就在那里，1922 年的 8 月，他经历了一次转化生命的精神体验。基金会在此后不久便成立起来，并且募集资金买下了这间松舍以及周围的六英亩土地。1978 年，围绕松舍建起了一栋漂亮的新房子，克里希那穆提保留了自己最初的卧室和一间小起居室。

他的口述录音不像他的书面作品那么完整，有时他的声音会因为离开录音机而显得很遥远。所以，与他的《笔记》和《日记》不同，为使表达清晰，录音需要进行一些轻微的编辑。从这些篇章中，读者可以非常近距离地接触到克里希那穆提，有时甚至可以进入他的意识之中。其中有几篇他还引入了一个假想的来访者，对他进行提问并引出谈话。

克里希那穆提教诲的精华就在这本书中，而多数时候他都是从对自然的描写开始的。很多读者不仅仅把他当作一位哲人，而且还是一位诗人，这些描写可以让他们整个身心都宁静下来，由直觉指引着融入下面的内容。书中有些重复之处，但是为了强调他的意指，这些重复似乎是必要的，它们能清楚地表明为什么对他来说，卸去了过去的所有负担，每一天都是崭新的。

奇怪的是，最后一篇，也许也是最美的一篇，是关于死亡的。这是我们最后一次听到克里希那穆提的独白。两年后，他在松舍的同一间卧室与世长辞。

克氏生前好友

玛丽·鲁琴斯

This book is unique in that it is the only one of Krishnamurti's publications which records words spoken into a tape—recorder while he was quite alone.

After the success of Krishnamurti's Journal, published in 1982, he was urged to continue it but, since by then his hand had become rather shaky (he was eighty—seven), it was suggested that instead of writing it, which would tire him, he should dictate it to himself. This idea appealed to him. However, he could not start at once because he was on the point of flying to India where he would have no time to himself. On his return to California, in February 1983, he dictated the first of the pieces contained in this volume into a new Sony tape—recorder.

All the dictations except one were recorded from his home, Pine Cottage, in the Ojai Valley, some eighty miles north of Los Angeles. He would dictate in the mornings, while in bed after breakfast, undisturbed.

Krishnamurti had first stayed at Pine Cottage with his brother in 1922, when it was lent to him by a friend, and it was there, on August'22, that he underwent a spiritual experience that transformed his life. Soon afterwards, a Trust was formed to which money was subscribed to buy the cottage and six acres of surrounding land. In 1978 a beautiful new house was built incorporating the cottage in which Krishnamurti retained his original bedroom and a small sitting—room.

His dictations were not as finished as his writings, and at times his voice would wander away from the recorder to become rather distant, so, unlike his Notebook and Journal, some slight editing has been necessary for the sake of clarity. The reader gets very close to Krishnamurti in these pieces—almost, it seems at moments, into his very consciousness. In a few of them he introduces an imaginary visitor who comes to question him and draw him out.

The gist of Krishnamurti's teaching is here, and the descriptions of nature with which he begins most of the pieces may for many, who regard him as a poet as well as a philosopher, quieten their whole being so that they become intuitively receptive to what follows. There are repetitions, but these seem somehow necessary in order to emphasize his meaning, and they clearly show how every day was a completely new day to him, free from all burdens of the past.

Strangely, the last piece, and perhaps the most beautiful, is about death. It is the last occasion on which we shall ever hear Krishnamurti discoursing to himself. Two years later he died in this same bedroom at Pine Cottage.

M.L.

CONTENTS

第一部分 | **加利福尼亚，欧亥**
OJAI, CALIFORNIA

第二部分 | 英国汉普郡，布洛克伍德公园
BROCKWOOD PARK, HAMPSHIRE

第三部分 | 加利福尼亚，欧亥
OJAI, CALIFORNIA

第一部分

加利福尼亚，欧亥

OJAI, CALIFORNIA

Friday, February 25, 1983

There is a tree by the river and we have been watching it day after day for several weeks when the sun is about to rise. As the sun rises slowly over the horizon, over the trees, this particular tree becomes all of a sudden golden. All the leaves are bright with life and as you watch it as the hours pass by, that tree whose name does not matter—what matters is that beautiful tree—an extraordinary quality seems to spread all over the land, over the river. And as the sun rises a little higher the leaves begin to flutter, to dance. And each hour seems to give to that tree a different quality. Before the sun rises it has a sombre feeling, quiet, far away, full of dignity. And as the day begins, the leaves with the light on them dance and give it that peculiar feeling that one has of great beauty. By midday its shadow has deepened and you can sit there protected from the sun, never feeling lonely, with the tree as your companion. As you sit there, there is a relationship of deep abiding security and a freedom that only trees can know.

Towards the evening when the western skies are lit up by the setting sun, the tree gradually becomes sombre, dark, closing in on itself. The sky has become red, yellow, green, but the tree remains quiet, hidden, and is resting for the night.

If you establish a relationship with it then you have relationship with mankind. You are responsible then for that tree and for the trees of the

1983 年 2 月 25 日，星期五

河边有棵树，我们已经在日出时分日复一日地观察了它好几个星期。朝阳慢慢从地平线升起，当它越过林梢时，这棵树刹那间变成了金黄色。所有的叶子都闪烁着生命的光芒，你就这么看着它，时光飞逝而过，但这棵树的名字并不重要，重要的是这棵美丽的树本身——似乎有一种非同寻常的品质散布在整片大地、整条河流之上。然后太阳又升高了些许，叶子开始颤动，开始跳舞。

这棵树似乎每个小时都具有一种不同的特质。在太阳升起前它有一种郁暗的感觉，很安静，很遥远，充满了庄严感。然后白天开始了，沾满了阳光的树叶在跳舞，赋予了它一种特别的感觉，有一种浩瀚的美感。中午时分，树影变深，你可以坐在树下遮阳，树是你的伙伴，你永远不会感觉孤独。当你坐在那里，有一种特别的连接，这连接里有一种深刻而持久的安全感，以及一种只有树木才懂得的自由。

黄昏时，西方的天空被落日点亮，这棵树又慢慢变得暗淡，再暗淡些，把自己包裹起来。天空变成了红色、黄色、绿色，但是这棵树安静如故，把自己隐藏起来，在夜里歇息着。

如果你和它建立了连接，那么你就和整个人类有了连接，然后你

world. But if you have no relationship with the living things on this earth you may lose whatever relationship you have with humanity, with human beings. We never look deeply into the quality of a tree; we never really touch it, feel its solidity, its rough bark, and hear the sound that is part of the tree. Not the sound of wind through the leaves, not the breeze of a morning that flutters the leaves, but its own sound, the sound of the trunk and the silent sound of the roots. You must be extraordinarily sensitive to hear the sound. This sound is not the noise of the world, not the noise of the chattering of the mind, not the vulgarity of human quarrels and human warfare but sound as part of the universe.

It is odd that we have so little relationship with nature, with the insects and the leaping frog and the owl that hoots among the hills calling for its mate. We never seem to have a feeling for all living things on the earth. If we could establish a deep abiding relationship with nature we would never kill an animal for our appetite, we would never harm, vivisect, a monkey, a dog, a guinea pig for our benefit. We would find other ways to heal our wounds, heal our bodies. But the healing of the mind is something totally different. That healing gradually takes place if you are with nature, with that orange on the tree, and the blade of grass that pushes through the cement, and the hills covered, hidden, by the clouds.

This is not sentiment or romantic imagination but a reality of a relationship with everything that lives and moves on the earth. Man has killed millions of whales and is still killing them. All that we derive from their slaughter can be had through other means. But apparently man loves to kill things, the fleeting deer, the marvellous gazelle and the great elephant. We love to kill each other. This killing of other human beings has never stopped throughout the history of man's life on this earth. If we

就会为那棵树和世界上所有的树负责。但是，如果你和地球上的生命没有建立连接的话，你可能就失去了和所有人类的连接。我们从未深入观察过一棵树的特质，我们从未真正触摸它，感觉它的坚实、它粗糙的树干，聆听来自这棵树的声音。这声音并不是穿过树叶的风声，也并非来自清晨拍动树叶的微风，而是树自己的声音，树干的声音，树根的寂静之声。你必须格外敏感才能听到这些声音。这声音并非来自这世界的噪声，并非思想喋喋不休的喧哗，也不是人们在争吵和战争中的粗鄙杂音，而是作为宇宙的一部分的声音。

有一点很奇怪，那就是我们和自然、和昆虫、和跳跃的青蛙，和在山间呼唤伙伴的猫头鹰几乎没有任何连接。我们似乎从不对地球上的生灵保有一份感情。如果我们能够和自然建立一份深刻而持久的联系，我们就不会为了口腹之欲猎杀动物，也不会为了自身的利益去伤害、去解剖一只猴子、一只青蛙和一只豚鼠，我们会找到疗伤和治愈身体的其他方法。而心灵的疗愈则是一件完全不同的事。当你和自然在一起，和树上的那只橙子在一起，和穿破水泥的青草叶片在一起，和隐于层云之下的山脉在一起时，这种疗愈就会渐渐地悄然发生。

这不是伤感或者浪漫的想象，而是和地球上生存着、活动着的万物的一种真实的连接。人类捕杀了数以百万计的鲸鱼，并且还在继续残杀。从屠杀它们而获取的东西，大可通过其他方式获得。但是显然人类热衷于杀戮，猎杀疾驰的鹿、漂亮的瞪羚和大象。我们也喜欢互相残杀。贯穿人类在地球上的整个历史，对他人的残杀就从未停止

could, and we must, establish a deep long abiding relationship with nature, with the actual trees, the bushes, the flowers, the grass and the fast moving clouds, then we would never slaughter another human being for any reason whatsoever. Organized murder is war, and though we demonstrate against a particular war, the nuclear, or any other kind of war, we have never demonstrated against war. We have never said that to kill another human being is the greatest sin on earth.

过。如果我们能够——我们也必须——和自然、和树木、和灌木丛、和花、和草、和快速飘过的云，建立一种深入持久的联系，那么我们就不会为了任何原因去杀害别人。有组织的谋杀就是战争，尽管我们通过游行示威反对某一场战争，核战争或其他战争，但是我们从不反对战争本身。我们从没说过杀害别人是世上最严重的罪行。

Monday 28th February, 1983

Flying at 41, 000 feet from one continent to another you see nothing but snow, miles of snow; all the mountains and the hills are covered with snow, and the rivers too are frozen. You see them wandering, meandering, all over the land. And far below, the distant farms are covered with ice and snow. It is a long, tiresome flight of eleven hours. The passengers were chattering away. There was a couple behind one and they never stopped talking, never looked at the glory of those marvellous hills and mountains, never looked at the other passengers. Apparently they were absorbed in their own thoughts, in their own problems, in their chatterings. And at last, after a tedious, calm flight, in the dead of winter, you land at the town on the Pacific.

After the noise and the bustle, you leave that ugly, sprawling, vulgar, shouting city and the endless shops selling almost all the same things. You leave all that behind as you go round the coast highway of the blue Pacific, following the seashore, on a beautiful road, wandering through the hills, meeting the sea often; and as you leave the Pacific behind and enter into the country, winding over various small hills, peaceful, quiet, full of that strange dignity of the country, you enter the valley. You have been there for the last sixty years, and each time you are astonished to enter into this valley. It is quiet, almost untouched by man. You enter into this valley which is almost like a vast cup, a nest.

1983 年 2 月 28 日，星期一

在四万一千英尺的高空从一个大洲飞往另一个大洲，你看到的就只有白雪，绵延不断的白雪，所有的山脉都被积雪覆盖，河流都冻成了冰。你看到河流在大地上蜿蜒而过。远远的下面，遥远的农场也被冰雪覆盖。这是一个历时十一个小时的冗长乏味的航班。旅客们喋喋不休地唠叨着。后面有一对夫妇，他们一直在说个不停，完全没有留意到那些瑰丽的群山，也从不关心其他乘客。显然，他们沉浸在自己的思绪里、自己的问题里、自己的唠叨里。最后，经过一段乏味沉闷的飞行，在冬天的尽头，你降落在了太平洋边的这个小镇上。

在一阵喧嚣忙乱之后，你离开了那个丑陋的、扩张着的、粗俗的、吼叫着的城市，离开了货品几乎千篇一律的、没完没了的商店。你把这些东西抛在身后，踏上蓝色太平洋岸边的公路，沿着海岸，走上了一条美丽的公路，在山间穿行，不时会看到海面，然后你把太平洋也留在了身后，进入乡下，蜿蜒穿过了很多小山。这些小山平静又安宁，充满了乡村特有的奇异庄严，随后你就进入了山谷。在过去的六十年中你一直待在这里，每次进入这座山谷时你都会被惊呆。这里很安静，几乎从未被人类所影响。你进入这个山谷，就像进入了一个

Then you leave the little village and climb to about 1, 400 feet, passing rows and rows of orange orchards and groves. The air is perfumed with orange blossom. The whole valley is filled with that scent. And the smell of it is in your mind, in your heart, in your whole body. It is the most extraordinary feeling of living in a perfume that will last for about three weeks or more. And there is a quietness in the mountains, a dignity. And each time you look at those hills and the high mountain, which is over 6, 000 feet, you are really surprised that such a country exists. Each time you come to this quiet, peaceful valley there is a feeling of strange aloofness, of deep silence and the vast spreading of slow time.

Man is trying to spoil the valley but it has been preserved. And the mountains that morning were extraordinarily beautiful. You could almost touch them. The majesty, the vast sense of permanency is there in them. And you enter quietly into the house where you have lived for over sixty years and the atmosphere, the air, is, if one can use that word, holy; you can feel it. You can almost touch it. As it has rained considerably, for it is the rainy season, all the hills and the little folds of the mountain are green, flourishing, full—the earth is smiling with such delight, with some deep quiet understanding of its own existence.

"You have said over and over again that the mind, or if you prefer it, the brain, must be quiet, must empty itself of all the knowledge it has gathered, not only to be free but to comprehend something that is not of time or thought or of any action. You have said this in different ways in most of your talks and I find this awfully difficult, not only to grasp the idea, the depth of it but the feeling of quiet emptiness, if I can use that word. I never could feel my way into it. I have tried various methods to end the chattering of the mind, the endless occupation with something or

大杯子、一个窝。

然后，你离开了那个小村子，穿过生着一排排橙树的果园和小树林，爬到了一千四百英尺的高度。空气中弥漫着橙花的味道，整个山谷都充满了这种香气。这芬芳弥漫在你的脑子里、你的心里、你的整个身体里。连续三个星期或者更长的时间，你都生活在这股香气里，这是最奇妙的感觉。群山之中有一种安静，一种庄严。每当你凝视那些小山和六千多英尺的高山，你都会非常惊讶竟然有这样的乡村。每次你来到这个宁静安详的山谷，就会有一种奇特的超然感，有一种深沉的寂静和时间放缓的广袤的延伸感。

人们正试图破坏这个山谷，但是它被保护了下来。那天清晨，群山显得格外美丽，你几乎能触碰到它们。它们有一种庄严感，一种永恒的广袤感觉。你轻轻地走进生活了六十多年的房子，那空气，那氛围——如果可以用这个词形容的话——是神圣的，你能感觉得到，你几乎能触摸得到。因为是雨季，刚刚下过大雨，所有的小山和高山的小侧面都是绿色的，郁郁葱葱，丰盈饱满，大地在欣喜地欢笑，带着一种对自身存在的安静而又深刻的领悟。

"你一次次地说过，心灵（如果你愿意，也可以叫作头脑），必须是安静的，必须清空它所积累的所有知识，不仅仅要自由，而且要理解一种不属于时间、思想以及任何行动的事物。在大多数讲话中你都用不同的方式说过这些，但是我发现这很难做到，不光是理解这个想法以及它的深度很难，而且理解安静的空无感觉也很难，如果我可以用这个词的话。我从未找到体会这些的途径。我试过很多方法来停

other, this very occupation creating its problems. And as one lives one is caught up in all this. This is our daily life, the tedium, the talk that goes on in a family, and if there isn't talking there is always the television or a book. The mind seems to demand that it should be occupied, that it should move from one thing to another, from knowledge to knowledge, from action to action with the everlasting movement of thought."

"As we pointed out, thought cannot be stopped by determination, by a decision of the will, or the urgent pressing desire to enter into that quality of quiet, still emptiness."

"I find myself envious for something which I think, which I feel, to be true, which I would like to have, but it has always eluded me, it has always gone beyond my grasp. I have come, as I have often come, to talk with you: why in my daily life, in my business life, is there not the stability, the endurance of that quietness? Why isn't this in my life? I have asked myself what am I to do. I also realize I cannot do much, or I can't do anything at all about it. But it is there nagging. I can't leave it alone. If only I could experience it once, then that very memory will nourish me, then that very remembrance will give a significance to a really rather silly life. So I have come to enquire, to probe into this matter: why does the mind—perhaps the word brain may be better—demand that it should be occupied?"

止喋喋不休的思想，不再被某些事情不断地占满心灵——这种占据本身就在制造问题，而人只要活着就会被这些东西攫住。这就是我们的日常生活——单调乏味，家人之间有些交谈，如果没有对话就看电视或者看书。心似乎要求被占据，把注意力从一件事转移到另一件事，从知识到知识，或者从行动到行动，思想一直在不停地活动着。"

"正如我们之前所指出的，意志力无法让思想停止，坚定的决心或者想要进入那种寂静的空无状态的迫切愿望也不能让思想止息。"

"我发现自己对某样我认为或者感觉是真实的并且想拥有的东西心怀羡妒，但它总是避开我，我抓不住它。我曾经来过，我现在也来和你探讨：在我的日常生活中，在我的事业生涯中，难道就不能有那种持久稳定的寂静吗？为什么我的生活里没有它？我问过自己该怎么办。我也意识到我做不了什么，或者说我对此完全无能为力。但是这个念头一直在那唠叨，我无法视而不见。只要我能体验一次那种寂静，那么那个记忆就能滋养我，那个回忆本身就能给这愚蠢的生命赋予一种意义。所以我来询问、来探索这个问题：为什么心灵（也许头脑这个词更好）要求被占据？"

Thursday 10th March, 1983

The other day as one was walking along a secluded wooded lane far from the noise and the brutality and the vulgarity of civilization, right away from everything that was put together by man, there was a sense of great quietness, enveloping all things—serene, distant and full of the sound of the earth. As you walked along quietly, not disturbing the things of the earth around you, the bushes, the trees, the crickets and the birds, suddenly round a bend there were two small creatures quarrelling with each other, fighting in their small way. One was trying to drive off the other. The other was intruding, trying to get into the other's little hole, and the owner was fighting it off. Presently the owner won and the other ran off. Again there was quietness, a sense o f deep solitude. And as you looked up, the path climbed high into the mountains, the waterfall was gently murmuring down the side of the path; there was great beauty and infinite dignity, not the dignity achieved by man that seems so vain and arrogant. The little creature had identified itself with its home, as we human beings do. We are always trying to identify ourselves with our race, with our culture, with those things which we believe in, with some mystical figure, or some saviour, some kind of super authority. Identifying with something seems to be the nature of man. Probably we have derived this feeling from that little animal.

One wonders why this craving, longing, for identification exists. One

1983 年 3 月 10 日，星期四

那天，漫步在一条人迹罕至的林荫道上，远离文明的喧嚣、残忍和粗俗，远离人为制造的一切，有一种囊括了万物的无限的静谧感——宁静而遥远，充满着大地的声音。你静静地漫步，不去打扰周围大地上的一切——灌木丛、树林、蟋蟀和鸟儿。然后你忽然蹲下身，发现那里有两个小生命在争吵，以它们细微的方式在打斗，其中一个正在努力驱赶另一个。一个是入侵者，企图进入另一个的巢穴，主人正在为此而战斗。现在主人大获全胜，另一个落荒而逃。

宁静又出现了，那是一种深沉的孤寂。这时你抬起头，小路向上延伸进入群山，瀑布在小路的一侧轻轻地呢喃而下。这里有一种浩瀚的美和无限的庄严，但不是人类求取的虚荣傲慢的庄严。那个小东西认为那个窝是它的家，就像我们人类一样。我们总是试图让自己归属于自己的种族、自己的文化，归属于我们相信的那些东西，某些神秘人物，或者某个救世主、某种超级权威。对某种事物的认同感似乎是人类的天性。也许我们的这种情感恰恰源于那个小小的动物。

你也许会问，为什么会存在对认同感的渴望和向往？有人认为认同感来自生理需要，来自生活必需品——衣服、食物、居所等等。但

can understand the identification with one's physical needs—the necessary things, clothes, food, shelter and so on. But inwardly, inside the skin as it were, we try to identify ourselves with the past, with tradition, with some fanciful romantic image, a symbol much cherished. And surely in this identification there is a sense of security, safety, a sense of being owned and of possessing. This gives great comfort. One takes comfort, security, in any form of illusion. And man apparently needs many illusions.

In the distance there is the hoot of an owl and there is a deep—throated reply from the other side of the valley. It is still dawn. The noise of the day has not begun and everything is quiet. There is something strange and holy where the sun arises. There is a prayer, a chant to the dawn, to that strange quiet light. That early morning, the light was subdued, there was no breeze and all the vegetation, the trees, the bushes, were quiet, still, waiting. Waiting for the sun to arise. And perhaps the sun would not come up for another half hour or so, and the dawn was slowly covering the earth with a strange stillness.

Gradually, slowly, the top most mountain was getting brighter and the sun was touching it, golden, clear, and the snow was pure, untouched by the light of day.

As you climbed, leaving the little village paths down below, the noise of the earth, the crickets, the quails and other birds began their morning song, their chant, their rich worship of the day. And as the sun arose you were part of that light and had left behind everything that thought had put together. You completely forgot yourself. The psyche was empty of its struggles and its pains. And as you walked, climbed, there was no sense of separateness, no sense of being even a human being.

The morning mist was gathering slowly in the valley, and that mist was you, getting more and more thick, more and more into the fancy, the

是内心里，我们总试图让自己归属于过去、传统，归属于某些奇异的浪漫形象，或者我们珍视的某个象征。毫无疑问，这种认同之中有一种安全感、保障感，一种被占有和占有的感觉，而这给人以巨大的安慰。人们从虚幻的形式中获取舒适和安全感。而人们显然需要各种各样的幻象。

　　远处有猫头鹰的鸣叫，随后从山谷的另一边传来一声深远的回应。此刻还是黎明，白天的喧闹还未开始，一切都是那么安静。太阳升起的地方有种奇特而神圣的东西，有一种对黎明、对那奇特而安静的光的祈祷和吟唱。清晨，光线柔和，没有一丝微风，所有的植被、树林、灌木丛，都那么静谧、安宁，都在等待着，等待朝阳升起。也许太阳在半个小时后才会升起，黎明用一种莫名的安详慢慢地覆盖着大地。

　　渐渐地，慢慢地，最高的山峰亮起来了，太阳在触碰它，金光闪闪，清晰可见，而白雪纯净依然，没有被日光所沾染。

　　你继续往上爬，把乡村小路留在身后，这里有大地的声音，蟋蟀、鹌鹑和另一些鸟儿唱起了它们的晨曲、它们的吟诵，还有它们对这一天的深深崇敬。当朝阳升起时，你就是那光线的一部分，把思想制造的一切都抛在了身后。你完全忘却了自己，心清空了它所有的挣扎和苦痛。在你漫步时、爬山时，没有分离感，甚至没有自己身为一个人的感觉。

　　晨雾在山谷里慢慢聚集，这雾就是你，越来越厚，越来越深地进入幻境和浪漫，进入生命的混沌状态。良久之后，你往山下走去，一

romance, the idiocy of one's own life. And after a long period of time you came down. There was the murmur of the wind, insects, the calls of many birds. And as you came down the mist was disappearing. There were streets, shops, and the glory of the dawn was fast fading away. And you began your daily routine, caught in the habit of work, the contentions between man and man, the divisions of identification, the division of ideologies, the preparations for wars, your own inward pain and the everlasting sorrow of man.

路上有风的呢喃，有昆虫和各种鸟儿的鸣叫。你下山时这雾就散去了。山下有街道、商店，黎明的辉煌迅速消失。然后你开始了一天的例行公事，被工作习惯、人与人之间的争夺、身份的划分、意识形态的划分、准备战争、你自己内心的痛苦和人类无尽的悲伤所牢牢俘获。

Friday 11th March, 1983

It was a cool fresh morning and there was the light that California alone has, especially the southern part of it. It is really quite an extraordinary light.

We have travelled probably all over the world, most of the world at least, have seen various lights and clouds in many parts of the earth. The clouds in Holland are very close; here in California the clouds against the blue sky seem to hold the light everlastingly—the light that great clouds have, with their extraordinary shape and quality.

It was a cool, very nice morning. And as you climbed the rocky path up to the great height and looked down into the valley and saw the row upon row of orange trees, avocados and the hills that surround the valley, it was as though you were out of this world, so completely lost were you to all things, to the weariness, to man's ugly reactions and actions. You left all that behind as you climbed up and up the very rocky path. You left behind far below you the vanity, the arrogance, the vulgarity of uniforms, decorations spread all over your chest, and the vanity and strange costumes of priests. You left all that behind.

And as you went up you nearly trod on a mother with her dozen or more little baby quails and they scattered with chirping into the bushes. As you went on up and looked back, the mother had again gathered them

1983 年 3 月 11 日，星期五

这是个清新凉爽的早晨，有种光是加州，特别是南加州所独有的。那真是一种非同寻常的光。

我们也许周游过全世界，至少是世界的大部分地方，见过地球的不同地区有着不同的光和云。荷兰的云很低，而在加州这里的蓝天上，云似乎永远都怀抱着这种光——大片大片的云才有的光芒，它们有着不可思议的轮廓和特质。

这是个凉爽而又美丽的清晨。当你爬上山路，到达顶峰，俯瞰山谷，看到一排排的橙树、鳄梨树，还有围绕着山谷的小山，感觉你好似离开了这个世界。你曾经把自己完全迷失在了琐事中、厌倦中，迷失在人类丑陋的反应和行为中。当你爬上崎岖的山路，你把这些都已抛下。你把虚荣、傲慢、划一的粗俗，把胸前挂满的饰物、神父的自负和奇装异服，都远远地抛在了下面。你把那一切全部抛在了身后。

你向上爬的时候，差一点儿就踩到了带着一群孩子的鹌鹑母亲，它们正鸣叫着稀稀拉拉地往灌木丛走去。你继续往上走去，然后再回头看时，那个母亲又把孩子们拢在了自己周围，它们在母亲的翅膀下非常安全。

round her and they were all quite secure under the wings of their mother.

You had to climb hour after hour to reach the great height. Some days you saw a bear a little way off and it paid no attention. And the deer across the gully, they too seemed unconcerned. At last you reached the height of a rocky plateau, and across the hills to the south—west you saw the distant sea, so blue, so quiet, so infinitely far away. You sat on a rock, smooth, cracked, where the sun must for century upon century, without any regret, have cracked it. And in the little cracks you saw tiny little living things scurrying about, and there was that utter silence, complete and infinite. A very large bird—they call it a condor—was circling in the sky. Apart from that movement there was nothing astir except these tiny little insects. but there was that silence that exists only where man has not been before; it was so peaceful.

You left everything behind in that little village so far below you. Literally everything: your identity, if you had any, your belongings, the possession of your experiences, your memories of things that had meant something to you—you left all that behind, down below there amidst the shining groves and orchards. Here there was absolute silence and you were totally alone.

It was a marvellous morning and the cool air which was becoming colder wrapped round you, and you were completely lost to everything. There was nothing and beyond nothing.

You should really forget the word meditation. That word has been corrupted. The ordinary meaning of that word—to ponder over, to consider, to think about—is rather trivial and ordinary. If you want to understand the nature of meditation you should really forget the word because you cannot possibly measure with words that which is not

你得爬好几个小时才能到达顶峰。有些天你会看到不远处有一只熊，但是它并没留意到你。小鹿跃过溪谷的时候也显得无忧无虑。最后你到达了山顶高台，向西南望去，越过群山，你能远远地看到大海，那么蓝，那么安静，那么遥不可及。你坐在一块开裂的光滑岩石上，是太阳经过几个世纪的不停照耀，才劈开了这些裂缝。然后从这些小裂缝里，你看到有很多细小的生命在匆忙奔走，此时有一种彻底的寂静，全然的、无限的寂静。一只很大的鸟，人们管它叫"神鹰"，正在空中盘旋。在那盘旋之外，除了这些小小的昆虫，没有一丝其他的骚动。然而，这种寂静只存在于人类没有到过的地方，一切都是那么安宁。

你把一切都远远地留在了山下的那个小村庄里。所有的一切，你的身份——如果你有的话——你的财产，你拥有的经验，你对往事的记忆，这些东西曾经对你而言有着某种意义，你把这些都远远抛在了身后，抛在了下面闪亮的树林和果园里。这里有绝对的寂静，你是完全地独自一人。

这是个奇妙非凡的清晨，正在变冷的凉爽空气包围着你，你把自己交付给了周围的一切。一片空无，却又超越了空无。

你真应该忘掉"冥想"这个词，它已然被败坏了。这个词通常的含义是指冥思苦想、思索、考虑，但这种含义是相当琐碎而平庸的。如果你想了解冥想的本质，你就应该把这个词完全忘掉，因为你不可能用语言来衡量无法衡量之物、超越一切量度之物。没有语言能传达它的含义，任何体系、思维模式、训练以及戒律都无法传达它的含

measurable, that which is beyond all measure. No words can convey it, nor any systems, modes of thought, practice or discipline. Meditation— or rather if we could find another word which has not been so mutilated, made so ordinary, corrupt, which has become the means of earning a great deal of money—if you can put aside the word, then you begin quietly and gently to feel a movement that is not of time. Again, the word movement implies time—what is meant is a movement that has no beginning or end. A movement in the sense of a wave: wave upon wave, starting from nowhere and with no beach to crash upon. It is an endless wave. Time, however slow it is, is rather tiresome. Time means growth, evolution, to become, to achieve, to learn, to change. And time is not the way of that which lies far beyond the word meditation. Time has nothing to do with it. Time is the action of will, of desire, and desire cannot in any way[word or words inaudible here]—it lies far beyond the word meditation.

Here, sitting on that rock, with the blue sky—it is astonishingly blue— the air is so pure, unpolluted. Far beyond this range is the desert. You can see it, miles of it. It is really a timeless perception of that which is. It is only that perception which can say it is.

You sat there watching for what seemed many days, many years, many centuries. As the sun was going down to the sea you made your way down to the valley and everything around you was alight, that blade of grass, that sumac, the towering eucalyptus and the flowering earth. It took time to come down as it had taken time to go up. But that which has no time cannot be measured by words. And meditation is only a word. The roots of heaven are in deep abiding silence.

义。冥想，或者如果我们能找到另一个没有变得那么残缺、庸常、腐败的词来代替它的话——这个词甚至变成了牟取暴利的工具——如果你能把这个词放在一边，那么你就能够开始安静地、轻轻地感知一种不属于时间的运动了。

"运动"这个词也意味着时间，而上面所说的是一种无始无终的运动，像海浪一样的运动：一波接着一波，没有来处也没有可以撞击的海滩，那是一种无尽的波浪。时间，无论多么缓慢，都极度令人生厌。时间意味着生长、进化、变成、到达、学习和改变。而时间绝非远远超越了"冥想"这个词的事物的运行方式，时间与它无关。时间是意志力的行动，是欲望的行动，而欲望无论如何都无法企及那种运动（注：此处的词语无法辨认）——它远远超越了"冥想"这个词。

在这里，坐在岩石上，和蓝天在一起，天惊人地蓝，空气是那么纯净，未被污染。群山遥远的另一边是沙漠，你能看到绵延不尽的沙漠。这真是一种对真相的超越时间的感知，而只有那种感知才能称为冥想。

你坐在那儿看着，好像很多天、很多年、很多世纪就此逝去。当夕阳落向大海，你开始朝山谷走去，你周围的一切，青草叶片、漆树、高大的桉树和开满鲜花的大地都被点亮了。下山需要花些时间，因为上山也花了不少时间。但是没有时间的那个事物是无法用语言衡量的，而冥想只是一个词而已。极乐的根源就在深切持久的寂静里。

Friday 11th March, 1983 (Continued)

It was really a most lovely clear beautiful morning. There was dew on every leaf. And as the sun rose slowly, quietly spreading over the beautiful land, there was great peace in this valley. The trees were full of oranges, small ones but many. Gradually the sun lit every tree and every orange. When you sat on that veranda overlooking the valley, there were the long shadows of the morning. The shadow is as beautiful as the tree. We wanted to go out, not in a car, but out among the trees, smell the fresh air and the scent of many oranges and the flowers, and hear the sound of the earth.

Later on one climbed right to the very top of the hill, overlooking the wide valley. The earth doesn't belong to anyone. It is the land upon which all of us are to live for many years, ploughing, reaping and destroying.

You are always a guest on this earth and have the austerity of a guest. Austerity is far deeper than owning only a few things. The very word austerity has been spoilt by the monks, by the sannyasis, by the hermits. Sitting on that high hill alone in the solitude of many things, many rocks and little animals and ants, that word had no meaning.

Over the hills in the far distance was the wide, shining, sparkling sea. We have broken up the earth as yours and mine—your nation, my nation, your flag and his flag, this particular religion and the religion of the distant man. The world, the earth, is divided, broken up. And for it we

1983 年 3 月 11 日，星期五（续）

这真是个极为清爽怡人的早晨，每片树叶都凝结着露珠。当朝阳慢慢升起，静静地照耀美丽的大地时，山谷里有一种广袤的寂静。树上结满了橙子，橙子很小，但是很多。渐渐地，太阳点亮了每一棵树和每颗橙子。当你坐在露台上俯瞰山谷，你会发现清晨那里会有长长的影子，这影子和树一般美丽。我们打算出去，不坐车，而是走在树下，嗅嗅清新的空气、橙子和花的香味，倾听大地的声音。

稍后，你爬到山顶最高处，俯瞰宽阔的山谷。大地不属于任何人，而正是在这片土地上，我们要生活经年，耕种、收割，以及破坏。

你始终是地球上的一位客人，有着一种客人的简朴。"简朴"的含义远远不止仅仅拥有少数几样东西而已。"简朴"这个词已被僧侣、遁世者和隐士们所败坏。在幽静而丰饶的野外，有着无数岩石，有着各种小动物和蚂蚁，独自坐在这样一座高山上，那个词已毫无意义。

在遥远的山那边，是闪耀着光芒的辽阔大海。我们把这个地球分割成了你的和我的，你的国家和我的国家，你的旗帜和他的旗帜，这种特定的宗教信仰和遥远的另一个人的宗教信仰。这个世界，这个地球，被分裂了、被打破了。我们为此而争论不休，政客们为维持这种

fight and wrangle, and the politicians exult in their power to maintain this division, never looking at the world as a whole. They haven't got the global mind. They never feel nor ever perceive the immense possibility of having no nationality, no division, they can never perceive the ugliness of their power, their position and their sense of importance. They are like you or another, only they occupy the seat of power with their petty little desires and ambitions, and so maintain apparently, as long as man has been on this earth, the tribal attitude towards life. They don't have a mind that is not committed to any issue, to any ideals, ideologies—a mind that steps beyond the division of race, culture, that the religions man has invented.

Governments must exist as long as man is not a light to himself, as long as he does not live his daily life with order, care, diligently working, watching, learning. He would rather be told what to do. He has been told what to do by the ancients, by the priests, by the gurus, and he accepts their orders, their peculiar destructive disciplines as though they were gods on this earth, as though they knew all the implications of this extraordinarily complex life.

Sitting there, high above all the trees, on a rock that has its own sound like every living thing on this earth, and watching the blue sky, clear, spotless, one wonders how long it will take for man to learn to live on this earth without wrangles, rows, wars and conflict. Man has created the conflict by his division of the earth, linguistically, culturally, superficially. One wonders how long man, who has evolved through so many centuries of pain and grief, anxiety and pleasure, fear and conflict, will take to live a different way of life.

As you sat quietly without movement, a bob cat, a lynx, came down. As the wind was blowing up the valley it was not aware of the smell of that

分裂的权力而扬扬得意，他们从不把世界看作一个整体，他们没有全球性的思维。

政客们从未感受到，也从未发觉没有国籍、没有分裂的无限可能性，他们永远无法洞察他们的权力、地位和自我重要性的丑陋。他们和你以及其他人一样，虽然位高权重，但同样被那些琐碎的小小欲望和野心满满占据，而只要人类还活在这个地球上，他们显然会继续维持这种看待生命的部落性态度。他们没有一颗不被某个特定问题、某种理想或意识形态攫住的心——这样的一颗心远远超越了种族和文化的分割，超越了人类所发明的各类宗教。

只要人还没有照亮自己，只要他还不能每天都生活在秩序、关怀、勤奋工作、觉察和学习之中，那么政府就必须存在。他宁愿别人告诉他做什么。古人、牧师、古鲁一直在告诉他做什么，他接受了他们的秩序，就好似这些人才懂得这格外复杂的生命的意义。

你坐在那里，树林就在脚下，你坐在一块岩石上——这块石头和地球上的其他生物一样有着自己的声音——凝望着清澈无瑕的蓝天，你会问到底要花多久，人类才能学会没有争吵、战争和冲突地活在地球上。人类因为从语言上、文化上肤浅地分割了地球而制造了诸多冲突。你会问，人类经过了漫长的进化，经过这么多世纪的痛苦和悲伤、焦虑和快乐、恐惧和冲突，还要花多久才能过上一种完全不同的生活？

你安静地坐着，一动不动，这时一只山猫，或者猞猁，走了下来。劲风从山谷里吹过，它没注意到有人类的气味。它咕噜咕噜地叫

human being. It was purring, rubbing itself against a rock, its small tail up, and enjoying the marvel of the earth. Then it disappeared down the hill among the bushes. It was protecting its lair, its cave or its sleeping place. It was protecting what it needs, protecting its own kittens, and watching for danger. It was afraid of man more than anything else, man who believes in god, man who prays, the man of wealth with his gun, with his casual killing. You could almost smell that bob cat as it passed by you. You were so motionless, so utterly still that it never even looked at you; you were part of that rock, part of the environment.

Why, one wonders, does man not realize that one can live peacefully, without wars, without violence; how long will it take him, how many centuries upon centuries to realize this? From the past centuries of a thousand yesterdays, he has not learned. What he is now will be his future.

It was getting too hot on that rock. You could feel the gathering heat through your trousers so you got up and went down and followed the lynx which had long since disappeared. There were other creatures: the gopher, the king snake, and a rattler (rattle—snake). They were silently going about their business. The morning air disappeared; gradually the sun was in the west. It would take an hour or two before it set behind those hills with the marvellous shape of the rock and the evening colours of blue and red and yellow. Then the night would begin, the night sounds would fill the air; only late in the night would there be utter silence. The roots of heaven are of great emptiness, for in emptiness there is energy, incalculable, vast and profound.

着，在一块石头上蹭着身体，小尾巴翘着，享受着大地的奇妙。然后它就消失在了山下的灌木丛中。它保护着自己的窝，保护着它的巢穴或者睡觉的地方。它是在保护它所需要的东西，保护它的幼崽，警惕着各种危险。它最害怕的是人类，这些人相信上帝，这些人祈祷，这些人拥有枪支和财富，而且随意杀生。那只猫鼬经过的时候，你几乎可以嗅到它的气味。你寂然不动，安静得它都不看你一眼，你就是那块岩石的一部分、环境的一部分。

你会好奇，为什么人类意识不到可以和平地生活，没有战争，没有暴力？要过多久、多少个世纪，人类才能意识到这一点？几个世纪过去了，千万个昨天过去了，人们没有明白这一点。人类现在如何，将来还会如何。

岩石开始变得炙热难耐，隔着裤子你能感觉到热量正在聚集。然后你起身往山下走去，跟随着那只早已消失不见的猫鼬。还有另一些动物，囊地鼠、王蛇、响尾蛇，它们正各自静静地忙碌着。清晨的空气消失了，太阳慢慢挪向西方。还得再过一两个小时太阳才会下山，那些山石有着不可思议的形状，傍晚时被染上了蓝、红、黄各种缤纷的色彩。然后夜色就会降临，夜晚的声音将充满在空气里，而只有深夜才有纯然的静寂。极乐的根源是浩瀚的空无，因为空无之中有巨大的能量，广袤、深远、不可估量。

Tuesday, March 15, 1983

This end of the valley, particularly on this lovely quiet morning, was peaceful, there was no sound of traffic. The hills were behind you and the tallest mountain in this region was over 6, 000 feet. This house is surrounded by orchards, bright yellow oranges, and the sky was blue without a single cloud. You could hear the murmur of bees among the flowers in the still quiet morning. The old oak tree* behind the house was a great age; the strong winds had broken many dead branches. It has survived many storms, many summers of great heat and the cold winters. Probably it could tell you a lot of stories but this morning it was very quiet, there was no breeze. Everything around you was full of green and bright oranges, yellow and shining, and perfume filled the air—the perfume of jasmine.

This valley is far from all the noise and the bustle of human traffic, of humanity, of all the ugly things that are going on in the world. The orange trees were just beginning to show their fresh young flowers. The scent of it would fill the valley in a week or two and there would be the hum of thousands of bees. It was a peaceful morning and beyond all this lay the sick world, a world that is becoming more and more dangerous, more and more corrupt, vastly dull in search of entertainment, religious and

---

*   The Californian evergreen holm oak.

1983 年 3 月 15 日，星期二

山谷的这头非常宁静，特别是在这个静谧怡人的清早，毫无车流的喧嚣。群山在你身后绵延，而这个地区最高的山峰超过了六千英尺。这座房子被果园环绕，树上结满了金黄的橙子，蓝天上没有一丝白云。在这个安宁静谧的清晨，你可以听到花丛中蜜蜂的嗡鸣。屋后的那棵老橡树 ① 已是高龄，劲风折断了它不少枯枝。它在无数暴风雨后幸存了下来，也经历了数不清的酷暑和寒冬。或许它想讲很多故事给你听，可今天早上它非常安静，四下没有一丝微风。你周围的一切都青翠欲滴，鲜亮的橙子金光闪闪，空气里弥漫着香气——那是茉莉的芬芳。

这条山谷远离一切喧嚣，远离人类，远离车流的熙熙攘攘，远离世间上演的一切丑恶。橙树刚刚开出娇嫩的花朵，橙花的香气一两周之内就会充满整条山谷，引来成千上万只嗡鸣的蜜蜂。这是一个安静的早晨，而远离这一切之外的，是那个病入膏肓的世界，一个正变得越来越危险、越来越腐败的世界，它正在人们对宗教与世俗娱乐的追

---

① 加州的常绿圣栎树。

otherwise. The superficiality of existence is thriving. Money seems to be the greatest value in life, and with it naturally goes power, position and the sorrow of it all.

"On such a beautiful morning I want to talk over with you a rather sad subject, frightening, the sense of apprehension that pervades humanity and myself. I would really like to understand, not merely intellectually or descriptively, why, with so many others, I dread the ending of life.

"We kill so easily—it is called blood sport, shooting birds for amusement to show off one's skill, chasing the fox, killing by the million the things of the sea; death seems to be everywhere. Sitting on this quiet veranda, looking at those bright yellow oranges, it is difficult—or rather it seems so unseemly—to talk over something that is so frightening. Man throughout all the ages has never really solved or understood the thing called death.

"Naturally I have studied various religious and scientific rationalizations, beliefs, and they assume realities; some of them are logical, comforting, but the fact remains that there is always the fear of the unknown.

"I was discussing this fact with a friend of mine whose wife has recently died. He was a rather lonely man and he was inclined not only to live in his memories but also to find out for himself through seances, mediums and all that whether his wife, whom he really loved, had just evaporated into thin air, or was there still a continuity of her in another dimension, in another world than this?

"He said, "Strangely enough I found that at one of these seances the medium mentioned my name and said that she had a message from my wife. And the message was something only known to her and me. Of

求中变得乏味无比。生命的肤浅甚嚣尘上。金钱似乎成了生活中最重要的东西，随之而来的自然是对权力、地位的追求，以及由此引发的无尽苦难。

"在这样美丽的一个早晨，我想和你探讨一个非常悲伤的话题——人类，包括我自己，心里充满的那种可怕的恐惧感。我真的想弄明白——而不只是从道理上或者字面上明白——我，连同其他很多人，为什么都惧怕生命的结束？

"我们如此轻易地杀生——而那被称为狩猎运动，为了炫耀自己的技术，为了取乐而射杀鸟儿、追赶狐狸，屠杀海洋里的万千生灵；死亡似乎无处不在。坐在这个安静的露台上，望着那些明黄的橙子，很难谈论如此可怕的事情——或者不如说看起来非常不合时宜。人类世世代代以来从未真正解决或者了解这件叫作死亡的事情。

"当然，我研究过宗教和科学上的各种合理化的解释和信仰，他们对事实进行了各种假定；其中有一些是符合逻辑、抚慰人心的，但事实上对未知的恐惧却一如既往地存在着。

"我也和我的一个朋友讨论过这件事情，他的妻子刚刚过世。他成了一个非常孤独的人，他不光是喜欢活在自己的回忆里，而且还通过降神会、灵媒以及诸如此类的东西，试图搞清楚他挚爱的妻子是不是就那样消失在了稀薄的空气中，还是说，她的生命在另一个维度中、另一个世界中得到了延续？

"他说，'奇怪的是，我发现，在其中一次降神会上，灵媒提到了我的名字，并且说她从我妻子那里捎来了一个讯息，而那是只有她

course the medium may have read my thoughts or my wife may exist. That thought was in the air, the thought of that secret which was between us. I have asked many people of their experiences. It all seems so vain and rather stupid, including the message from my wife which was so trivial, so deeply meaningless." I don't want to discuss with you whether there is an entity of a person which continues after death. That is not my interest. Some say there is a continuity, others say there is total annihilation. This contradiction—annihilation, total ending of a person or the continuity of that individual—has been in all literature, from the ancients to the present day. But to me, all this is beside the point. Its validity is still in the realm of speculation, superstition, belief and the desire for comfort, hope. I am really not concerned with all that. I really mean this. I am at least quite certain of that. But I would like to have a dialogue with you, if I may, about what is the meaning of it all—this whole business of living and dying. Is it all utterly meaningless, vague, without any depth, without any significance whatsoever? Millions have died and millions will be born and continue and die. I am one of those. I always ask myself: what is the meaning of living and dying? The earth is beautiful, I have travelled a great deal, talked to many people who are supposed to be wise and learned, but they too die.

"I have come a long way so perhaps you would be good enough to take time and have the quiet patience to talk over this subject with me."

"Doubt is a precious thing. It cleanses, purifies the mind. The very questioning, the very fact that the seed of doubt is in one, helps to clarify our investigation. Not only doubting what all the others have said, including the whole concept of regeneration, and the Christian belief and dogma of resurrection, but also the Asiatic world's acceptance that there is continuity. In doubting, questioning all that, there is a certain freedom

和我才知道的事情。当然了，也许是那个灵媒读出了我的念头，要么就是我妻子确实是存在的。那个念头，那个仅限于我俩之间的秘密，就在空中。我也问了很多人他们的经验如何。这些看起来都是那么徒劳无益、那么愚蠢，包括来自我妻子的讯息，都太微不足道了，根本毫无意义。'我不知该如何与你探讨这个问题：人死后生命究竟是否能够继续？我对此不感兴趣。这种矛盾——人是寂灭了、彻底终结了还是延续了下来——从古至今一直存在于各种文献中。但是在我看来，这些都偏离了重点。

"这些说法的合理性依然局限在了臆测、迷信和信仰的范畴内，局限在了对慰藉和希望的渴求之中。我对这些都毫不关心，我此话当真。至少我对此笃信不疑。但是，如果可以，我还是想跟你谈一谈这件事的意义何在——这整个生与死的问题。它是不是真的毫无意义、晦涩不清，是不是真的没有任何深度、没有任何意义？无数人死去，又有无数人降生，然后接着死去，而我也是其中之一。我总是问自己：生与死的意义究竟何在？大地如此美丽，我周游世界，和许多貌似智慧和博学的人交谈过，可他们也会死。

"我远道而来，希望你也许能行行好，能花些时间安静地、耐心地和我谈谈这个问题。"

"质疑是一项非常宝贵的品质，它能够净化和涤荡心灵。质疑本身，质疑的种子在你心里种下，这个事实本身就会让我们的探索清晰起来。不只是质疑其他人所说的一切，包括整个重生的概念以及基督教对复活的信仰和教义，也要质疑整个亚洲世界对死后生命可以延

which is necessary for our enquiry. If one can put all that aside, actually, not merely verbally but negate all that deep within oneself, then one has no illusion. And it is necessary to be totally free from any kind of illusion—the illusions that are imposed upon us and the illusions that we create for ourselves. All illusions are the things that we play with, and if one is serious then they have no place whatsoever, nor does faith come into all this.

"So having set aside all that, not for the moment but seeing the falseness of all that, the mind is not caught in the falsehood that man has invented about death, about god, about all the rituals that thought has created. There must be freedom of opinion and judgement, for then only can one deliberately, actually, hesitantly explore into the meaning of daily living and dying—existence and the end of existence. If one is prepared for this, or if one is willing, or even better if one is actually, deeply concerned to find out the truth of the matter (living and dying is a very complex problem, an issue that requires a very careful examination) where should we begin? With life or with death? With living or with the ending of that which we call living?"

"I am over fifty, and have lived rather extravagantly, keeping an interest in many, many things. I think I would like to begin—I am rather hesitant, I am rather doubtful where I should begin."

"I think we ought to begin with the beginning of existence, man's existence, with one's existence as a human being."

"I was born into a fairly well—to—do family, carefully educated and brought up. I have been in several businesses and I have sufficient money; I am a single man now. I have been married, had two children, who all died in a car accident. And I have never married again. I think I should like to begin with my childhood. From the beginning, like every other child

续的信念。在对一切的质疑、怀疑之中，就有一种我们的探究所必需的自由。如果你可以把那一切真正抛开，不只是嘴上说说，而是否定自己内心深处的那一切，那么你就扫清了一切幻觉。而彻底摆脱一切形式的幻觉是非常必要的——别人强加给我们的那些幻觉，以及我们自己制造的幻觉。所有的幻觉都是我们玩弄的东西，而如果你是认真的，那么它们就没有了任何地位，信仰也不会乘虚而入。

"那么，把那一切抛开之后，不是暂时抛开，而是看清了那一切的虚假之后，心就不会被困在那些虚假之中了——人类就死亡、神明以及思想制造的各种仪式所发明的那些虚假之物。你必须具备摆脱了观点和评判的自由，因为只有此时你才能主动地、实际地、小心翼翼地探究司空见惯的生与死的真谛——生命以及生命的结束。如果你准备好了，如果你愿意，或者不如说，如果你真的殷切希望弄清这个问题的真相（生与死是个非常复杂的问题，是一个需要仔细审视的课题），那么我们应该从哪里开始呢？从生开始还是从死开始？从生命开始，还是从我们所谓生命的了结开始？"

"我已经五十多岁了，一直过着相当奢侈的生活，对很多很多事情都兴致勃勃。我想我希望——关于从哪里开始，我相当犹豫，相当迟疑。"

"我想我们应当从生命、人生的开端讲起，从你作为一个人存在开始。"

"我出生在一个非常富有的家庭，然后被悉心教导、培养成人。我做过一些生意，财富充裕，但我现在是孤身一人了。我结过婚，有

in the world, poor or rich, there was a well developed psyche, the self—centred activity. It is strange, as you look back upon it, that it begins from very early childhood, that possessive continuity of me as J. Smith. He went through school, expanding, aggressive, arrogant, bored, then into college and university. And as my father was in a good business I went into his Company. I reached the top, and on the death of my wife and children, I began this enquiry.

As happens to all human beings, it was a shock, a pain—the loss of the three, the memories associated with them. And when the shock of it was over I began to enquire, to read, to ask, to travel in different parts of the world, talking the matter over with some of the so—called spiritual leaders, the gurus. I read a great deal but I was never satisfied. So I think we ought to begin, if I may suggest, with the actual living—the daily building up of my cultivated, circumscribed mind. And I am that. You see, my life has been that. My life is nothing exceptional. Probably I would be considered upper middle class, and for a time it was pleasurable, exciting, and at other times dull, weary, and monotonous. But the death of my wife and children somehow pulled me out of that. I haven't become morbid but I want to know the truth of it all, if there is such a thing as truth about living and dying."

"How is the psyche, the ego, the self, the I, the person, put together? How has this thing come into being, from which arises the concept of the individual, the "me", separate from all others? How is this momentum set going—this momentum, this sense of the I, the self? We will use the word "self" to include the person, the name, the form, the characteristics, the ego. How is this self born? Does the self come into being with certain characteristics transmitted from the parents? Is the self merely a series of

过两个孩子，但他们都在一次车祸中丧生了。此后我没再结婚。我想我应该从我的童年开始说起。就像世上的其他任何一个孩子一样，无论贫富，从一开始，我们都有一个充分发展的心智，有着自我中心的行为。当你回溯过去，你会发现，作为 J. 史密斯延续下来的占有欲强烈的我，从童年初期就存在了，这很奇怪。他上了学，膨胀、好斗、傲慢、无聊，然后又上了学院和大学。而由于我父亲生意做得很好，我就进了他的公司。我到达了人生的巅峰，然后我妻子和孩子的死，让我开始了这场探寻。

"就像对所有人一样，这是一场打击、一次剧痛——痛失三位亲人，以及与他们息息相关的诸多回忆。当打击过后，我开始了探究、阅读和询问，我周游世界各地，与一些所谓的灵性导师、古鲁探讨这个问题。我涉猎广泛，但从未觉得满足。所以，如果可以，我想我们应该从实际的生活开始——我那颗被培植出来的受限的心是如何日渐强大的。而我就是它。你知道，我的生活就是它。我的生活没什么优越的。也许在别人看来，我属于上层社会，而曾经一度那种生活让人觉得很快乐、很刺激，但其余的时候则是枯燥、乏味、单调的。但是我妻子和儿子的死或多或少把我从这种生活中拉了出来。我心理上并没有变得病态，但我想知道这一切的真相，如果关于生与死存在所谓真相的话。"

"心智、自我、自己、我、这个人，是如何产生的？这个东西是如何出现的？——从中就产生了与他人相分离的个体、'我'的概念。这种动力、这种自我感是如何启动的？我们用'自我'这个词来

reactions? Is the self merely the continuity of centuries of tradition? Is the self put together by circumstances, through accidents, happenings? Is the self the result of evolution—evolution being the gradual process of time, emphasizing, giving importance to the self? Or, as some maintain, especially the religious world, does the outward shell of the self really contain within itself the soul and the ancient concept of the Hindus, of the Buddhists? Does the self come into being through the society which man has created, which gives strength to the formula that you are separate from the rest of humanity?

All these have certain truths in them, certain facts, and all these constitute the self. And the self has been given tremendous importance in this world. The expression of the self in the democratic world is called freedom, and in the totalitarian world, that freedom is suppressed, denied and punished. So would you say that instinct begins in the child with the urge to possess? This also exists in the animals, so perhaps we have derived from the animals this instinct to possess. Where there is any kind of possession there must be the beginning of the self. And from this instinct, this reaction, the self gradually increases in strength, in vitality, and becomes well—established. The possession of a house, the possession of land, the possession of knowledge, the possession of certain capacities— all this is the movement of the self. And this movement gives the feeling of separateness as the individual.

"Now you can go much further into details: is the you, the self, separate from the rest of mankind? Are you, because you have a separate name, a separate physical organism, certain tendencies different from another's, perhaps a talent—does that make you an individual? This idea that each one of us throughout the world is separate from another, is that

涵盖这个人，他的姓名、外形、性格与自我。这个自我是如何产生的？自我是不是带着从父母那里继承来的某些个性形成的？自我是不是只是一系列的反应？自我是不是只是千百年来传统的延续？自我是通过发生的事故、事件由环境形成的吗？自我是进化的结果吗？——进化就是渐进的时间过程，强调了自我，赋予了它重要性。还是说，就像有些人声称的那样——特别是宗教界——自我的外壳真的包含着灵魂，包含着印度教徒、佛教徒所秉持的那个古老概念吗？自我是不是通过人类建立的这个社会形成的？而社会加强了这个观念——你是分离于其他人而存在的。

"这些都具有某种真实性、某种事实性的东西，这些都构成了自我。而自我在这个世界上被赋予了超乎寻常的重要性。自我在民主世界的表达被称为自由，而在极权主义的世界，那种自由受到了压制、否定和惩罚。那么你会不会说，那种本能从小孩子就开始了，并且表现为占有的欲望？这种本能在动物身上也存在，所以或许我们这种占有的本能是从动物那里得来的。哪里有任何形式的占有，自我就必然会在哪里出现。而借助这种本能、这种反应，自我的力量和生命力会逐渐强大，进而变得根深蒂固。占有房子、土地、知识和某些能力——这些都是自我的活动，而这种活动带来了我们都是个体的分离感。

"现在你可以探究得更细致一些：你、自己，与其他人是分开的吗？因为你有个单独的名字、单独的身体，有些与众不同的性情，或许还有某种天赋——这些就让你成为一个个体了吗？我们全世界的每一个人都与他人是分开的，这个想法是事实吗？还是说，这整个概念

an actuality? Or may the whole concept be illusory just as we have divided the world into separate communities, nations, which is really a glorified form of tribalism? This concern with oneself and the community being different from other communities, other selves—is that in actuality real?

Of course you may say it is real because you are an American, and others are French, Russian, Indian, Chinese and so on. This linguistic, cultural, religious difference has brought about havoc in the world—terrible wars, incalculable harm. And also, of course, in certain aspects there is great beauty in it, in the expression of certain talents, as a painter, as a musician, as a scientist and so on. Would you consider yourself as a separate individual with a separate brain which is yours and nobody else's? It is your thinking, and your thinking is supposedly different from another's. But is thinking individual at all? Or is there only thinking, which is shared by all humanity, whether you are the most scientifically talented person or the most ignorant, primitive?

"All these questions and more arise when we are considering the death of a human being. So would you, looking at all this—the reactions, the name, the form, the possessiveness, the impulse to be separate from another, sustained by society and by religion—would you in examining all this logically, sanely, reasonably, consider yourself to be an individual? This is an important question in the context of the meaning of death."

"I see what you are driving at. I have an intuitive comprehension, cognizance, that as long as I think that I am an individual, my thinking is separate from the thinking of others—my anxiety, my sorrow is separate from the rest of humanity. I have a feeling—please correct me—that I have reduced a vast complex living of the rest of mankind to a very small, petty little affair. Are you saying in effect that I am not an individual at all? My

都是虚幻的，就像我们把世界分割成了社团、国家一样？而国家实际上不过是一种美化了的部落主义。对自己的这种关心，认为自己的社团与其他社团、其他自我不同——这是千真万确的事实吗？

"当然，你也许会说那是真实的，因为你是一个美国人，而其他人是法国人、俄罗斯人、印度人、中国人等。这种语言上、文化上、宗教上的差异造成了世界上的混乱——可怕的战争和不计其数的伤害。当然了，在某些方面也存在着非凡的美，在某些天赋的表达中，比如作为一个画家、一个音乐家、一个科学家等。你会认为自己是一个分离的个体，有着一个不属于别人而只属于你自己的独立的大脑吗？那是你的思想，而你的思想看起来似乎与别人不同。但思想究竟是不是独特的？还是说存在的只有思想而已，它为全人类所共有，无论你极具科学天赋还是极其蒙昧无知？

"当我们思考人的死亡问题时，这些问题以及更多的问题就会出现。那么，当你看着这一切——所有的反应、名字、外形、占有欲、与他人分离开来的冲动，这些都被社会和宗教维系着——当你合乎逻辑地、理性地、清醒地审视这一切时，你还会认为自己是一个个体吗？在探讨死亡的含义时，这是一个非常重要的问题。"

"我明白你所指向的意思了。我有一种直觉的理解和认识，那就是只要我认为自己是个个体，我的思想就与别人的思想隔离开了——我的焦虑、我的哀伤与其他人是隔离开的。我有一种感觉——请纠正我——我把整个人类广阔而复杂的生命缩减成了一件非常狭窄、非常琐碎的小事情。你实际上是不是说，我根本不是一个个体？我的思想

thinking is not mine? And my brain is not mine, separate from others? Is this what you are hinting at? Is this what you are maintaining? Is this your conclusion?"

"If one may point out, the word 'conclusion' isn't justified. To conclude means to shut down, to end—conclude an argument, conclude a peace after a war. We are not concluding anything; we are just pointing out, because we must move away from conclusions, from finality and so on. Such an assertion limits, brings a narrowness into our enquiry. But the *fact*, the observable rational fact, is that your thinking and the thinking of another are similar. The expression of your thinking may vary; you may express something in one way if you are an artist, and another person, who is not an artist, may express it in another way. You judge, evaluate, according to the expression, and the expression then divides you into an artist and a football player. But you, as an artist, and he, as a football player, *think*. The football player and the artist suffer, are anxious, have great pain, disappointment, apprehension; one believes in god and the other doesn't believe in god, one has faith and the other has no faith, but this is common to all human beings, though each one may think he is different.

You may think my sorrow is entirely different from another's, that my loneliness, my desperation, are wholly opposite to another's. Our tradition is that, our conditioning is that, we are educated to that—I am an Arab, you are a Jew, and so on. And from this division there arises not only individuality but the communal racial difference. The individual identifying himself with a community, with a nation, with a race, with a religion invariably brings conflict between human beings. It is a natural law. But we are only concerned with the effects, not with the causes of war, causes of this division.

不是我的？我的大脑也不是我的，和别人也不是分开的？这就是你暗示的意思吗？这就是你的主张吗？这是你的结论吗？"

"恕我冒昧指出，'结论'这个词并不恰当。下结论意味着关闭和结束——下定论断，战后缔结和平。我们不是在下定任何结论，我们只是在指出事实，因为我们必须远离结论、定局之类的东西。那种定论会带来局限，会让我们的探索变得狭隘。然而，**事实**，可以观察的合理的事实是，你的思想和另一个人的思想是相似的。你的思想可能有各种不同的表达方式，如果你是个艺术家，你也许会用一种方式表达一件事情，而另一个人不是艺术家，他就会用另一种方式来表达。你会根据表达方式来评估、来判断，于是表达方式就把你们划分成了艺术家和足球运动员。然而，作为艺术家的你和作为足球运动员的他，**都思考**。足球运动员和艺术家都受苦，都焦虑，都经受着巨大的痛苦、失望和恐惧。一个人相信上帝而另一个人不信，一个人有信仰而另一个人没有，但思想这件事对于所有人类来说都是共有的，尽管每个人可能都认为自己与众不同。

"你也许认为，我的忧伤与别人迥然不同，我的孤独、我的绝望与别人完全相反。我们的传统就是这样，我们所受的制约就是这样，我们接受的教育就是这样——我是个阿拉伯人，而你是个犹太人，诸如此类。而从这种划分中不仅仅产生了个体性，还产生了群体之间的种族分别。一个人让自己与群体、国家、种族、宗教相互认同，这不可避免地会造成人与人之间的冲突，这是自然规律。但是我们只关心结果，却不关心战争的根源、这种分裂的根源。

"So we are merely pointing out, not asserting, not concluding, that you, sir, are the rest of humanity, psychologically, deeply. Your reactions are shared by all humanity. Your brain is not yours, it has evolved through centuries of time. You may be conditioned as a Christian, believe in various dogmas, rituals; another has his own god, his own rituals, but all this is put together by thought. So we are questioning deeply whether there is an individual at all. We are the whole of humanity; we are the rest of mankind. This is not a romantic, fantastic, statement, and it is important, necessary, when we are going to talk over together the meaning of death.

"What do you say to all this, sir?"

"I must say I am rather puzzled by all these questions. I am not certain why I have always considered myself to be separate from you or from somebody else. What you say seems to be true but I must think it over, I must have a little time to assimilate all that you have said so far."

"Time is the enemy of perception. If you are going to think over what we have talked about so far, argue with yourself, discuss what has been said, analyse what we have talked over together, it is going to take time. And time is a brand new factor in the perception of that which is true. Anyhow, shall we leave it for the moment?"

He came back after a couple of days and he seemed more quiet and rather concerned. It was a cloudy morning and probably it was going to rain. In this part of the world they need much more rain because beyond the hills there is a vast desert. It gets very cold here at night because of that.

"I have come back after a couple of days of quiet thinking. I have a house by the sea, I live by myself. It is one of those little seaside cottages and you have in front of you the beach and the blue Pacific, and you can walk for miles on the beach. I generally go for long walks either in the

"所以，我们只是在这里指出来——而不是下断语、下结论——先生，从心理上、从深层上讲，你就是其他人类。你的反应由全体人类所共有。你的大脑不是你自己的，它是经过千百年时间的进化而来的。你也许受到了身为基督教徒的制约，相信各种教条和仪式；而另一个人有他自己的神明、他自己的仪式，但这一切都是由思想拼凑而成的。所以我们在深深地质疑个体究竟是否存在。我们就是整个人类，我们就是其他人类。这不是一个浪漫的、异想天开的说法，而当我们要一起探讨死亡的含义时，这一点是非常重要、必不可少的。

"对于以上所说，你有什么看法，先生？"

"我必须承认，我自己对这些问题都感到相当困惑。我不确定为什么我总是认为自己和你或者别人是分开的。你说的话听起来很对，但是我必须把它想清楚，我必须花些时间来吸收你之前所说的这些话。"

"时间是洞察的敌人。如果你要努力思考我们刚才说的那些话，和你自己争论，或者讨论、分析我们一起谈到的内容，那是要花时间的。而对于洞察真相来说，时间是一个全新的因素。不管怎样，我们可以先把这个问题暂且搁下吗？"

几天之后他又来了，看起来更加安静，同时也思虑重重。那是个浓云密布的早晨，天也许会下雨。地球的这个部分需要更多的雨水，因为山那边就是广袤的沙漠。这里的夜晚因此而变得很冷。

"经过了几天安静的思考之后，我又回来了。我在海边有座房子，我一个人住在那里。那是海滨小屋中的一座，屋前就是海滩和蓝色的太平洋，你可以沿着海滩走上几英里。在见过你之后，有一天我

morning or evening. After seeing you the other day I took a walk along the beach, probably about five miles or more, and I decided to come back and see you again. I was at first very disturbed. I couldn't quite make out what you were saying, what you were pointing out to me. Though I am rather a sceptical person about these matters, I allowed what you were saying to occupy my mind. It wasn't that I was inwardly accepting or denying it, but it intrigued me, and I purposely use the word "allow"—to allow it to enter into my mind.And after some deliberation I took a car and drove along by the coast and then turned inland and came here. It is a beautiful valley. I am glad to find you here. So could we continue with what we were talking about the other day?

"If I understand it clearly, you were pointing out that tradition, long conditioned thinking, can bring about a fixation, a concept that one readily accepts, perhaps not with a great deal of thought—accepts the idea that we are separate individuals; and as I thought more about it—I am using the word "thought" in its ordinary sense, thinking, rationalizing, questioning, arguing—it was as though I was having a discussion with myself, a prolonged dialogue, and I think I really do grasp what is involved in that. I see what we have done with the marvellous world we live in. I see the whole historical sequence. And after considerable to and fro of thought I really do understand the depth and the truth of what you said. So if you have time I would like to go much further into all this. I really came to find out, as you know, about death, but I see the importance of beginning with one's comprehension of oneself, and through the door of the self—if one can use the word—come to the question of what is death."

"As we were saying the other day, we share, all humanity shares, the sunlight [he had not said this]; that sunlight is not yours or mine. It is the

沿着海边散步，可能大约走了五英里或者更远，然后我就决定要再回来见你。起初我感觉非常不安，我不太明白你说的话，不明白你向我指出的内容。尽管对于这些问题我抱着非常怀疑的态度，我还是允许你的话占据了我的心。这并不是说我内心接受了或者拒绝了你说的话，而是它让我着迷。我故意用了'允许'这个词——允许它进入我的心。深思熟虑之后，我上了车，沿着海岸线一路驶来，然后转向内陆，接着就来到了这里。这是一座美丽的山谷。我很高兴能在这里找到你。我们可以继续那天的话题吗？

"如果我清楚地理解了你的意思，你指出的是传统、局限良久的思想会造成一种僵化，一个人们也许不假思索就愿意接受的概念——接受这个概念：我们是分离的个体；而由于我对此进行了更多的思考——我用'思考'这个词指的是通常的含义，思考、推理、质疑、讨论——就好像我在跟自己讨论一样，那是一次长长的对话，我认为我真的领会了其中的含义。我看到了我们在自己所生活的这个神奇妙的世界上都做了什么，我看到了这整个历史的进程。在进行了反反复复的大量思考之后，我真的领悟了你所说的话的深度和真相。所以，如果你有时间的话，我希望能够更深入地探讨这些问题。如你所知，我来实际上是想弄清楚死亡的真相，但是我发现了从对自己的了解开始的重要性，穿过自我这扇门——如果我可以用这个词的话——就可以探究死亡是什么这个问题了。"

"正如我们那天所说，我们所有的人类，都共享着阳光（注：他并没有这么说过）；阳光不属于你也不属于我。它就是我们所有人共

life—giving energy which we all share. The beauty of a sunset, if you are watching it sensitively, is shared by all human beings. It is not yours setting in the west, east, north or south; it is the sunset that is important. And our consciousness, in which is included our reactions and actions, our ideas and concepts and patterns, systems of belief, ideologies, fears, pleasures, faith, the worship of something which we have projected, our sorrows, our griefs and pain—all this is shared by all human beings. When we suffer we have made it into a personal affair. We shut out all the suffering of mankind. Like pleasure; we treat pleasure as a private thing, ours, the excitement of it and so on. We forget that man—including woman, of course, which we needn't repeat—that man has suffered from time beyond all measure. And that suffering is the ground on which we all stand. It is shared by all human beings.

"So our consciousness is not actually yours or mine; it is the consciousness of man, evolved, grown, accumulated through many, many centuries. In that consciousness is the faith, the gods, all the rituals man has invented. It is really an activity of thought; it is thought that has made the content—behaviour, action, culture, aspiration; the whole activity of man is the activity of thought. And this consciousness is the self, is the "me", the I, the ego, the personality and so on. I think it is necessary to understand this very deeply, not merely argumentatively, logically but deeply, as blood is in all of us, is part of us, is the essence, the natural process of all human beings. When one realizes this our responsibility becomes extraordinarily important. We are responsible for everything that is happening in the world as long as the content of our consciousness continues. As long as fear, nationalities, the urge for success, you know the whole business of it—as long as that exists we are part of humanity, part of the human movement.

享的那种孕育生命的能量。夕阳的美，如果你敏锐地观察，是由全人类所共享的。无论落在东西南北哪个方向，它都不属于你，重要的是那轮落日。而我们的意识，其中囊括了我们的反应和行动，我们的观点、概念和模式，我们信仰和意识形态的体系，我们的恐惧、欢愉和信念，对我们投射出来的事物的膜拜，我们的悲伤、不幸和痛苦——这一切都为全人类所共有。而当我们受苦时，我们却把它变成了一件个人的事情。我们将人类的所有苦难拒之门外。就像欢愉一样，我们把它当成了一件私人的事情，当成了我们自己的刺激等。我们忘了人类——当然也包括女人，这无须重申——自远古以来就一直在受苦。而这种苦难就是我们所有人立足的基础，它为所有人类所共有。

"所以说我们的意识实际上并不是你的或我的；它是人类的意识，经过了千百年来的进化、成长和积累。那个意识中有人类发明的信仰、神明以及所有的仪式。它实际上是一种思想活动，是思想造出了这些内容——行为、活动、文化、渴望；人类的所有活动都是思想的活动。而这个意识就是自我，就是那个'我'、那个自己、那个人格等。我认为需要非常深刻地理解这一点，不只是从辩论和逻辑的角度，而是深刻地理解，就像我们所有人身上流淌的血液一样，是我们的一部分、我们的精髓，是全人类身上发生的一个再自然不过的进程。当你认识到这一点，我们的责任就会显得无比重大。只要我们意识的内容还在延续，我们就要为世界上所发生的一切负责。只要恐惧、国家、对成功的渴望还存在——你知道这所有的把戏——只要这些存在，我们就是人类的一部分、人类运动的一部分。

"This is utterly important to understand. It is so: the self is put together by thought. Thought is not, as we have said, yours or mine; thinking is not individual thinking. Thinking is shared by all human beings. And when one has really deeply seen the significance of this, then I think we can understand the nature of what it means to die.

"As a boy you must have followed a small stream gurgling along a narrow little valley, the waters running faster and faster, and have thrown something, such as a piece of stick, into the stream and followed it, down a slope, over a little mound, through a little crevasse—followed it until it went over the waterfall and disappeared. This disappearance is our life.

"What does death mean? What is the very word, the threatening feeling about it? We never seem to accept it."

"了解这一点真的极其重要，那就是：自我由思想所造。正如我们所说，思想不是你的也不是我的；思想不是个人的，思想由全人类所共有。而当你真正深刻地看到了其中的含义，那么我想我们就可以了解死亡的含义和本质了。

"小时候，你肯定沿着小峡谷里一条潺潺的小溪走过，溪水越流越快，你会把一些东西，比如一根木棍丢到溪水里，然后跟着它一路走下去，越过山坡，跨过小丘，穿过裂缝——跟着它，直到它跨越瀑布消失无踪。这种消失就是我们的生命。

"死亡意味着什么？这个词本身，关于它的这种威胁感究竟是什么？我们似乎从未接受它。"

Wednesday, March 16, 1983

(Continuing the dialogue of the 15th)

"Man has killed man in different states of mind. He has killed him for religious reasons, he has killed him for patriotic reasons, for peace, killed him through organized war. This has been our lot, killing each other endlessly.

"Sir, have you considered this kind of killing, what sorrow has come to man—the immense sorrow of mankind which has gone on through the ages, the tears, the agony, the brutality, the fear of it all? And it is still going on. The world is sick. The politicians, whether left, right, centre, or totalitarian, are not going to bring about peace. Each one of us is responsible, and being responsible we must see that the slaughter comes to an end so that we live on this earth, which is ours, in beauty and peace. It is an immense tragedy which we do not face or want to resolve. We leave it all to the experts; and the danger of experts is as dangerous as a deep precipice or a poisonous snake.

"So leaving all that aside, what is the meaning of death? What to you, sir, does death mean?"

"To me it means that all I have been, all that I am, suddenly comes to an end through some disease, accident or old age.Of course I have read and talked to Asiatics, to Indians, for whom there is a belief in reincarnation. I

1983 年 3 月 16 日，星期三

（继续 15 日的对话）

"人类曾在各种不同的心态下互相残杀。他为了宗教原因杀害别人，为了爱国主义的原因、为了和平，通过有组织的战争去杀害别人。这一直是我们的命运——无止境地互相残杀。

"先生，你有没有思考过这种杀戮行为？人类遭遇了怎样的悲伤——世世代代以来人类所经历的无尽悲伤，以及所有的泪水、痛苦、残暴与恐惧？而这一切还在继续。这个世界已经病入膏肓。政客们，无论是左派、右派、中间派还是极权主义者，都不会带来和平。我们每个人都对此负有责任，而要负责我们就必须确保结束这场屠杀，这样我们才能在这个属于我们大家的地球上活得美丽、活得和平。这是一个我们不去面对也不想解决的巨大悲剧。我们把它留给了专家去解决，而专家就像深不见底的悬崖或者毒蛇一样危险。

"抛开这一切，死亡的意义又是什么呢？先生，对你来说，死亡意味着什么？"

"对我来说，死亡就意味着我过去曾是的一切、我现在所是的一切，因为疾病、意外或者年迈而突然结束了。当然，我读了不少书，

don't know whether this is true or not, but as far as I can understand, death means the ending of a living thing; the death of a tree, the death of a fish, death of a spider, death of my wife and children, a sudden cutting off, a sudden ending of that which has been living with all its memories, ideas, pain, anxiety, joys, pleasures, seeing the sunset together—all that has come to an end. And the remembrance of all that, not only brings tears but also the realization of one's own inadequacy, one's own loneliness. And the idea of separation from one's wife and children, from the things that one has worked for, cherished, remembered, held on to, the attachments and the pain of attachment—all that and more ceases suddenly. I think we generally mean that; death means that. It is to me the ending.

"There's a picture of my wife and the children on the piano in my cottage by the sea. We used to play the piano together. There is the remembrance of them in the picture on the piano, but the actuality has gone. Remembrance is painful, or remembrance may give one pleasure, but the pleasure is rather fading because sorrow is overriding. All that to me means death.

"We had a very nice Persian cat, a very beautiful thing. And one morning it had gone. It was on the front porch. It must have eaten something—there it was, lifeless, meaningless; it will never purr again. That is death. The ending of a long life, or the ending of a new born baby. I had a small new plant once which promised to grow into a healthy tree. But some thoughtless, unobservant person passed by, trod on it, and it will never be a great tree. That is also a form of death. The ending of a day, a day that has been poor or rich and beautiful, can also be called death. The beginning and the ending."

也跟亚洲人、印度人探讨过这个问题，他们抱有轮回转世的信仰。我不知道那个信念是真是假，但据我的理解，死亡意味着一样活着的东西终止了；一棵树的死，一条鱼的死，一个蜘蛛的死，我妻子和孩子的死，那是一种突然的切断、突然的结束，过去一直活着的东西，有着无数的记忆、思绪、痛苦、焦虑、喜悦、快乐，一起看日落——这一切都结束了。对此的所有回忆，不仅仅带来了眼泪，也让我意识到了自己的贫乏和孤独。而想到与妻子、孩子的别离，离开了我一直为之奋斗、视若珍宝、念念不忘、紧紧依附的那些东西，各种依附，还有依附带来的痛苦——那些东西都突然终结了。我想我们通常所说的死亡就是这个含义。对我来说，它就是结束。

"在我海边的小屋里，钢琴上放着我妻子和孩子的照片。我们过去经常一起弹钢琴。钢琴上的照片里有对他们的回忆，可他们本人已经故去。回忆是痛苦的，或者回忆也能给我带来片刻欢愉，但那种欢愉正在褪去，因为悲痛正汹涌而来。这一切对我来说都意味着死亡。

"我们养过一只非常漂亮的波斯猫，小东西非常美丽。可一天早上它也死了，就在前门廊那里。它肯定吃了什么东西——它就躺在那里，毫无生气，毫无意义，它再也不会咕噜咕噜叫了。这就是死亡。年迈生命的死，或者新生婴儿的死。我曾经种下一棵小植物，它本应长成一棵健硕的树。但是有个粗心大意、毫不留心的人经过的时候践踏了它，它再也不会长成一棵大树了。这也是一种死亡。一天的结束，无论是贫穷还是富有、美好的一天，它的结束也可以称为死亡。先是开始，然后结束。"

"Sir, what is living? From the moment one is born until one dies, what is living? It is very important to understand the way we live—why we live this way after so many centuries. It is up to you, is it not, sir, if it is one constant struggle? Conflict, pain, joy, pleasure, anxiety, loneliness, depression, and working, working, working, labouring for others or for oneself; being self—centred and perhaps occasionally generous, envious, angry, trying to suppress the anger, letting that anger go rampant, and so on. This is what we call living—tears, laughter, sorrow, and the worship of something that we have invented; living with lies, illusions and hatred, the weariness of it all, the boredom, the inanities: this is our life. Not only yours but the life of all human beings on this earth, hoping to escape from it all. This process of worship, agony, fear has gone on from the ancient of days until now—labour, strife, pain, uncertainty, confusion, and joy and laughter. All this is part of our existence.

"The ending of all this is called death. Death puts an end to all our attachments, however superficial or however deep. The attachment of the monk, the sannyasi, the attachment of the housewife, the attachment to one's family, every form of attachment must end with death.

"There are several problems involved in this: one, the question of immortality. Is there such a thing as immortality? That is, that which is not mortal, for mortal implies that which knows death. The immortal is that which is beyond time and is totally unaware of this ending. Is the self, the "me", immortal? Or does it know death? The self can never become immortal. The "me", the I, with all its qualities is put together through time, which is thought; that self can never be immortal. One can invent an idea of immortality, an image, a god, a picture and hold to that and derive comfort from it, but that is not immortality.

"先生，什么是活着？一个人从生到死，活着又是什么？了解我们的生活方式，这非常重要——我们为什么过了千百年之后还是这样活着。生活是不是一场不停的挣扎，这取决于你，不是吗，先生？冲突、痛苦、喜悦、快乐、焦虑、孤独、沮丧，还有不停地工作、工作、工作，为了别人或者为了自己辛苦劳作；一直自私自利——也许偶尔闪现一丝慷慨——嫉妒、愤怒，试图压抑愤怒，或者让愤怒猖狂爆发，等等等等。这就是我们所谓的生活——泪水、欢笑、悲伤，还有对我们所发明的东西的膜拜；与谎言、幻觉和仇恨生活在一起，还有所有的枯燥、乏味、浅薄：这就是我们的生活。这不只是你的生活，这个地球上所有人类的生活都是如此，都希望能够从中逃离。这个膜拜、痛苦和恐惧的过程，自远古时代一直延续到了现在——辛劳、挣扎、痛苦、不确定、困惑，还有喜悦和欢笑。这一切都是我们生命的一部分。

"这一切的终结被称为死亡。死亡结束了我们所有的依附，无论层次深浅。僧侣、隐士的依附，家庭主妇的依附，对自己家庭的依附，所有形式的依附都必定会随着死亡而终结。

"其中涉及几个问题，首先是不朽的问题。究竟存在不朽这回事吗？也就是不会灭亡的东西，因为灭亡就意味着死亡。不朽是超越时间的，它完全不知道这种终结。自我、'我'是不朽的吗？还是说它是知道死亡的？自我永远无法变得不朽。'自我'、我，连同他所有的品质，都是由时间即思想所造；自我永远无法不朽。你可以发明不朽的概念、形象、神明和画面，然后紧抓不放，从中获得慰藉，但那

"Secondly (this is a little bit more complex): is it possible to live with death? Not morbidly, not in any form of self—destructiveness. Why have we divided death from living? Death is part of our life, it is part of our existence—the dying and the living, and the living and dying. They are inseparable. The envy, the anger, the sorrow, the loneliness, and the pleasure that one has, which we call living, and this thing called death—why separate them? Why keep them miles apart? Yes, miles of time apart. We accept the death of an old man. It is natural. But when a young person dies through some accident or disease, we revolt against it. We say that it is unfair, it shouldn't be. So we are always separating life and death. This is a problem which we should question, understand—or not treat as a problem, but look at, see the inward implications of, not deceptively.

"Another question is the issue of time—the time involved in living, learning, accumulating, acting, doing, and the ending of time as we know it; the time that separates the living from the ending. Where there is separation, division, from here to there, from "what is" to "what should be", time is involved. Sustaining this division between that which is called death and that which is called life, is to me a major factor.

"When there is this division, this separation, there is fear. Then there is the effort of overcoming that fear and the search for comfort, satisfaction, for a sense of continuity. (We are talking about the psychological world not the physical world or the technical world.) It is time that has put the self together and it is thought that sustains the ego, the self. If only one could really grasp the significance of time and division, the separation, psychologically, of man against man, race against race, one type of culture against another. This separation, this division, is brought about by thought and time, as living and dying. And to live a life with death means

并不是不朽。

"其次（这个问题要稍微复杂一些），有没有可能与死亡一起生活？但不是死气沉沉地活着，也不是采取任何一种自我毁灭的生活方式。我们为什么把死亡和生命割裂开来？死亡就是我们生命的一部分，就是我们存在的一部分——死与生，生与死，它们是不可分割的。一个人拥有的嫉妒、愤怒、悲伤、孤独和快乐，我们称之为生活，而这件事情我们叫作死亡——为什么要把它们分开？为什么把它们远远分开？是的，隔着广袤的时间。我们接受年迈者的亡故，认为这很正常。但是，当一个年轻人因为意外或者疾病而去世，我们就感到十分厌恶。我们说这不公平，事情不应该这样。所以说我们总是把生死分离开来。这是我们应该质问和了解的一个问题——或者不是把它当作一个问题，而是去看一看，毫不自欺地看看它内在的含义。

"另一个问题则是时间的问题——时间包含在了生活、学习、积累、行动、做事当中，还有我们所知道的时间的终结，以及把生与死隔离开来的时间。而哪里有由此及彼、从'现在如何'到'应该如何'的隔离和分裂，时间就会涉入。维系所谓的死亡和所谓的生活之间的这种分离，在我看来是一个主要的因素。

"哪里有这种分裂和隔离，哪里就会有恐惧。然后你就会努力去战胜那种恐惧，同时寻求安慰和满足，寻求一种延续感。（我们在这里谈的是心理世界，而不是物理世界或者科技世界。）正是时间造就了自我，正是时间维系了我、自我。你真的需要领会心理上的分裂和隔离的含义，人对抗人，种族对抗种族，一种文化对抗另一种文化。

a profound change in our whole outlook on existence. To end attachment without time and motive, that is dying while living.

"Love has no time. It is not my love opposed to your love. Love is never personal; one may love another but when that love is limited, narrowed down to one person, then it ceases to be love. Where there really is love there is no division of time, thought and all the complexities of life, all the misery and confusion, the uncertainties, jealousies, anxieties involved. One has to give a great deal of attention to time and thought. Not that one must live only in the present, which would be utterly meaningless. Time is the past, modified and continuing as the future. It's a continuum and thought holds on, clings to this. It clings to something which it has itself created, put together.

"Another question is: as long as human beings represent the entire humanity—you are the entire humanity, not representing it, just as you are the world and the world is you—what happens when you die? When you or another die, you and the other are the manifestation of that vast stream of human action and reaction, the stream of consciousness, of behaviour and so on: you are of that stream. That stream has conditioned the human mind, the human brain, and as long as we remain conditioned by greed, envy, fear, pleasure, joy and all the rest of it, we are part of this stream. Your organism may end but you are of that stream, as you are, while living, that stream itself. That stream, changing, slow at times, fast at others, deep and shallow, narrowed by both sides of the bank and breaking through the narrowness into a vast volume of water—as long as you are of that stream there is no freedom. There is no freedom from time, from the confusion and the misery of all the accumulated memories and attachments. It is only when there is the ending of that stream, the ending, not you stepping out

生与死之间的这种隔离、这种分裂，是由思想和时间造成的。而与死亡生活在一起就意味着我们对生命的整个视角发生了深刻的改变。终结依附而不牵涉时间和动机，这就是活着的时候就死去。

"爱没有时间。它不是与你的爱相对立的我的爱。爱永远不是个人化的；你也许爱着别人，然而，当那份爱仅仅局限于一个人时，那就不再是爱了。哪里存在真正的爱，哪里就不会有时间、思想的划分，也不会有生活中所有的纷繁复杂——其中所包含的所有不幸、困惑、不确定、嫉妒和焦虑。你必须仔细审视时间和思想。这并不是说你必须活在当下，那将是毫无意义的。时间就是过去，稍做调整然后延续到将来。这是一种延续，而思想就依附其上，紧抓不放。它紧紧抓住它自己制造出来的、拼凑出来的东西。

"另一个问题则是：只要人们代表着全人类——你就是整个人类，而不是代表它，因为你就是世界，世界就是你——那么你死去时会发生什么？当你或另一个人死去，你和另一个人就是人类行动和反应的巨大洪流、意识的洪流、行为的洪流等的显现：你就属于那条洪流。那条洪流制约了人类的心灵、人类的大脑，而只要我们继续被贪婪、嫉妒、恐惧、快乐、喜悦以及诸如此类的东西所局限，我们就是这条洪流的一部分。你的身体也许会终结，但你依然属于那条洪流，就像活着的时候你就是那条洪流本身一样。那条洪流一直在变化，时慢时快，有深有浅，时而被堤岸变窄，时而冲破堤岸汇成巨流——但是只要你还属于那条洪流，就没有自由可言，就没有从时间、从累积的所有记忆和依附的困惑和苦难中解脱出来的自由。只有当终结了那

of it and becoming something else, but the ending of it, only then is there quite a different dimension. That dimension cannot be measured by words. The ending without a motive is the whole significance of dying and living. The roots of heaven are in living and dying."

条洪流——终结，不是你从中迈了出来然后变成了别的什么，而是终结它——只有此时才会出现一个截然不同的维度。这个维度无法用言语度量。毫无动机地终结，就是生与死的全部意义。极乐的根源就在生死之中。"

Thursday, March 17, 1983

The clouds were very low this morning. It rained last night, not too much but it has left the earth watered, rich, nourished. Considering, on a morning like this with the hills floating among the clouds and with those skies, the enormous energy that man has expended on this earth, the vast technological progress in the last fifty years, all the rivers more or less polluted and the waste of energy in this everlasting entertainment, it all seems so strange and so sick.

On the veranda this morning time is not very near to man, time as movement, time as going from here to there, time to learn, time to act, time as a means of changing from this to that in the ordinary things of life. One can understand that time is necessary to learn a language, to learn a skill, to build an aeroplane, to put together a computer, to travel around the world; the time of youth, the time of old age, time as the setting of the sun and of the sun rising slowly over the hills, the long shadows and the growth of a slowly maturing tree, time to become a good gardener, a good carpenter and so on. In the physical world, in physical action, time to learn becomes necessary and useful.

Is it that we carry over, extend, the same usage of time into the psychological world? Extend this way of thinking, acting, learning into the world inside the skin, into the area of the psyche, as hope, as becoming

1983 年 3 月 17 日，星期四

这天早上，云层很低。昨晚刚下过雨，雨不大，但足以灌溉土地，让大地显得富饶、肥沃。群山在云层里蜿蜒出没，绵延到天边，在这样的一个清晨，思考人类在这个地球上所耗费的能量，过去五十年来巨大的科技进步，所有的河流都遭遇了不同程度的污染，人们把能量浪费在了无止境的消遣娱乐之中，这看起来都是那么奇怪、那么病态。

在今天清早的露台上，时间似乎远离了人类——作为运动的时间，由此及彼的时间，用来学习、行动的时间，时间是日常生活中实现从这到那的改变所用的工具。你能明白学习一门语言、一门技术，建造飞机、组装电脑、周游世界，都是需要时间的；年轻的时间，年迈的时间，太阳落下又缓缓爬上山顶的时间，一棵日渐成熟的树垂下长影和成长所需的时间，成为一名优秀的园丁、一名好木匠等需要的时间。在物理世界中，在身体活动中，学习的时间是必要的、有用的。

然而，我们是不是把时间的这种用途原样照搬到了、延伸到了心理世界？把这种思考、行动和学习的方式，以希望、成为什么和自

something, as self improvement? It sounds rather absurd—the changing from this to that, from "what is"to "what should be" . Time is necessary, one thinks, to change the whole complex quality of violence into that which is not violent.

Sitting quietly by yourself, overlooking the valley, wide and long, you could almost count the rows of orange trees, the beautifully kept orchards. Seeing the beauty of the earth, of the valley, does not involve time, but the translation of that perception on to a canvas or into a poem needs time. Perhaps we use time as a means of escaping from "what is" , from what we are, from what the future will be for ourselves and for the rest of mankind.

Time in the psychological realm is the enemy of man. We want the psyche to evolve, grow, expand, fulfil, turn itself into something more than what it is. We never question the validity of such a desire, of such a concept; we easily, perhaps happily, accept that the psyche can evolve, flourish, and that one day there will be peace and happiness. But actually there is no psychological evolution.

There is a hummingbird going from flower to flower, brightness in this quiet light, with such vitality in that little thing. The rapidity of the wings, so fantastically rhythmical, steady; it seems it can move forward and backward. It is a marvellous thing to watch it, to feel the delicacy, the bright colour, and wonder at its beauty, so small, so rapid and so quickly gone. And there is a mockingbird on the telephone wire. Another bird is sitting on the top of that tree overlooking the whole world. It has been there for over half an hour, never moving, but watching, moving its little head to see that there is no danger. And it too has gone now. The clouds are beginning to move away from the hills, and how green the hills are.

As we were saying, there is no psychological evolution. The psyche

我改善的形式，延伸到了体肤之内的世界，延伸到了心理领域？这听起来真的非常荒唐——从这变成那，从"现在如何"变成"应当如何"。人们以为，从这整个错综复杂的暴力变成非暴力，时间是必不可少的。

独自安静地坐着，俯瞰宽阔绵长的山谷，你几乎能数出橙树和打理得很漂亮的果园有多少排。望着美丽的大地和山谷，并不涉及时间，但是要把这份感知诉诸画布或者诗篇，就需要时间了。也许我们把时间当成了一种手段，用来逃避"现在如何"，逃避我们实际的样子，逃避面对我们自己以及全人类的未来将会如何。

心理世界的时间是人类的敌人。我们希望心智能够进化、成长、扩张、达成，把它变成某种超越它自身现状的东西。我们从不质疑这种愿望、这个概念的合理性；我们轻易地，或许还很开心地就接受了心智能够进化、茁壮成长，相信和平跟幸福终有一天会到来。然而事实上根本不存在心理上的进化。

有一只蜂鸟流连于花丛之中，在安详的晨光中显得格外明亮。那个小东西身上有着如此非凡的活力，快速扇动的翅膀，有着令人叹为观止的韵律感和稳定感；它看起来似乎可以随意地前后移动。看着它，感受它的优雅和明亮的色泽，真是一件奇妙的事，你会讶异于它的美，它是如此小巧、如此迅捷，然后又如此快速地消失在你的视野。电话线上站着一只知更鸟，另一只小鸟则坐在树顶俯瞰着全世界。它已经在那里待了半个多小时了，从未离开，只是看着，偶尔动动它的小脑袋，看看是不是有危险。现在它也飞走了。云层开始飘离

can never become or grow into something which it is not. Conceit and arrogance cannot grow into better and more conceit, nor can selfishness, which is the common lot of all human beings, become more and more selfish, more and more of its own nature. It is rather frightening to realize that the very word "hope" contains the whole world of the future. This movement from "what is" to "what should be" is an illusion, is really, if one can use the word, a lie. We accept what man has repeated throughout the ages as a matter of fact, but when we begin to question, doubt, we can see very clearly, if we want to see it and not hide behind some image or some fanciful verbal structure, the nature and the structure of the psyche, the ego, the "me". The "me" can never become a better me. It will attempt to, it thinks it can, but the "me" remains in subtle forms. The self hides in many garments, in many structures; it varies from time to time, but there is always this self, this separative, self—centred activity which imagines that one day it will make itself something which it is not.

So one sees there is no becoming of the self, there is only the ending of selfishness, of anxiety, of pain and sorrow which are the content of the psyche, of the "me". There is only the ending of that, and that ending does not require time. It isn't that it will all end the day after tomorrow. It will only end when there is the perception of its movement. To perceive not only objectively, without any prejudice, bias, but to perceive without all the accumulations of the past; to witness all this without the watcher— the watcher is of time and however much he may want to bring about a mutation in himself, he will always be the watcher; remembrances, however pleasurable, have no reality, they are things of the past, gone, finished, dead: only in observing without the observer, who is the past, does one see the nature of time and the ending of time.

群山，而那些小山是多么青翠！

正如我们所说，心理上不存在进化。心智永远无法变成或者成长为某种它所不是的东西。自负和傲慢无法成长为更优越、更严重的自负，自私——这一全人类共同的命运——也无法变得越来越自私，越来越合乎它的本质。意识到"希望"这个词本身就包含了未来的整个世界，真是一件相当可怕的事。从"现在如何"到"应当如何"的这种运动，是一个幻觉，实际上是一个谎言——如果我可以使用这个词的话。我们把人类世世代代以来重复的模式当作事实接受了下来，但是当我们开始质疑、开始怀疑，我们就能看得很清楚，如果我们想看清楚心智、自我、"我"的本质和结构，不想躲在某个形象或者某个异想天开的说法背后的话。"我"永远无法变成一个更好的我。它试图这么做，它以为自己能做到，但"我"还是以微妙的形式留存了下来。自我藏在各种外衣、各种架构之下；它随时在变化，但始终存在这个自我，这种分裂性的、自我中心的活动，想象着自己终有一天会变成一副与如今不同的样子。

所以你看到了自我成为什么并不存在，存在的只有自私、焦虑、痛苦和悲伤的终结，这些都是心智、"我"的内容。存在的只有它的终结，而这种终结是不需要时间的。并不是它会在后天终结，而是只有当你洞察了它的活动时，它才会终结。不仅要客观地洞察，不带任何偏见和成见，还要抛开过去的所有积累；见证一切而没有一个观察者——观察者是属于时间的，无论他多么希望让自身发生突变，他依然始终是个观察者；无论回忆有多么愉快，都没有丝毫真实性，它们是属于过去

The hummingbird has come back again. A ray of sunlight through the broken clouds has caught it, flashing its colours and the long thin beak and the rapidity of those wings. The pure watching of that little bird, without any reaction, just watching it, is to watch the whole world of beauty.

"I heard you the other day saying that time is the enemy of man. You explained something briefly about it. It seems such an outrageous statement. And you have made other similar statements. Some of them I have found to be true, natural, but one's mind never easily sees that which is actual, the truth, the fact, I was asking myself, and I have asked others too, why our minds have become so dull, so slow, why we cannot instantly see whether something is false or true? Why do we need explanations which seem so obvious when you have explained them? Why don't I, and any of us, see the truth of this fact? What has happened to our minds? I would like, if I may, to have a dialogue about it with you, to find out why my mind isn't subtle, quick. And can this mind, which has been trained and educated, ever become really, deeply, subtle, rapid, seeing something instantly, the quality and the truth or the falseness of it?"

"Sir, let's begin to enquire why we have become like this. It surely has nothing to do with old age. Is it the way of our life—the drinking, the smoking, the drugs, the bustle, the weariness, the everlasting occupation? Outwardly and inwardly we are occupied with something. Is it the very nature of knowledge? We are trained to acquire knowledge—through college, university, or in doing something skilfully. Is knowledge one of the factors of this lack of subtlety? Our brains are filled with so many facts, they have gathered so much information, from the television and from every newspaper and magazine, and they are recording as much as they can; they are absorbing, holding. So is knowledge one of the factors that

的、消失的、完结的、死去的东西：只有在没有观察者的观察中——观察者就是过去——你才能发现时间的本质以及时间的终结。

那只蜂鸟又飞了回来。一束穿破云层的阳光俘获了它，它多彩的毛色、狭长的尖喙以及飞快挥动的双翼显得光彩夺目。纯粹地看着那只小鸟，没有任何反应，只是观察它，就是在看着这整个美丽的世界。

"那天我听你说到了时间是人类的敌人，你也简要地解释了一下。可那是如此骇人听闻的一个说法，而且你也说过其他一些类似的话。其中有一些我发现是真实的、合理的，但我的心从来没有如此简单地看到真实的东西，看到事实、真相，于是我问自己，我也问过别人，为什么我们的心变得如此愚钝、如此迟缓？为什么我们就不能立刻看到某件事情的虚假或真实？你都解释得如此清楚了，我们为什么还需要解释？为什么我，以及我们每一个人，都看不到这个事实的真实性？我们的心出了什么问题？如果可以，我希望和你谈谈这个问题，好弄清楚我的心为什么不敏锐、不迅捷。还有，这颗受过训练和教育的心，究竟能不能真正变得敏锐、迅捷，能够即刻看清事实，看清事物的本质，看清它的真实或者虚假？"

"先生，我们先从探究我们为什么会变成这样开始。毫无疑问，这跟上了年纪没有任何关系。喝酒、抽烟、吸毒、奔忙、疲倦以及不停被占据，这是不是我们的生活方式？我们的内在和外在都被某种东西占据着。那是知识的本性吗？我们接受的训练就是获取知识——在学院里、大学里，或者在娴熟地做事的过程中。知识是不是缺乏敏感性的因素之一？我们的大脑塞满了太多的数据，它们从电视上、从各

destroys subtlety? But you can't get rid of your knowledge or put it aside; you have to have knowledge. Sir, you have to have knowledge to drive a car, to write a letter, to carry out various transactions; you even have to have some kind of knowledge of how to hold a spade. Of course you do. We have to have knowledge in the world of everyday activity.

"But we are speaking of the knowledge accumulated in the psychological world, the knowledge that you have gathered about your wife, if you have a wife; that very knowledge of having lived with your wife for ten days or fifty years has dulled your brain, has it not? The memories, the pictures are all stored there. We are talking of this kind of inward knowledge. Knowledge has its own superficial subtleties: when to yield, when to resist, when to gather and when not to gather, but we are asking: doesn't that very knowledge make your mind, your brain, mechanical, repetitious from habit? The encyclopaedia has all the knowledge of all the people who have written in it. Why not leave that knowledge on the shelf and use it when necessary? Don't carry it in your brain.

"We are asking: does that knowledge prevent the instant comprehension, instant perception, which brings about mutation, the subtlety that isn't in the words? Is it that we are conditioned by the newspapers, by the society in which we live—which, by the way, we have created, for every human being from past generations to the present has created this society whether in this part of the world or any other part? Is it conditioning by religions that has shaped our thinking? When you have strong beliefs in some figure, in some image, that very strength prevents the subtlety, the quickness.

"Are we so constantly occupied that there is no space in our mind and heart—space both outwardly and inwardly? We need a little space, but you cannot have space physically if you are in a crowded city, or crowded in

种报纸杂志上收集了太多的信息，然后竭尽所能地记录；它们在不停地吸收、抓取。所以知识是不是破坏敏感性的一个因素？但是你不能把知识清除或者把它抛在一边；你必须具备知识。先生，你必须有知识才能开车、写信、进行各种操作；连如何握着铁锹你都需要某种知识。毫无疑问你需要知识。我们在日常活动的领域内必须具备知识。

　　"但我们现在谈的是心理领域累积的知识，关于你的妻子你所收集的知识，如果你有个妻子的话；与你妻子一起生活了十天或者五十年，这个认识本身就钝化了你的大脑，不是吗？各种记忆、画面都储存在那里。我们谈的是这种内心的知识。知识有它自身浅层的敏感性：何时顺从，何时抗拒，何时收集，何时不要收集。但我们在问：难道不正是那些知识让你的心灵、你的头脑因为习惯而变得机械、变得千篇一律吗？百科全书里有所有编撰人的所有知识。为什么不把那些知识束之高阁，只在必要的时候才使用呢？不要把它们一直带在脑子里。

　　"我们问的是：那种知识是不是妨碍了会带来突变的即刻的领悟、即刻的洞察，妨碍了言语所无法包含的敏感性？是不是因为我们被报纸、被我们所生活的社会局限了？——而社会恰好是我们建立的，因为从过去的世世代代到现在的每一个人一起建立了这个社会，无论在世界的这个地区还是其他地区。是不是各种宗教的制约塑造了我们的思想？当你对某个人物、某种形象拥有强大的信仰，那种力量本身就阻碍了敏感和迅捷的发生。

　　"是不是因为我们被牢牢占据着，所以我们的头脑和心中没有空间——内在和外在的空间？我们需要一点空间，但如果你身处拥挤的

your family, crowded by all the impressions you have received, all the pressures. And psychologically there must be space—not the space that thought may imagine, not the space of isolation, not the space that divides human beings, politically, religiously, racially, not the space between continents, but an inward space that has no centre. Where there is a centre there is a periphery, there is a circumference. We are not talking of such space.

"And is another reason why we are not subtle, quick, because we have become specialists? We may be quick in our own specialization, but one wonders, if one is trained, specialized, whether there is any comprehension of the nature of sorrow, pain, loneliness and so on. Of course you cannot be trained to have a good, clear mind; the word "trained" is to be conditioned. And how can a conditioned mind ever be clear?

"So all these may be the factors, sir, that prevent us from having a good, subtle, clear mind."

"Thank you, sir, for seeing me. Perhaps, and I hope that, some of what you have said—not that I have understood it completely—but that some of the things you have said may take seed in me and that I will allow that seed to grow, to flourish without interfering with it.Perhaps then I may see something very rapidly, comprehend something without tremendous explanations, verbal analysis and so on. Goodbye, sir."

城市或者家里很拥挤，被你接收到的各种印象、各种压力所充塞，那么你就没有身体上的空间。而心理上你必须拥有空间——不是思想能想象的空间，不是隔绝的空间，不是从政治上、宗教上、种族上划分了人类的空间，也不是各大洲之间的空间，而是没有中心的内在的空间。只要有中心，就会有周边，就会有外围。我们说的不是那种空间。

"我们不敏感的另一个原因，是不是我们变成了专家？我们也许在自己的专业领域很敏锐，但你会好奇，如果受到了专门化的训练，那么你究竟还能不能领悟悲伤、痛苦、孤独等的本质。毫无疑问，你无法被训练得拥有一颗优秀、清晰的心；'受到训练'的意思就是受到局限。而一颗受限的心又如何能够清晰呢？

"所以，先生，这些或许都是妨碍我们拥有一颗优秀、敏锐、清晰的心的因素。"

"谢谢你能见我，先生。也许——我也希望如此——你说的某些话会在我心里播下种子，我也会允许那颗种子茁壮成长，而不去干扰它——即使我没有完全理解你的话。或许随后我就能够非常迅捷地看到某些事情、领悟某些事情，而不需要庞杂的解释、文字上的分析之类的东西。再见，先生。"

Friday, March 18, 1983

At the bird feeder there were a dozen or more birds chirping away, pecking at the grains, struggling, fighting each other, and when another big bird came they all fluttered away. When the big bird left again they all came back, chattering, quarrelling, chirping, making quite a lot of noise. Presently a cat went by and there was a flurry, a screeching and a great to—do. The cat was chased away—it was one of those wild cats, not a pet cat; there are a great many of those wild ones around here of different sizes, shapes and colours. At the feeder all day long there were birds, little ones and big ones, and then a blue jay came scolding everybody, the whole universe, and chased the other birds away—or rather they left when it came. They were very watchful for cats. And as the evening drew close all the birds went away and there was silence, quiet, peaceful. The cats came and went, but there were no birds.

That morning the clouds were full of light and there was promise in the air of more rain. For the past few weeks it had been raining. There is an artificial lake and the waters were right to the top. All the green leaves and the shrubs and the tall trees were waiting for the sun, which hadn't appeared bright as the Californian sun is; it had not shown its face for many a day.

One wonders what is the future of mankind, the future of all those children you see shouting, playing—such happy, gentle, nice faces—what is their future? The future is what we are now. This has been so historically

1983 年 3 月 18 日，星期五

野鸟喂食器那里有十几只鸟儿在叽叽喳喳地叫着，啄食着谷粒，互相争抢，互相打斗，而当另一只大鸟飞来时，它们就都扑棱棱飞走了。那只大鸟离开之后，它们又都飞了回来，聒噪着，争吵着，啁啾不断，发出不少噪声。不久后有一只猫经过，引起了一场骚动、一阵尖叫和一场喧闹。然后猫被赶走了——那是一只野猫，不是宠物猫；这周围有很多体型、身材和颜色各异的野猫。喂食器那里整天都聚集着很多鸟儿，大小不一，然后来了一只蓝色的松鸦，训斥着所有人，训斥着整个宇宙，把其他的鸟儿都赶走了——或者不如说是它来的时候它们就都离开了。它们都对猫非常警惕。随着夜幕降临，所有的鸟儿都飞走了，只剩下一片寂静、安详、和平。野猫们来来去去，但是再也没有鸟儿的踪影。

那天早上，云层中霞光四射，空气中弥漫着大雨将至的味道。过去几周一直阴雨连绵。附近有片人工湖，湖水已然溢满堤岸。所有的绿叶、灌木和大树都在等待朝阳升起，这些天它没有像加州本来的太阳那么明亮地现身，好多天都没露过面了。

你会好奇人类的未来会怎样，所有那些孩子的未来会怎样？——你看着他们喧哗、玩耍，这些如此开心、温柔、漂亮的脸庞——他

for many thousands of years—the living and dying, and all the travail of our lives. We don't seem to pay much attention to the future. You see on television endless entertainment from morning until late in the night, except for one or two channels, but they are very brief and not too serious. The children are entertained. The commercials all sustain the feeling that you are being entertained. And this is happening practically all over the world.

What will be the future of these children? There is the entertainment of sport—thirty, forty thousand people watching a few people in the arena and shouting themselves hoarse. And you also go and watch some ceremony being performed in a great cathedral, some ritual, and that too is a form of entertainment, only you call that holy, religious, but it is still an entertainment—a sentimental, romantic experience, a sensation of religiosity. Watching all this in different parts of the world, watching the mind being occupied with amusement, entertainment, sport, one must inevitably ask, if one is in any way concerned: what is the future? More of the same in different forms? A variety of amusements?

So you have to consider, if you are at all aware of what is happening to you, how the worlds of entertainment and sport are capturing your mind, shaping your life. Where is all this leading to? Or perhaps you are not concerned at all? You probably don't care about tomorrow. Probably you haven't given it thought, or, if you have, you may say it is too complex, too frightening, too dangerous to think of the coming years—not of your particular old age but of the destiny, if we can use that word, the result of our present way of life, filled with all kinds of romantic, emotional, sentimental feelings and pursuits, and the whole world of entertainment impinging on your mind. If you are at all aware of all this, what is the future of mankind?

们的未来会怎样？未来就是我们现在的样子。数千年来的历史一直如此——生生死死，还有我们生活的所有艰辛。我们似乎不太关注未来。从清晨到深夜，你都会看到电视上放着没完没了的娱乐节目，除了一两个频道，但它们的节目都非常简短，看起来也不太认真。孩子们也被娱乐着。那些商业广告都维持着你正在被娱乐的感觉。而这就是全世界真实发生着的事情。

这些孩子的未来会怎样？还有体育运动的娱乐——三四万人观看着竞技场上的那几个人，喊哑了自己的嗓子。同时你也跑去观看大教堂里举行的某些仪式，而那也是一种娱乐形式，只是你谓之以神圣、虔诚，但那依然是一种娱乐——一种多愁善感的、浪漫的体验，一种笃信宗教的感受而已。看着世界各地发生的这一切，看着人心被娱乐、消遣、体育运动所占据，你必然会问，如果你对此有那么一点儿关心的话：未来会怎样？只是换汤不换药地继续老样子吗？只会有样式更丰富的消遣吗？

所以你必须思考——如果你对发生在自己身上的事有那么一点儿觉知的话——娱乐与游戏的世界是如何捕获你的心、塑造你的生活的。这一切将通往哪里？还是说你根本不关心这些？你也许并不关心明天。也许你想都没想过，或者，如果你思考过，你也许会说，一想到未来的岁月，就觉得太复杂、太可怕、太危险了——不是你个人的年迈，而是人类的命运，如果我们可以用这个词的话，我们如今的生活方式会有怎样的结果，这种生活充斥着各种浪漫的、情绪化的、多愁善感的感受和追求，而这整个娱乐业在侵害着你的心灵。如果你对

As we said earlier, the future is what you are now. If there is no change—not superficial adaptations, superficial adjustments to any pattern, political, religious or social, but the change that is far deeper, demanding your attention, your care, your affection—if there is not a fundamental change, then the future is what we are doing every day of our life in the present. Change is rather a difficult word. Change to what? Change to another pattern? To another concept? To another political or religious system? Change from this to that? That is still within the realm, or within the field of "what is". Change to that is projected by thought, formulated by thought, materialistically determined.

So one must enquire carefully into this word change. Is there a change if there is a motive? Is there a change if there is a particular direction, a particular end, a conclusion that seems sane, rational? Or perhaps a better phrase is "the ending of what is". The ending, not the movement of "what is" to "what should be". That is not change. But the ending, the cessation, the—what is the right word?—I think ending is a good word so let's stick to that. The ending. But if the ending has a motive, a purpose, is a matter of decision, then it is merely a change from this to that. The word decision implies the action of will. "I will do this"; "I won't do that". When desire enters into the act of the ending, that desire becomes the cause of ending. Where there is a cause there is a motive and so there is no real ending at all.

The twentieth century has had a tremendous lot of changes produced by two devastating wars, and the dialectical materialism, and the scepticism of religious beliefs, activities and rituals and so on, apart from the technological world which has brought about a great many changes, and there will be further changes when the computer is fully developed—you are just at the beginning of it. Then when the computer takes over, what is

这一切有那么一点儿觉知的话，那么人类的未来会怎样？

正如我们之前所说，未来就是你现在的样子。如果没有改变——不是对任何一种政治、宗教或社会模式进行浅层的调整、表面的适应，而是在更为深入的层面上改变，而这需要你的关注、你的关怀、你的爱——如果没有一场根本的转变，那么未来就依然是我们现在每天的生活中所做的事情。"改变"是一个很难理解的词。变成什么？变成另一种模式吗？变成另一个概念？另一个政治或宗教体系？从这变成那吗？这些依然落在了"现在如何"的范畴或者领域内。变成那些，是思想所投射、思想所构造的，是思想以物质主义的方式确定的。

所以你必须仔细探究"改变"这个词。如果有动机，那改变还存在吗？如果有一个特定的方向、特定的目标，有一个看起来理智、合理的结论，那还存在改变吗？或者也许可以说，有一个更好的说法来表达，那就是"现状的终结"。终结，而不是从"现在如何"变成"应该如何"。那不是改变。而终结、止息——恰当的词是什么？——我想"终结"是一个合适的词，所以让我们紧扣这个词：终结。然而，如果终结有个动机、有个目的，是一个决定，那么它就只是从这到那的改变。"决定"这个词隐含着意志力的行为。"我要这么做。""我不会那么做。"当欲望进入了终结的行动，那个欲望就成了终结的原因。而只要有原因，就会有动机，因此根本就不存在真正的终结。

20 世纪因为两场毁灭性的战争，因为辩证唯物主义，因为对宗教信仰、宗教活动和仪式等的怀疑，还因为带来很多变化的科技界，而发生了巨大的改变。当计算机充分发展起来，还会发生更进一步的变化——

going to happen to our human minds? That is a different question which we should go into another time.

When the industry of entertainment takes over, as it is gradually doing now, when the young people, the students, the children, are constantly instigated to pleasure, to fancy, to romantic sensuality, the words restraint and austerity are pushed away, never even given a thought. The austerity of the monks, the sannyasis, who deny the world, who clothe their bodies with some kind of uniform or just a cloth—this denial of the material world is surely not austerity. You probably won't even listen to this, to what the implications of austerity are. When you have been brought up from childhood to amuse yourself and escape from yourself through entertainment, religious or otherwise, and when most of the psychologists say that you must express everything you feel and that any form of holding back or restraint is detrimental, leading to various forms of neuroticism, you naturally enter more and more into the world of sport, amusement, entertainment, all helping you to escape from yourself, from what you are.

The understanding of the nature of what you are, without any distortions, without any bias, without any reactions to what you discover you are, is the beginning of austerity. The watching, the awareness, of every thought, every feeling, not to restrain it, not to control it, but to watch it, like watching a bird in flight, without any of your own prejudices and distortions—that watching brings about an extraordinary sense of austerity that goes beyond all restraint, all the fooling around with oneself and all this idea of self—improvement, self—fulfilment. That is all rather childish. In this watching there is great freedom and in that freedom there is the sense of the dignity of austerity. But if you said all this to a modern group of students or children, they would probably look out of the window in

你现在只是处于它的初始阶段而已。然后，当计算机占据了主导，我们人类的心智将会怎样？这是另一个问题了，我们改天再探讨。

当娱乐业占据了主导，就像它现在正逐渐展现的那样，当年轻人、学生、孩子都不断被怂恿着去沉浸在享乐、幻想、罗曼蒂克的感受中，克制和简朴这些词就被远远推开了，甚至连想都不想一下。僧人、托钵僧的简朴——他们摒弃了俗世，用某种制服或者一块布条包裹身体——这种对物质世界的摒弃无疑不是简朴。你可能甚至不愿意听这些，听听简朴的含义是什么。当你从小被抚养长大的方式，就是通过宗教或非宗教的消遣来娱乐自己、逃避自己，同时多数心理学家都说你必须表达出你的一切感受，任何形式的保留或克制都是有害的，会导致各种各样的神经质，你自然就会越来越深地沉溺于嬉戏、娱乐和消遣的世界，它们都在帮助你逃避自己，逃避你实际的样子。

了解你自身现状的本质，不做任何扭曲，不带任何偏见，对你所发现的自己不做任何反应，就是简朴的开始。观察和觉知每个想法、每个感受，不压抑，不控制，而只是看着它，就像看着一只飞翔的小鸟，不带有自己的任何偏见和曲解——这种观察就带来了一份非凡的简朴感，它超越了一切克制、一切自欺的愚行以及所有自我改善、自我实现的想法。那些都太幼稚了。这份观察中有一种辽阔的自由，而那种自由中就有一种简朴的庄严。但是，如果你跟一群当代的学生或者孩子说这些，他们很可能会无聊地望向窗外，因为这个世界已经完全臣服于对享乐的追求了。

一只浅褐色的大松鼠从树上爬了下来，跳到喂食器上，啃去了几颗

boredom because this world is bent on its own pursuit of pleasure.

A large fawn—coloured squirrel came down the tree and went up to the feeder, nibbled at a few grains, sat there on top of it, looked around with its large beady eyes, its tail up, curved, a marvellous thing. It sat there for a moment or so, came down, went along the few rocks and then dashed to the tree and up, and disappeared.

It appears that man has always escaped from himself, from what he is, from where he is going, from what all this is about—the universe, our daily life, the dying and the beginning. It is strange that we never realize that however much we may escape from ourselves, however much we may wander away consciously, deliberately or unconsciously, subtly, the conflict, the pleasure, the pain, the fear and so on are always there. They ultimately dominate. You may try to suppress them, you may try to put them away deliberately with an act of will but they surface again. And pleasure is one of the factors that predominate; it too has the same conflicts, the same pain, the same boredom. The weariness of pleasure and the fret is part of this turmoil of our life. You can't escape it, my friend. You can't escape from this deep unfathomed turmoil unless you really give thought to it, not only thought but see by careful attention, diligent watching, the whole movement of thought and the self. You may say all this is too tiresome, perhaps unnecessary.

But if you do not pay attention to this, give heed, the future is not only going to be more destructive, more intolerable but without much significance. All this is not a dampening, depressing point of view, it is actually so. What you are now is what you will be in the coming days. You can't avoid it. It is as definite as the sun rising and setting. This is the share of all man, of all humanity, unless we all change, each one of us, change to something that is not projected by thought.

谷粒，然后坐在上面，瞪着晶亮如珠的大眼睛环顾四周，弯弯的尾巴高高翘起，这真是个不可思议的小东西。它在那里坐了一会儿，然后跳下来，沿着几块石头走去，接着就蹿到了高高的树上，消失不见了。

人似乎一直在逃避自己，逃避自己真实的样子，逃避面对他要去向哪里、这一切都是怎么回事——整个世界，我们的日常生活，所有的生生灭灭，究竟是怎么回事。奇怪的是，我们从未意识到我们对自己的逃避有多么严重，我们偏离得有多么远，无论是有意识地、故意地还是无意识地、不易察觉地这么做，而冲突、欢愉、痛苦和恐惧等等一直都在那里。它们最终占据了统治地位。你也许试图压制它们，或者企图借助意志力的行为，刻意把它们弃置一旁，但它们还是会浮出水面。而欢愉就是主导因素之一，它也面临着同样的冲突、同样的痛苦、同样的乏味。欢愉导致的乏味和烦恼就是我们混乱生活的一部分。你无法逃避它，我的朋友。你无法逃避这种深刻的、无法测度的混乱，除非你真正地思考它，不仅仅是思考，而且要通过用心的关注、勤奋的观察去看清思想和自我的所有活动。你或许会说这些都太无聊了，可能也没什么必要。

然而，如果你不关注、不关心这些，那么未来就不仅仅会变得更具毁灭性、更加难以忍受，而且还会变得毫无意义。这并不是一种悲观的、沮丧的观点，而是事实就是如此。你现在的样子就会是你来日的样子。你无法避开这一点，它就像日出日落一样笃定。这是所有人、全人类共同的命运，除非我们，我们每一个人都发生改变，成为某种并非思想所投射的东西。

Friday, March 25, 1983

It is the second day of a spring morning. It's lovely. It is extraordinarily beautiful here. It rained last night heavily and everything is again washed clean and all the leaves are shining bright in the sunlight. There is a scent in the air of many flowers and the sky is blue, dotted with passing clouds. The beauty of such a morning is timeless. It isn't this morning: it is the morning of the whole world. It is the morning of a thousand yesterdays. It is the morning that one hopes will continue, will last endlessly. It is a morning that is full of soft sunlight, sparkling, clear, and the air is so pure here, fairly high up the valley. The orange trees and the bright yellow oranges have been washed clean and they are shining as though it was the first morning of their birth. The earth is heavy with the rain and there is snow on the high mountains. It is really a timeless morning.

Across the valley the far mountains enclosing this valley are eager for the sun, for it has been a cold night, and all the rocks and the pebbles and the little stream seem to be aware and full of life.

You sit quietly far from everything and look at the blue sky, feel the whole earth, the purity and the loveliness of everything that lives and moves on this earth—except man of course. Man is what he is now after many thousands of centuries of time. And he will go on perhaps in the same manner; what he is now is what he will be tomorrow and a thousand

1983 年 3 月 25 日，星期五

这是春日的第二个早晨，天气怡人，这片地方也美丽非凡。昨夜下过一场大雨，万物又被涤荡一清，所有的树叶都在阳光下闪闪发亮。空气中弥漫着各种花香，天空湛蓝，点缀着几朵缓缓飘过的白云。这样一个美丽的清晨是永恒的。它并不是今天的早晨，它是全世界的早晨，是一千个昨日的早晨。它是你希望能够延续下去，能够永远持续的清晨。这是一个充满了闪亮而清澈的柔软日光的早晨，这里的空气是如此纯净，高高地飘浮在山谷上空。橙树和明黄色的橙子被洗刷得干干净净，它们熠熠放光，就好像这是它们有生以来的第一个清晨。大地在雨后显得很厚重，高山上覆盖着积雪。这真是一个一切时间都静止了的清晨。

跨越山谷的另一边，环抱着山谷的远山渴望着太阳的到来，因为昨夜很冷，而所有的山岩、卵石和小溪似乎都十分警醒，洋溢着勃勃生机。

你静静地坐着，远离一切，遥望着蓝天，感受着整个大地，感受生活在这片土地上的万物的那份纯净和美丽——当然除了人类以外。千万年之后，人类还是他现在的样子。他也许还会继续现在的生活方式，他现在如何，明天以及千万个明天还会如何。时间、进化把他带

tomorrows. Time, evolution, has brought him to what he is now. The future is what he is unless, of course, there is a deep abiding mutation of his whole psyche.

Time has become extraordinarily important to man, to all of us— time to learn, time to have a skill, time to become and time to die, time both outwardly in the physical world and time in the psychological world. It is necessary to have time to learn a language, to learn how to drive, to learn how to speak, to acquire knowledge. If you had no time you couldn't put things together to bring about a house; you must have time to lay brick upon brick. You must have time to go from here to where you want to go. Time is an extraordinary factor in our life—to acquire, to dispense, to be healed, to write a simple letter. And we seem to think we need psychological time, the time of what has been, modified now and continuing in the future. Time is the past, the present and the future. Man inwardly pins his hope on time; hope is time, the future, the endless tomorrows, time to become inwardly—one is "this", one will become "that". The becoming, as in the physical world, from the little operator to the big operator, from the nonentity to the highest in some profession—to become.

We think we need time to change from "this" to "that". The very words "change" and "hope" intrinsically imply time. One can understand that time is necessary to travel, to reach a port, to reach land after a long flight to the desired place. The desired place is the future. That is fairly obvious and time is necessary in that realm of achieving, gaining, becoming proficient in some profession, in a career that demands training. There, time seems not only necessary but must exist. And in the world of the psyche this same movement, this becoming, is extended. But is there psychological becoming at all? We never question that. We have accepted it as natural.

到了如今的样子，而未来就是他现在的样子，当然，除非他的整个心智发生一场深刻而持久的突变。

时间对于人类来说，对于我们所有人来说，都已变得太过重要——学习、掌握技能、成为什么都需要时间，死去也需要时间，既有外在物质世界的时间，也有心理世界的时间。学习一门语言，学习如何开车，学习如何说话以及获取知识，都需要时间。如果你没有时间，你就不能把东西砌在一起盖出房子；你必须花时间一砖一瓦地把房子垒起来。从这里去到你想去的地方，你也必须花时间。时间是我们生活中一个非同寻常的因素——获得、分发、疗愈、写一封短信，都需要时间。而我们似乎以为我们也需要心理上的时间，过去如何，现在稍做调整然后延续到未来，这样的时间。时间就是过去、现在和未来。人类从内心把希望寄托在了时间上；希望就是时间，就是未来和永无止境的明天，就是从内在成为什么——你现在是"这个"，你要变成"那个"。在外部世界中，从一个小职员成为一名大佬，从无名氏成为行业的翘楚——总是想成为什么。

我们以为我们需要时间来从"这"变成"那"。"改变"和"希望"这个词本身就隐含了时间。你能明白需要时间来旅行、靠岸，需要时间在长途飞行之后到达目的地。目的地就是未来。这是显而易见的，而在获取成就、实现目标的领域中，在某些行业中，在需要训练的职业中变得技艺娴熟，都需要时间。在那里，时间看起来不仅仅是需要的，而是必不可少的。而这种运动、这种成为活动，延伸到了心理世界中。然而心理上的成为究竟是不是存在？我们从未质疑这一

The religions, the evolutionary books, have informed us that we need time to change from "what is" to "what should be". The distance covered is time. And we have accepted that there is a certain pleasure and pain in becoming non—violent when one is violent, that to achieve the ideal needs an enormous amount of time. And we have followed this pattern all the days of our life, blindly, never questioning. We don't doubt.We follow the old traditional pattern. And perhaps that is one of the miseries of man—the hope of fulfilment, and the pain that that fulfilment, that hope, is not achieved, is not come by easily.

Is there actually time in the psychological world—that is, to change that which is to something totally different? Why do ideals, ideologies, whether political or religious, exist at all? Is it not one of the divisive concepts of man that has brought about conflict? After all, the ideologies, the left, right or centre, are put together by study, by the activity of thought, weighing, judging, and coming to a conclusion, and so shutting the door on all fuller enquiry. Ideologies have existed perhaps as long as man can remember. They are like belief or faith that separate man from man. And this separation comes about through time. The "me", the I, the ego, the person, from the family to the group, to the tribe, to the nation. One wonders if the tribal divisions can ever be bridged over. Man has tried to unify nations, which are really glorified tribalism.You cannot unify nations. They will always remain separate. Evolution has separate groups. We maintain wars, religious and otherwise. And time will not change this. Knowledge, experience, definite conclusions, will never bring about that global comprehension, global relationship, a global mind.

So the question is: is there a possibility of bringing about a change in "what is", the actuality, totally disregarding the movement of time? Is

点，我们理所当然地接受了这一点。

各种宗教、各种进化论的书籍，都告诉我们需要时间从"现在如何"变成"应当如何"。跨越的这个距离就是时间。而我们接受了这一点：如果你暴力，在变得不暴力的过程中，就有着某种苦与乐，而实现那个理想需要大量的时间。于是我们在生活中天天盲目地遵循这个模式，从不质疑。我们不怀疑，我们跟随着传统的古老模式。然而，或许这正是人类的苦难之一——希望得到满足，当那种满足感、那个希望无法实现、无法轻易到来时，痛苦就出现了。

在心理世界中，时间——也就是，把现状变成完全不同的样子——真的存在吗？理想、意识形态，无论是政治上的还是宗教上的，究竟为什么会存在？这不正是造成了冲突的分裂性的人类观念之一吗？归根结底，各种意识形态，无论是左派、右派还是中间派，都是通过研究、通过思想活动产生的——权衡、判断然后得出结论，从而关闭了所有更充分的探索的大门。意识形态也许自人类有史以来就存在了，它们就像信念或者信仰一样分割了人与人，而这种分割就来自时间。"我"、自己、自我、这个人，从家庭到群体，再到部落，再到国家。我想知道部族间的分割究竟能不能弥合。人们试图团结各个国家，而国家实际上不过是美化了的部落主义。你无法把国家团结起来，它们将会永远保持分裂。进化分割了各个群体。我们维系着宗教和世俗的战争，而时间无法改变这一点。知识、经验和确定的结论，永远无法带来那种全球化的领悟和关系，无法造就一颗放眼全球的心。

所以问题就在于：有没有可能为"现在如何"、为事实带来一种

there a possibility of changing violence—not by becoming non—violent, that is merely the opposite of "what is" ? The opposite of "what is" is merely another movement of thought. Our question is: can envy, with all its implications, be changed without time being involved at all, knowing that the word change itself implies time—not even transformed, for the very word transform means to move from one form to another form—but to radically end envy without time?

Time is thought. Time is the past. Time is motive. Without any motive can there be—and we will use the word—change? Does not the very word motive already imply a direction, a conclusion?And when there is a motive there is actually no change at all. Desire is again a rather complex thing, complex in its structure. Desire to bring about a change, or the will to change, becomes the motive and therefore that motive distorts that which has to be changed, that which has to end. The ending has no time.

Clouds are slowly gathering around the mountain, clouds are moving to blot out the sun and probably it will rain again, as yesterday. For here in this part of the world it is the season of rain. It never rains in the summer time; when it is hot and dry, this valley is desert. Beyond the hills the desert lies out there, open, endless and bleak. And at other times it is very beautiful, so vast in its space. The very vastness of it makes it a desert. When the spring disappears it gets hotter and hotter and the trees seem to wither and the flowers have gone and the dry heat makes all things clean again.

"Why do you say, sir, that time is unnecessary for change?"

"Let us together find out what is the truth of the matter, not accepting what one has said, or disagreeing, but together have a dialogue to explore into this matter. One is trained to believe and it is the tradition that time

改变，彻底消除时间的活动？有没有可能改变暴力？——但不是变成非暴力，那只是"现在如何"的反面而已。"现在如何"的反面只不过是另一种思想活动。我们的问题是：嫉妒，连同它所有的含义，能不能改变而完全不牵涉时间，同时明白"改变"这个词本身就隐含了时间——甚至不是转变，因为"转变"（transform）这个词就意味着从一种形式变成另一种形式——无须时间就彻底终结嫉妒？

　　时间就是思想，时间就是过去，时间就是动机。如果没有任何动机——我们就用这个词——那么能有改变吗？难道"动机"这个词本身不就已经隐含了一个方向、一个结论吗？而只要有动机，那么实际上就根本没有任何改变。同时，欲望也是一件相当复杂的事情，它的结构非常复杂。想要引发改变的欲望，或者希望改变的意志，会变成动机，进而动机会扭曲那个必须改变、必须终止的对象。而终止是没有时间的。

　　云层慢慢聚集到了山那边，完全遮住了太阳，也许很快又会下雨，就像昨天一样。因为在这里，地球的这个部分，现在正是雨季。夏季从不下雨，那时天气炎热干燥，这座山谷一片荒芜，群山的另一边是开阔、无垠、荒凉的沙漠。而其他时候这里非常美丽，有着广袤的空间。它的那种广袤把它变成了一座荒漠。当春天过去，这里会变得越来越热，树木似乎凋萎了，花儿也谢掉了，干热的气息让一切又再次变得洁净。

　　"你为什么说，先生，改变是不需要时间的？"

　　"让我们一起来弄清事情的真相，既不要接受我说的话，也不要

is necessary for change. That is correct, is it not? Time is used to become from what one is to something greater, to something more. We are not talking about the physical time, the time necessary to gain a physical skill, but rather we are considering whether the psyche can become more than what it is, better than what it is, reach a higher state of consciousness. That is the whole movement of measurement, comparison. Together we are asking, are we not, what does change imply? We live in disorder, confused, uncertain, reacting against this and for that. We are seeking reward and avoiding punishment. We want to be secure, yet everything we do seems to bring about insecurity. This, and more, brings about disorder in our daily life. You can't be disordered in business, for example, or negligent. You have to be precise, think clearly, logically. But we do not carry that same attitude into the psychological world. We have this constant urge to move away from "what is", to become something other than the understanding of "what is", to avoid the causes of disorder."

"That I understand," the questioner said. "We do escape from "what is". We never consider carefully, diligently, what is going on, what is happening now in each one of us. We do try to suppress or transcend "what is". If we have a great deal of pain, psychologically, inwardly, we never look at it carefully. We want immediately to erase it, to find some consolation. And always there is this struggle to reach a state where there is no pain, where there is no disorder. But the very attempt to bring about order seems to increase disorder, or bring about other problems."

"I do not know if you have noticed that when the politicians try to resolve one problem, that very resolution multiplies other problems. This again is going on all the time."

"Are you saying, sir, that time is not a factor of change? I can vaguely

反对，而是一起通过对话来探索这个问题。我们所受的教育就是相信改变是需要时间的，这也是传统的看法。确实如此，不是吗？需要用时间从你现在的样子变成某个更伟大、更如何的人。我们说的不是物理时间，获得身体技能所需的时间，而是考虑心智能不能变成超越它现状、优于它现状的样子，达到一个更高的意识状态。这全都是衡量和比较的活动。而我们是在一起探询改变意味着什么，不是吗？我们生活在失序中，困惑、不确定，对各种事情不停反应。我们寻求奖赏，避开惩罚。我们希望自己安全，可我们所做的一切似乎都带来了不安全。而这为我们的日常生活带来了失序。比如说，在生意上你就不能杂乱无序或者粗心大意。你必须精确，必须清晰地、合乎逻辑地思考。但我们没有把同样的态度带入内心世界。我们一直抱有一种离开'现状'的渴望，想成为别的什么，而不是去了解'现状'，避免失序的根源。"

"这一点我明白，"提问者说。"我们确实会逃避'现在如何'。我们从没认真地、勤恳地思考我们每个人身上此刻发生着什么。我们确实试图压制或者超越'现状'。如果我们在心理上、精神上遭受着巨大的痛苦，我们从不仔细地去看它。我们希望立刻消除它，找到某种慰藉。而且我们始终在努力达到一种没有痛苦、没有失序的状态。然而，似乎正是引入秩序的努力本身增加了失序，或者带来了另外的问题。"

"我不知道你有没有注意到，当政客们试图解决一个问题时，正是那个解决方案成倍地引发了更多的问题。这种事情也一直在发生着。"

comprehend this but I am not quite sure I really understand it. You are saying in fact that if I have a motive for change, that very motive becomes a hindrance to change, because that motive is my desire, my urge to move away from that which is unpleasant or disturbing to something much more satisfactory, which will give me greater happiness. So a motive or a cause has already dictated, or shaped the end, the psychological end. This I understand. I am getting a glimmer of what you are saying. I am beginning to feel the implication of change without time."

"So let us ask the question: is there a timeless perception of that "which is"? That is, to look at, to observe "what is" without the past, without all the accumulated memories, the names, the words, the reactions—to look at that feeling, at that reaction, which we call, let us say, envy. To observe this feeling without the actor, the actor who is all the remembrance of things that have happened before.

"Time is not merely the rising of the sun and the setting, or yesterday, today and tomorrow. Time is much more complicated, more intricate, subtle. And really to understand the nature and the depth of time one has to meditate upon whether time has a stop—not fictitious time nor the imagination that conjures up so many fantastic, romantic probabilities—but whether time, really, actually, in the field of the psyche, can ever come to an end? That is really the question. One can analyse the nature of time, investigate it, and try to find out whether the continuity of the psyche is a reality or the desperate hope of man to cling to something that will give him some sort of security, comfort. Does time have its roots in heaven? When you look at the heavens, the planets and the unimaginable number of stars, can that universe be understood by the time—bound quality of the mind? Is time necessary to grasp, to understand, the whole movement of the cosmos and of the human being—to see instantly

"你是不是说，先生，时间并非改变的因素？我能模糊地理解这一点，但不太确定我是不是真的理解了。你实际上说的是，如果我的改变有个动机，那个动机本身就会成为改变的障碍，因为那个动机就是我逃离的欲望，我想逃离令人不快或者令人不安的东西，躲到令我更满足、带给我更多快乐的东西那里去。所以说动机或者原因已经掌控了或者塑造了一个目标，心理上的目标。这一点我理解了。我稍稍明白了一点你所讲的内容。我开始体会到无须时间的改变意味着什么。"

"所以我们来问问这个问题：有没有一种无须时间的对'现状'的洞察？也就是说，去看、去观察'现状'，而不带着过去，不带着积累的所有记忆、名称、言语和反应——只是看着那种感受、那个反应，比如说'嫉妒'。观察这种感受而没有行动者——行动者就是对以前所发生事情的所有记忆。

"时间不只是日升日落，不只是昨天、今天和明天。时间要复杂得多，微妙得多。而若要真正了解时间的本质和深度，你就必须冥想，看看时间能否停止——不是虚构的时间或者捏造出各种异想天开、罗曼蒂克的可能性的想象——而是心理领域的时间究竟能不能真正停止？这才是真正的问题。你可以分析时间的本质，探究它，然后试着弄清心智的延续究竟是一个真相，还是只是人类孤注一掷的希望，希望紧紧抓住某个能带给他某种舒适和安全感的东西。时间是根植于天堂的吗？当你凝望天空，凝望行星和数不尽的满天星斗，那浩瀚的宇宙可以被受限于时间的心灵所领悟吗？领会、懂得宇宙和人类

that which is always true?

"One should really, if one may point out, hold it in your mind, not think about it, but just observe the whole movement of time, which is really the movement of thought. Thought and time are not two different things, two different movements, actions. Time is thought and thought is time. Is there, to put it differently, the total ending of thought? That is, the ending of knowledge? Knowledge is time, thought is time, and we are asking whether this accumulating process of knowledge, gathering more and more information, pursuing more and more the intricacies of existence, can end? Can thought, which is after all the essence of the psyche, the fears, the pleasures, the anxieties, the loneliness, the sorrow and the concept of the I—I as separate from another—this self—centred activity of selfishness, can all that come to an end? When death comes there is the ending of all that. But we are not talking about death, the final ending, but whether we can actually perceive that thought, time, have an ending.

"Knowledge after all is the accumulation through time of various experiences, the recording of various incidents, happenings, and so on; this recording is naturally stored in the brain, this recording is the essence of time. Can we find out when recording is necessary, and whether psychological recording is necessary at all? It is not dividing the necessary knowledge and skill, but beginning to understand the nature of recording, why human beings record and from that recording react and act. When one is insulted or psychologically hurt by a word, by a gesture, by an action, why should that hurt be recorded? Is it possible not to record the flattery or the insult so that the psyche is never cluttered up, so that it has vast space, and the psyche that we are conscious of as the "me", which again is put together by thought and time, comes to an end? We are always afraid of something that we have never seen, perceived—

的全部运动——即刻看到永恒的真相——需要时间吗？

"容我冒昧指出，你真的应该把它装在你心里，不是思考它，而只是观察时间的整个运动，它实际上就是思想的运动。思想和时间并非两样东西，并非两种不同的运动、活动。时间就是思想，思想就是时间。换句话说，思想能不能彻底终结？也就是说，知识能不能彻底终结？知识就是时间，思想就是时间，而我们问的是，这个知识的积累过程，收集越来越多的信息，追逐生活中越来越多的错综复杂的细节，这个过程能终止吗？思想，归根结底就是心智的核心，就是恐惧、欢愉、焦虑、孤独、悲伤以及'我'这个概念的核心——我与他人是分开的——这种自我中心的、自私的活动，这一切能停止吗？当死亡来临，这一切就都终止了。但是我们谈的不是死亡，那种最终的结束，而是我们能否真正地洞察并终结思想与时间。

"毕竟知识就是假以时日积累起来的各种经验，对发生的各种事件等的记录；这种记录自然而然地储存在了大脑中，这种记录就是时间的本质。我们能不能弄清楚何时需要记录，以及心理上的记录究竟是否必要？这不是在划分哪些知识和技能是必要的，而是开始了解记录的本质，人类为什么要记录，然后再根据那种记录来反应和行动。当你受到了侮辱，或者因为一句话、一个手势、一个行为而受到了心理上的伤害，为什么那个伤害要被记录下来？有没有可能不去记录奉承或者侮辱，这样心智就不会被充塞，于是它就拥有了广袤的空间？而我们作为'我'意识到的心智，也是由思想和时间塑造的，它能不能就此终止？我们总是畏惧我们从未见过、从未感知的事物——未

something not experienced. You can't experience truth. To experience there must be the experiencer. The experiencer is the result of time, accumulated memory, knowledge and so on.

"As we said at the beginning, time demands quick, watchful, attentive understanding. In our daily life can we exist without the concept of the future? Not concept—forgive me, not the word concept—but can one live without time, inwardly? The roots of heaven are not in time and thought."

"Sir, what you say has actually, in daily life, become a reality. Your various statements about time and thought seem now, while I am listening to you, so simple, so clear, and perhaps for a second or two there is the ending and stopping of time. But when I go back to my ordinary routine, the weariness and the boredom of it all, even pleasure becomes rather wearisome—when I go back I will pick up the old threads.It seems so extraordinarily difficult to let go of the threads and look, without reaction, at the way of time. But I am beginning to understand (and I hope it is not only verbally) that there is a possibility of not recording, if I may use your word. I realize I am the record. I have been programmed to be this or that. One can see that fairly easily and perhaps put all that aside. But the ending of thought and the intricacies of time need a great deal of observation, a great deal of investigation. But who is to investigate, for the investigator himself is the result of time? I catch something. You are really saying; just watch without any reaction, give total attention to the ordinary things of life and there discover the possibility of ending time and thought. Thank you indeed for this interesting talk."

曾经历的事物。然而你是无法经历真理的。若要经历就必须有个经历者，而经历者就是时间、累积的记忆、知识等的产物。

"正如我们一开始所说，对时间需要加以快速、警醒、细心的了解。在我们的日常生活中，我们能够活着而丝毫没有未来的概念吗？不是概念——请原谅，不是概念这个词——而是我们的内心能抛开时间活着吗？极乐的根源不在时间和思想当中。"

"先生，你所说的话，实际上在我的日常生活中已经变成了现实。当我此刻听你讲话时，你关于时间和思想的很多表述，在这一刻对我来说是如此简单、如此清晰，也许有那么一两秒钟思想终结了、停止了。然而，当我回到日常的例行公事中，各种枯燥、乏味又再度出现，连快乐都变得相当令人疲倦——当我回去之后，我又会重蹈覆辙。抛开旧有的模式去看时间的运作方式，而不做任何反应，这真是太难了。但是，我已经开始理解（我希望不仅仅是字面上理解了）存在着一种不记录的可能性，如果我可以借用你的词汇的话。我意识到我就是记录本身。我被设定的程序就是要成为这个或那个。我们很容易就可以看到这一点，也许还可以摒弃这些。但是，思想的终结和思想的复杂性则需要大量的观察、大量的探究。然而又是谁在探究呢？因为探究者本身就是时间的产物。我有点儿明白了。你实际上是说，只是观察而不做任何反应，全神贯注于生活中平常的事情，在那里发现终结时间和思想的可能性。真的非常感谢你这番有趣的谈话。"

Thursday, March 31, 1983

It had been raining all day and the clouds hung low over the valley and the hills and the mountains. You couldn't see the hills at all. It is a rather gloomy morning but there are new leaves, new flowers, and the little things are growing fast. It is spring and there is all this cloud and gloom. The earth is recovering from the winter and in this recovery there is great beauty. It has been raining almost every day for the last month and a half; there have been great storms and winds, destroying many houses and land sliding down the hillside. All along the coast there is great destruction. In this part of the country everything seems to have been so extravagant. It is never the same from winter to winter. One winter you may have hardly any rain, and in other winters there may be most destructive rain, huge monstrous waves, the roads awash, and though it was spring the elements were never graceful with the land.

There are demonstrations all over the country against particular kinds of war, against nuclear destruction. There are pros and cons. The politicians talk about defence, but actually there is no defence;there is only war, there is only killing millions of people. This is rather a difficult situation. It is a great problem which man is facing. One side wants to expand in its own way, the other is aggressively pushing, selling arms, bringing about certain definite ideologies and invading lands.

1983 年 3 月 31 日，星期四

雨下了一整天，云层低垂在山谷、丘陵和群山之上。你根本看不到远处的丘陵。这真是一个阴郁的早晨，但是嫩叶和鲜花正在绽放，各种小生命正茁壮成长。春天已经来临，浓云和幽暗笼罩着四周。大地正从冬日中复苏过来，而这复苏中有着惊人的美。一个半月以来，几乎每天都在下雨；暴风雨摧毁了许多房屋，造成了山体滑坡和泥石流，整条海岸线都损失惨重。在这里的乡间，一切都显得无比夸张，而且每个冬天都各不相同。一个冬天几乎没下一滴雨，而另一些冬天则雨灾深重，浊浪滔天，道路被淹，尽管已是春天，风雨却从未对大地展现仁慈。

近来全国上下都在示威反对某种特定形式的战争，反对核战争。支持与反对的意见不绝于耳。政客们说要防御，但实际上根本没什么防御，只有战争，只有对数百万人的屠杀。时局非常凶险，这是人类所面临的巨大难题。一个国家想以自己的方式扩张，而另一个国家也在强势推进，贩卖武器，树立某种意识形态，并且侵占土地。

人类如今提出了一个问题，这个问题他本应在多年前就向自己提出了，而不是等到最后一刻。人倾尽一生都在为战争做准备，而不幸

Man is now posing a question he should have put to himself many years ago, not at the last moment. He has been preparing for wars all the days of his life. Preparation for war seems unfortunately to be our natural tendency. Having come a long way along that path we are now saying: what shall we do? What are we human beings to do? Actually facing the issue, what is our responsibility? This is what is really facing our present humanity, not what kinds of instruments of war we should invent and build. We always bring about a crisis and then ask ourselves what to do. Given the situation as it is now, the politicians and the vast general public will decide with their national, racial, pride, with their fatherlands and motherlands and all the rest of it.

The question is too late. The question we must put to ourselves, in spite of the immediate action to be taken, is whether it is possible to stop all wars, not a particular kind of war, the nuclear or the orthodox, and find out most earnestly what are the causes of war. Until those causes are discovered, dissolved, whether we have conventional war or the nuclear form of war, we will go on and man will destroy man.

So we should really ask:what are essentially, fundamentally, the causes of war? See together the true causes, not invented, not romantic, patriotic causes and all that nonsense, but actually see why man prepares to murder legally—war. Until we research and find the answer, wars will go on. But we are not seriously enough considering, or committed to, the uncovering of the causes of war. Putting aside what we are now faced with, the immediacy of the issue, the present crisis, can we not together discover the true causes and put them aside, dissolve them? This needs the urge to find the truth.

Why is there, one must ask, this division—the Russian, the American, the British, the French, the German and so on—why is there this division

的是，备战似乎是我们天生的本性。我们沿着这个方向一路走来，到如今才问：我们该怎么办？我们人类该怎么办？切实地面对着这个问题，我们的责任是什么？这才是当今我们人类所真正面临的问题，而不是我们应该发明和制造哪种战争武器。我们总是引发危机，然后再问自己该怎么办。政客们和广大的普通民众将会根据当前的局势，带着他们民族自豪感、种族自豪感，以他们的祖国等之类的名义，来决定该如何行动。

这个问题来得太迟了。尽管需要采取一些迫切的行动，但我们必须向自己提出的问题是：有没有可能停止所有战争——而不是某一种战争，核战争或传统战争——并且抱着极其热切的态度去弄清楚战争的根源是什么。除非发现并消除了这些根源，否则，无论是传统战争还是核战争，我们都会继续发动下去，而人类将会毁灭彼此。

所以我们实际上应该问：战争最根本、最本质的根源是什么？一起来看看战争真正的根源，不是臆想出来的原因，不是罗曼蒂克的、爱国主义的原因以及诸如此类的废话，而是真正去弄清楚人类为什么热衷于合法地谋杀——也就是发动战争。除非我们探究并找到答案，否则战争还将继续。但是我们的思考不够认真、不够投入，无法揭开战争的根源。先抛开我们现在所面临的、最紧迫的问题和当前的危机，我们能不能一起去探究战争真正的根源，进而抛弃它们、消除它们？而这需要我们有发现真相的迫切愿望。

我们必须问一问，为什么存在这种划分——俄国人、美国人、英国人、法国人、德国人等——为什么人与人、种族与种族之间会存在

between man and man, between race and race, culture against culture, one series of ideologies against another? Why? Why is there this separation? Man has divided the earth as yours and mine—why? Is it that we try to find security, self protection, in a particular group, or in a particular belief, faith? For religions also have divided man, put man against man—the Hindus, the Muslims, the Christians, the Jews and so on. Nationalism, with its unfortunate patriotism, is really a glorified form, an ennobled form, of tribalism. In a small tribe or in a very large tribe there is a sense of being together, having the same language, the same superstitions, the same kind of political, religious system. And one feels safe, protected, happy, comforted. And for that safety, comfort, we are willing to kill others who have the same kind of desire to be safe, to feel protected, to belong to something. This terrible desire to identify oneself with a group, with a flag, with a religious ritual and so on, gives us the feeling that we have roots, that we are not homeless wanderers. There is the desire, the urge, to find one's roots.

And also we have divided the world into economic spheres, with all their problems. Perhaps one of the major causes of war is heavy industry. When industry and economics go hand in hand with politics they must inevitably sustain a separative activity to maintain their economic stature. All countries are doing this, the great and the small. The small are being armed by the big nations—some quietly, surreptitiously, others openly. Is the cause of all this misery, suffering, and the enormous waste of money on armaments, the visible sustenance of pride, of wanting to be superior to others?

It is our earth, not yours or mine or his. We are meant to live on it, helping each other, not destroying each other. This is not some romantic

这种划分，文化对抗着文化，一套意识形态对抗着另一套？为什么？为什么会有这种分割？人类把地球分割成了你的和我的——为什么？是不是因为我们试图在某个群体或某个信念、信仰中找到安全，实现自我保护？因为各派宗教也分裂了人类，让人们互相对抗——印度教徒、穆斯林、基督教徒、犹太人等。民族主义，以及它不幸的爱国主义，实际上是一种被美化、被高尚化了的部落主义。人们无论在一个小部落里还是一个非常庞大的部落里，都有一种在一起的感觉，说着同样的语言，信奉着同样的迷信，有着同一种政治和宗教体制。我们在里面觉得安全、快乐、舒适，感觉受到了保护。于是为了那种安全和舒适，我们就愿意去杀害其他那些同样渴望安全的人，他们也希望受到保护，有所归属。让自己与某个群体、某个旗帜、某种宗教仪式等相认同的可怕欲望，给了我们一种感觉——我们有了根基，我们不再是无家可归的流浪汉。人的内心都有这种找到自己根基的渴望和冲动。

同时，我们也把这个世界划分成了很多经济圈，这也带来了无数的问题。或许战争的主要根源之一就是重工业。当工业界和经济界与政界携手共进时，他们必然会维持一种分裂性的活动，以确保他们的经济地位。所有的国家都在这么做，无论大小。小国被大国所武装——有的在悄无声息地暗中操作，其他的则在明目张胆地进行。这所有的苦难、不幸，以及浪费在军备上的大量金钱，其根源是不是由自豪感和超越他人的渴望在大力支撑着？

这是我们的地球，不是你的、我的或者他的。我们活在地球上是

nonsense but the actual fact. But man has divided the earth, hoping thereby that in the particular he is going to find happiness, security, a sense of abiding comfort. Until a radical change takes place and we wipe out all nationalities, all ideologies, all religious divisions, and establish a global relationship—psychologically first, inwardly before organizing the outer— we shall go on with wars. If you harm others, if you kill others, whether in anger or by organized murder which is called war, you, who are the rest of humanity, not a separate human being fighting the rest of mankind, are destroying yourself.

This is the real issue, the basic issue, which you must understand and resolve. Until you are committed, dedicated, to eradicating this national, economic, religious division, you are perpetuating war, you are responsible for all wars whether nuclear or traditional.

This is really a very important and urgent question: whether man, you, can bring about this change in yourself—not say, "If I change, will it have any value? Won't it be just a drop in a vast lake and have no effect at all?What is the point of my changing?" That is a wrong question, if one may point out. It is wrong because you are the rest of mankind. You are the world, you are not separate from the world. You are not an American, Russian, Hindu or Muslim. You are apart from these labels and words, you are the rest of mankind because your consciousness, your reactions, are similar to the others. You may speak a different language, have different customs, that is superficial culture— all cultures apparently are superficial—but your consciousness, your reactions, your faith, your beliefs, your ideologies, your fears, anxieties, loneliness, sorrow and pleasure, are similar to the rest of mankind. If you change it will affect the whole of mankind.

要互相帮助的，而不是互相毁灭。这不是什么浪漫的胡话，而是真切的事实。但是人类划分了地球，希望因此能在某个局部找到幸福、安全以及一种持久的舒适感。除非我们发生一场根本的转变，消除所有的国籍、所有的意识形态、所有的宗教派系，并且在建立外在的组织之前，首先从心理上、从内在建立起一种全球化的关系——否则我们还将继续混战下去。如果你伤害他人，如果你杀害他人，无论是因为愤怒还是通过有组织的屠杀，也就是战争，那么你——你就是整个人类，而不是一个在对抗其他人类的人——就是在摧毁你自己。

这才是真正的问题、最根本的问题，你必须加以了解并将其解决。除非你真的非常用心、非常投入，去根除国家、经济和宗教上的这些划分，否则你就是在无止境地延续战争，你就对所有的战争都负有责任，无论是核战争还是传统战争。

这真的是一个非常重要而又十分紧迫的问题：人类，你，能否在自己身上触发这场改变——而不说，"如果我改变了，那又有什么价值呢？那难道不就像是大湖里的一滴水，所以毫无影响吗？我的改变又有什么意义呢？"请恕我指出，这是一个错误的问题。它之所以是错误的，是因为你就是整个人类。你就是世界，你与世界是分不开的。你不是什么美国人、俄国人、印度教徒或者穆斯林。抛开这些标签和名词，你就是整个人类，因为你的意识、你的反应和其他人是相似的。你也许说着另一种语言，有着不同的习俗。这些都是肤浅的文化——显然所有的文化都是肤浅的——但你的意识，你的反应，你的信念，你的信仰，你的意识形态，你的恐惧，你的焦虑、孤独、悲伤和快乐，

This is important to consider—not vaguely, superficially—in enquiring into, researching, seeking out, the causes of war. War can only be understood and put an end to if you and all those who are concerned very deeply with the survival of man, feel that you are utterly responsible for killing others. What will make you change? What will make you realize the appalling situation that we have brought about now? What will make you turn your face against all division—religious, national, ethical and so on? Will more suffering? But you have had thousands upon thousands of years of suffering and man has not changed; he still pursues the same tradition, same tribalism, the same religious divisions of "my god" and "your god".

The gods or their representatives are invented by thought; they have actually no reality in daily life. Most religions have said that to kill human beings is the greatest sin. Long before Christianity, the Hindus said this, the Buddhists said it, yet people kill in spite of their belief in god, or their belief in a saviour and so on; they still pursue the path of killing. Will the reward of heaven change you or the punishment of hell? That too has been offered to man. And that too has failed. No external imposition, laws, systems, will ever stop the killing of man. Nor will any intellectual, romantic, conviction stop wars. They will stop only when you, as the rest of humanity, see the truth that as long as there is division in any form, there must be conflict, limited or wide, narrow or expansive, that there must be struggle, conflict, pain. So you are responsible, not only to your children, but to the rest of humanity. Unless you deeply understand this, not verbally or ideationally or merely intellectually, but feel this in your blood, in your way of looking at life, in your actions, you are supporting organized murder which is called war. The immediacy of perception is far more important than the immediacy of answering a question which is the outcome of a

与其他人类都是相似的。如果你改变了，那将会影响整个人类。

思考、探求、追究、找出战争的根源——但不是模糊地、肤浅地探究——这非常重要。只有当你以及那些深切关注人类命运的人，感受到了自己要对杀害别人负有全部责任时，战争才能得以了解和终结。什么能让你改变？什么才能让你认识到，是我们一手造就了如今这番可怕的境地？什么才能让你背弃所有的分别——宗教、国家、伦理等方面的分别？是更多的苦难吗？可是你已然历经了千千万万年的苦难，而人类还是没有改变；他还在追随着同样的传统、同样的部落主义、同样的宗教分别——"我的上帝"和"你的上帝"。

神明或者他们的代言人都是思想发明出来的；他们在日常生活中完全没有任何真实性。大部分宗教都说过杀人是最严重的罪行。早在基督教出现之前，印度教徒就这么说过，佛教徒也这么说过，但人类照样杀戮，完全无视他们对上帝、对救世主等的信仰，依然走上了屠杀的道路。天堂的奖赏或者地狱的惩罚会改变你吗？这些东西也都给过人类了，而且也都失败了。没有哪个外在的规则、法律、体制能够阻止人类的杀戮。任何思想上的、浪漫的信念也都无法制止战争。只有当你，也就是整个人类，看到了这个真相——只要有任何形式的分别，就必然会有冲突，无论那种分别宽或窄、大或小，都必然会导致斗争、冲突、痛苦——战争才会停止。所以你不仅仅要对自己的孩子负责，你还要对整个人类负责。除非你深刻地理解了这一点，不是从字面上、观念上，也不是仅仅从道理上理解，而是这种感受融入了你的血液，融入了你看待生活的方式，融入了你的行动中，否则你就是

thousand years of man killing man.

The world is sick and there is no one outside you to help you except yourself. We have had leaders, specialists, every kind of external agency, including god—they have had no effect; they have in noway influenced your psychological state. They cannot guide you. No statesman, no teacher, no guru, no one can make you strong inwardly, supremely healthy. As long as you are in disorder, as long as your house is not kept in a proper condition, a proper state, you will create the external prophet, and he will always be misleading you. Your house is in disorder and no one on this earth or in heaven can bring about order in your house. Unless you yourself understand the nature of disorder, the nature of conflict, the nature of division, your house, that is you, will always remain in disorder, at war.

It is not a question of who has the greatest military might, but rather it is man against man, man who has put together ideologies, and these ideologies, which man has made, are against each other. Until these ideas, ideologies, end and man becomes responsible for other human beings, there cannot possibly be peace in the world.

在支持有组织的屠杀，也就是所谓的战争。即刻洞察这一点，远远比立刻回答一个因为人类数千年来互相残杀而造成的问题重要多了。

这个世界已病入膏肓，除了你自己，外面没有人能帮你。我们有过领袖、专家，有过各种外在的代理人，包括上帝——他们都没有奏效；他们完全没有影响你的内心状态。他们无法引领你。没有哪个说法、哪个导师、哪个古鲁、哪个人能让你内心变得坚强，变得无比健康。只要你身处混乱，只要你自己的房子没有保持在恰当的秩序、恰当的状况，你就会树立起外在的先知，而他必定会引你误入歧途。你的房子一片混乱，上天入地都没有人能为你的房子带来秩序。除非你自己懂得了混乱的本质、冲突的本质、分裂的本质，否则你的房子——也就是你——将会一直混乱下去，一直征战不休。

谁拥有最强大的军事实力并不是问题，人与人彼此对抗才是症结所在，是人类建立了各种意识形态，然后这些意识形态之间相互对立。除非这些观念、这些意识形态全部消失，人们为其他人类负起责任来，否则世界上就不可能有和平。

Monday, April 18*, 1983

It is a new day and the sun won't be up for an hour or so. It is quite dark and the trees are silent, waiting for the dawn and the sun to rise behind the hills. There ought to be a prayer for dawn. It comes so slowly, penetrating the whole world. And here in this quiet secluded house, surrounded by orange trees and a few flowers, it is extraordinarily quiet. There are no birds as yet singing their morning song. The world is asleep, at least in this part of the world, far from all civilization, from the noise, the brutality, the vulgarity and the talk of politicians.

Slowly, with great patience, the dawn begins in the deep silence of the night. It was broken by the mourning dove and the hoot of an owl. There are several owls here, they were calling to each other. And the hills and the trees are beginning to awaken. In silence the dawn begins, it gets lighter and lighter, and the dew is on the leaf and the sun is just climbing over the hill. The first rays of the sun are caught in those tall trees, in that old oak that has been there for a very, very long time. And the mourning dove begins with its soft mournful call. Across the road, across the orange trees, there is a peacock calling. Even in this part of the world there are peacocks, at least

---

*　Between this date and March 31 Krishnamurti had been to New York where he gave two talks at the Felt Forum, Madison Square Garden, and attended a seminar organized by Dr David Shainberg.

1983 年 4 月 18 日，[①] 星期一

新的一天到来了，大约一小时之后太阳才会升起。天很黑，树林都静悄悄的，等待着黎明来临，等待朝阳从山后升起。空气里似乎有一种对黎明的祈祷，等它慢慢降临，穿透整个世界。而在这座偏僻的房子里——它被橙树和花儿所环绕——有一种出奇的安静。鸟儿们还没有唱起晨曲，世界依然在沉睡，至少世界的这个地方，远离了所有文明，远离了喧嚣、残忍、粗俗以及政客们的高谈阔论。

慢慢地，怀着极大的耐心，黎明从夜晚深沉的寂静中缓缓步出。夜的寂静被鸽子忧伤的咕哝和猫头鹰的叫声打破。这里有好几只猫头鹰，它们彼此呼唤着对方。群山和树林开始苏醒。黎明在寂静中降临，天光愈来愈亮，叶子上缀满露珠，太阳刚刚爬上山顶。第一束阳光被那些高大的树木所遮挡，被那棵早已在那里矗立久远的老橡树所俘获。那只忧伤的鸽子开始了它柔声的哀鸣。穿过马路，跨过橙树林，有一只孔雀在鸣叫。连世界的这个地方都有孔雀，至少有那么几只。白天开始了。这真是奇妙的一天，如此清新而又生机勃勃，洋溢

---

① 3 月 28 日到 31 日期间，克里希那穆提到纽约的费尔特论坛和麦迪逊花园广场进行了两次演讲，并出席了由大卫·辛伯格组织的一场研讨会。

there are a few of them. And the day has begun. It is a wonderful day. It is so new, so fresh, so alive and full of beauty. It is a new day without any past remembrances, without the call of another.

There is great wonder when one looks at all the beauties—those bright oranges with the dark leaves, and the few flowers, bright in their glory. One wonders at this extraordinary light which only this part of the world seems to have. One wonders as one looks at the creation which seems to have no beginning and no end—a creation not by cunning thought, but the creation of a new morning. This morning it is as it has never been before, so bright, so clear. And the blue hills are looking down. It is the creation of a new day as it has never been before.

There is a squirrel with a long bushy tail, quivering and shy in the old pepper tree which has lost many branches; it is getting very old. It must have seen many storms, as the oak has in its old age, quiet, with a great dignity. It is a new morning, full of an ancient life; it has no time, no problems. It exists and that in itself is a miracle. It is a new morning without any memory. All the past days are over, gone, and the voice of the mourning dove comes across the valley, and the sun is now over the hill, covering the earth. And it too has no yesterday. The trees in the sun and the flowers have no time. It is the miracle of a new day.

"We want continuity, " said the man. "Continuity is part of our life. Continuity of generation after generation, of tradition, of the things we have known and remembered. We crave continuity and we must have it. Otherwise what are we? Continuity is in the very roots of our being. To be is to continue. Death may come, there may be an end to many things but there is always the continuity. We go back to find our roots, our identity. If one has kept one's beginning as a family, probably

着美。这是崭新的一天，丝毫没有过去的记忆，也没有他人的希冀。

当你凝望着所有的美景——那些被黝黯的枝叶所映衬的鲜亮的橙子，还有光华四射的花朵，你会感到无比讶异，讶异于似乎只有地球的这个部分才拥有的那种不可思议的光线。当你注视着那似乎无始又无终的创造——并非由狡猾的思想所为，而是诞生一个崭新的清晨的创造——你会感到十分惊奇。这似乎是一个前所未有的早晨，如此明亮，如此清新。蓝色的远山俯瞰着大地，崭新的一天诞生了，这一天史无前例。

有一只拖着毛茸茸长尾的松鼠，颤抖着害羞地躲在那棵老胡椒树上，那棵胡椒树已经脱落了不少枝叶，正变得老迈不堪。它必定目睹了无数风雨，就像那株老橡树一样，安静，而又无比庄严。这是一个崭新的清晨，充盈着古老的生命力；它超越了时间，它没有问题。它就这样存在着，这本身就是一个奇迹。这是一个抛开了所有记忆的早晨。过去的所有日子都结束了、远去了，鸽子忧伤的叫声穿越山谷而来，而此时太阳已经高悬在山顶之上，照耀着整个大地。它也没有昨天。阳光下的树木和花朵没有时间，而崭新的一天本身就是个奇迹。

"我们都希望事物延续下去，"那个男人说。"延续就是生命的一部分——一代接一代的延续，传统的延续，我们已知和记忆中的那些事物的延续。我们渴望延续，我们必须拥有它，否则我们又是什么呢？延续性正是我们存在的根本，存在就是延续。死亡也许会来临，很多事情都可能终结，但始终存在一种延续性。我们追溯过去，找寻自己的根本、自己的身份。如果你认为自己的存在是从家庭开始的，

one can trace it, generation after generation for many centuries, if one is interested in that kind of thing. The continuity of the worship of god, the continuity of ideologies, the continuity of opinions, values, judgements, conclusions—there is a continuity in all the things one has remembered. There is a continuity from the moment we are born until we die, with all the experiences, all the knowledge that man has acquired. Is it an illusion?"

"What has continuity? That oak, probably two hundred years old, has a continuity until it dies or is chopped down by man. And what is this continuity which man wants, craves for? The name, the form, the bank account, the things remembered? Memory has a continuity, remembrances of that which has been. The whole psyche is memory and nothing else. We attribute to the psyche a great many things—qualities, virtues, ignoble deeds, and the exercise of many clever acts in the outer and the inner world. And if one examines diligently, without any bias or conclusion, one begins to see that our whole existence with the vast network of memories, remembrances, the things that have happened before, all have continuity. And we cling to that desperately."

The squirrel has come back. It has been away for a couple of hours; now it is back on the branch nibbling at something, watching, listening, extraordinarily alert and aware, alive, quivering with excitement. It comes and goes without telling you where it is going and when it is coming back. And as the day is getting warmer, the dove and the birds have gone. There are a few pigeons flying from one place to another in a group. You can hear their wings beating in the air. There used to be a fox here—one hasn't seen it for a long time. Probably it has gone away for ever. There are too many people about. There are plenty of rodents but people are dangerous. And

也许你就可以一代一代地追溯回去，如果你对这类事情感兴趣的话。膜拜神明的延续，意识形态的延续，观点、价值观、评判和结论的延续——人所记得的一切之中都有一种延续性。延续性从生到死都一直存在着，无论是经验，还是人获得的所有知识。这是一个幻觉吗？"

"什么有延续性？那棵橡树，也许有两百年了，在它死掉或者被人砍倒之前，确实存在一种延续性。而人类想要的、渴望的这种延续性又是什么？是名声、外形、银行账户，还有记忆中的一切吗？记忆也有一种延续性，能够记得过去的事情。整个心智就只是记忆而已，别无其他。我们赋予了心智很多内容——品质、美德、卑劣的行径，还有在外部和内心世界里耍的各种花招。如果你勤勉地审视这一点，不带任何偏见或结论，你就能看到我们的整个存在，连同记忆、回忆和过去所发生的一切，那张巨网确实存在一种延续性。而我们无可救药地攀附于它。"

那只松鼠又回来了。它离开了几个小时，现在它又回到了树枝上，碎碎地咬着什么，观察，聆听，极为警醒和觉察，生机勃勃，兴奋地颤抖着。它来来去去，完全不知会你它要去往哪里以及何时回来。随着天气越来越热，鸽子和鸟儿们都离开了。鸽子成群结队地从一处飞向另一处，你能听到它们的翅膀在空中拍动的声音。这里以前曾有一只狐狸——已经好久没见过它了。也许它永远地消失了。周围的人太多了。这里有很多啮齿类动物，可是人类太危险了。而这是一只害羞的小松鼠，它就像燕子一样让人捉摸不定。

尽管除了记忆没有任何延续性可言，然而，在整个人身上，在大

this is a shy little squirrel and wayward as the swallow.

Although there is no continuity except memory, is there in the whole human being, in the brain, a place, a spot, an area small or vast, where memory doesn't exist at all, which memory has never touched? It is a remarkable thing to look at all this, to feel your way sanely, rationally, see the complexity and the intricacies of memory, and its continuity which is, after all, knowledge. Knowledge is always in the past, knowledge is the past. The past is vast accumulated memory as tradition. And when you have trodden that path diligently, sanely, you must inevitably ask: is there an area in the human brain, or in the very nature and structure of a human being, not merely in the outer world of his activities but inwardly, deep in the vast quiet recesses of his own brain, something that is not the outcome of memory, not the movement of a continuity?

The hills and the trees, the meadows and the groves, will continue as long as the earth exists unless man in his cruelty and despair destroys it all. The stream, the spring, from which it comes, have a continuity, but one never asks whether the hills and beyond the hills have their own continuity.

If there is no continuity what is there? There is nothing. One is afraid to be nothing. Nothing means not a thing—nothing put together by thought, nothing put together by memory, remembrances, nothing that you can put into words and then measure. There is most certainly, definitely, an area where the past doesn't cast a shadow, where time, the past or the future or the present, has no meaning. We have always tried to measure with words something that we don't know. What we do not know we try to understand and give it words and make it into a continuous noise. And so we clog our brain which is already clogged with past vents, experiences, knowledge. We

脑里，有没有一块地方、一个空间、一块面积，无论大小，记忆是根本不存在的，那里是记忆所从未沾染的？审视这个问题，理智地、清醒地感受自己的行为方式，看清记忆的复杂和微妙之处，以及它所谓的延续性——归根结底，记忆不过是知识而已——这真是一件了不起的事情。知识永远属于过去，知识就是过去。过去就是积攒起来的庞大记忆，也就是传统。而当你勤劳地、理智地踏过那条路，你就必然会问：人类的大脑中，或者人类的本质或者结构中，不仅仅是他外在的行为，而且在他大脑广阔宁静的深处，有没有那么一块地方，不是记忆的产物，也不属于延续的活动？

群山和密林，草地和树丛，只要地球存在，它们就会继续存在，除非人类的残忍和绝望将它们摧毁殆尽。溪流和春日作为它们的源头，确实有一种延续性，但人们从不问群山以及群山之外，它们自身是否会延续。群山和密林，草地和树丛，只要地球存在，它们就会继续存在，除非人类的残忍和绝望将它们摧毁殆尽。溪流和春日作为它们的源头，确实有一种延续性，但人们从不问群山以及群山之外，它们自身是否会延续。

如果没有延续性，那还剩下什么？只剩下空无。但人害怕空无，空无意味着一无所有——没有思想所造的一切，没有记忆、回忆所造的一切，没有你可以诉诸言语然后加以度量的一切。毫无疑问，确实存在着一片地方，过去没有在那里投下一丝阴影，在那里，时间——过去、未来、现在——没有丝毫意义。我们总是企图用语言衡量某种我们所不懂的事物。我们试图理解我们不知道的东西并诉诸语言，

think knowledge is psychologically of great importance, but it is not. You can't ascend through knowledge; there must be an end to knowledge for the new to be. New is a word for something which has never been before. And that area cannot be understood or grasped by words or symbols: it is there beyond all remembrances.

然后再把它变成一种持续的噪声。同时，我们也用以往的事件、经验和知识来充塞我们早已拥挤不堪的大脑。我们以为知识在心理上无比重要，但事实并非如此。你无法借助知识来超越；知识必须止息，新事物才能诞生。"新事物"一词指的是前所未有的东西。而这片领域是词语或者符号所无法理解或者领会的，它的存在超越了所有的记忆。

Tuesday, April 19, 1983

This winter there has been constant rain, day after day, practically for the last three months. It is rather an extravagance of California—either it doesn't rain at all or it rains to drown the land. There have been great storms and very few sunny days. It has been raining all yesterday and this morning the clouds are low down on the hills and it is rather gloomy. All the leaves are beaten down by the rain of yesterday. The earth is very wet. The trees and that magnificent oak must be asking where the sun is.

On this particular morning with the clouds hiding the mountains and the hills almost down to the valley, what does it mean to be serious? What does it mean to have a very quiet, serious mind—or, if you will, brain? Are we ever serious? Or do we always live in a world of superficiality, walking to and fro, fighting, quarrelling, violent over something utterly trivial? What does it mean to have a brain that is very awake, not limited by its own thoughts, memories and remembrances? What does it mean to have a brain that is free from all the turmoil of life, all the pain, all the anxiety and the endless sorrow? Is it ever possible to have a totally free mind, free brain, not shaped by influences, by experience and the vast accumulation of knowledge?

Knowledge is time; learning means time. To learn to play the violin takes infinite patience, months of practice, years of dedicated

1983 年 4 月 19 日，星期二

这个冬天一直在持续降水，日复一日，一连下了三个月的雨。这是加州的一种相当夸张的气候——要么滴雨未落，要么豪雨成灾。连日来暴风雨不断，鲜见太阳露脸。昨天一直阴雨连绵，今天早上云层也低低地压在山顶，天气非常阴郁。昨天的大雨让树叶低垂，土地泥泞潮湿。树林和那棵大橡树肯定在问太阳哪里去了。

在这个特别的早上，乌云遮住了群山和丘陵，几乎布满了整片山谷，我们来问一问：认真究竟意味着什么？拥有一颗非常安静、非常认真的心——或者说大脑，如果你愿意这么说的话——究竟是什么意思？我们可曾认真过？还是说，我们一直生活在一个非常肤浅的世界里，来来回回地逡巡、打斗、争吵，因为琐碎不堪的事情而暴力连连？拥有一颗非常醒觉的大脑，不被它自己的思想、记忆和回忆所局限，这是什么意思？拥有一颗摆脱了生活的一切混乱、一切痛苦、一切焦虑以及无尽悲伤的头脑，这究竟意味着什么？究竟有没有可能拥有一颗全然自由的心、全然自由的头脑，不被各种影响、经验以及累积的庞大知识所塑造？

知识就是时间，学习就意味着时间。学习拉小提琴需要无限的耐

concentration. Learning to acquire a skill, learning to become an athlete or to put together a good engine or to go to the moon—all this requires time. But is there anything to learn about the psyche, about what you are—all the vagaries, the intricacies of one's reactions and actions, the hope, the failure, the sorrow and joy—what is there to learn about all that? As we said, in a certain area of one's physical existence, gathering knowledge and acting from that knowledge, requires time. Is it that we carry that same principle, extend that same movement of time into the psychological world? There too we say we must learn about ourselves, about our reactions, our behaviour, our elations and depressions, ideations and so on; we think that all that requires time too.

You can learn about the limited, but you cannot learn about the unlimited. And we try to learn about the whole field of the psyche, and say that needs time. But time may be an illusion in that area, it may be an enemy. Thought creates the illusion, and that illusion evolves, grows, extends. The illusion of all religious activity must have begun very, very simply, and now look where it is—with immense power, vast properties, great accumulation of art, wealth, and the religious hierarchy demanding obedience, urging you to have more faith. All that is the expansion, the cultivation and the evolution of illusion which has taken many centuries. And the psyche is the whole content of consciousness, is the memory of all things past and dead. We give such importance to memory. The psyche is memory. All tradition is merely the past. We cling to that and want to learn all about it, and think that time is necessary for that as in the other area.

I wonder if one ever asks whether time has a stop—time to become, time to fulfil? Is there anything to learn about all that? Or can one see that the whole movement of this illusory memory, which appears so real, can

心，需要数月的练习和经年的专注投入。学会一门技能，学习成为一名运动员、组装一台优良的引擎或者登上月球——这些都需要时间。然而，关于心智，关于你实际是什么——你所有的反应和行动、希望和挫败、忧伤和欢乐，这些反复无常、复杂微妙之处——关于这些，又有什么可学的？正如我们所说，在我们实际生活的某些领域，收集知识然后根据那些知识去行动，确实需要时间。然而，我们是不是把同样的原则、同样的时间运动照搬到了、延展到了心理世界？我们说在那里也必须了解自己，了解自己的反应、行为、喜怒哀乐、意识形态等；我们以为这些也都需要时间。

你可以了解有限的事物，但你无法了解无限。而我们试图了解整个心理领域，并且说这也需要时间。但是在那个领域，时间也许是个幻象，也许是个敌人。思想制造了幻象，而那些幻象得到了进化、成长和延展。所有虚幻的宗教活动最初必定都非常非常单纯，但是看看它现在到了什么地步——无边的权力，庞大的产业，积累了大量的艺术品和财富，要求服从的宗教等级，敦促你抱有更多的信仰。这些都在扩展、培植和助长人们千百年来抱有的幻觉。而心智就是意识的全部内容，就是对过去的、已死的一切的回忆。可我们是如此看重记忆。心智就是记忆，所有的传统都只是过去。我们攀附其上，希望了解它的全部，并且以为那也需要时间，就像在另一个领域中一样。

我想知道你可曾问过时间——成为什么、实现什么的时间——究竟能否停止？关于这一切，有什么可了解的吗？或者说，你能否看清这虚幻的记忆的整个活动，无论看起来多么真实，都是可以停止的？

end? If time has a stop, then what is the relationship between that which lies beyond time and all the physical activities of the brain as memory, knowledge, remembrances, experiences? What is the relationship between the two? Knowledge and thought, as we have often said, are limited. The limited cannot possibly have any relationship with the unlimited but the unlimited can have some kind of communication with the limited, though that communication must always be limited, narrow, fragmentary.

One might ask, if one is commercially minded, what is the use of all this, what is the use of the unlimited, what can man profit by it? We always want a reward. We live on the principle of punishment and reward, like a dog which has been trained; you reward him when he obeys. And we are almost similar in the sense that we want to be rewarded for our actions, for our obedience and so on. Such demand is born out of the limited brain. The brain is the centre of thought and thought is ever limited under all circumstances. It may invent the extraordinary, theoretical, immeasurable, but its invention is always limited. That is why one has to be completely free from all the travail and toil of life and from self—centred activity for the unlimited to be.

That which is immeasurable cannot be measured by words. We are always trying to put the immeasurable into a frame of words, and the symbol is not the actual. But we worship the symbol, therefore we always live in a limited state.

So with the clouds hanging on the treetops and all the birds quiet, waiting for the thunderstorm, this is a good morning to be serious, to question the whole of existence, to question the very gods and all human activity. Our lives are so short and during that short period there is nothing to learn about the whole field of the psyche, which is the movement of

如果时间停止，那么超越时间的事物，与记忆、知识、回忆、经验等这些大脑的物质活动，它们之间的关系如何？两者之间有什么关系？知识和思想，正如我们常说的，是局限的。局限的事物与无限不可能有丝毫的关系，而无限与有限的事物可以产生某种沟通，尽管那种沟通也必然是局限的、狭隘的、破碎的。

如果一个人唯利是图，那他也许会问，这些又有什么用，无限又有什么用，人能从中获取什么利益？我们总是希望得到回报。我们仰仗奖惩的原则而活，就像一条受训的狗一样；当他顺从，我们就奖励他。我们也希望因为我们的行为、我们的顺从等而得到奖赏，在这一点上，我们几乎如出一辙。这种需求就脱胎于那颗受限的大脑。大脑是思想的中心，而思想在任何情况下都是局限的。它也许能发明出不可思议的、理论上的、无法衡量的事物，但它的发明始终是局限的。这就是为什么人必须彻底摆脱生活的所有苦痛和辛劳，摆脱自我中心的活动，这样无限才能得以发生。

那不可度量者无法由言语来衡量。我们总是企图把不可度量者装入言辞的框架，但符号并非真实之物。然而我们膜拜符号，因此总是活在局限的境地中。

此时，层云就压在树顶，所有的鸟儿都安静下来，等待着暴风雨来临。这是一个绝佳的早晨，可以认真地思考这整个人生的问题，质疑各种神明以及人类的所有行为。我们的生命是如此短暂，在这短短的人生中，关于心智的整个领域，也就是记忆的活动，没什么可了解的；我们只能观察它。观察而没有丝毫思想活动，抛开时间，抛开

memory; we can only observe it. Observe without any movement of thought, observe without time, without past knowledge, without the observer who is the essence of the past. Just watch. Watch those clouds shaping and reshaping, watch the trees, the little birds. It is all part of life. When you watch attentively, with diligence, there is nothing to learn; there is only that vast space, silence and emptiness, which is all—consuming energy.

过去的知识，抛开作为过去的核心的观察者，只是去观察。观察那些
云朵的成形与重塑，观察树木，观察小鸟，这些都是生命的一部分。
当你勤勉地、全神贯注地观察，就没什么可了解的；只有那广袤的空
间、寂静和空无，而那就是强大无比的能量。

Wednesday, April 20, 1983

At the end of every leaf, the large leaves and the tiny leaves, there was a drop of water sparkling in the sun like an extraordinary jewel. And there was a slight breeze but that breeze didn't in any way disturb or destroy that drop on those leaves that were washed clean by the late rain. It was a very quiet morning, full of delight, peaceful, and with a sense of benediction in the air. And as we watched the sparkling light on every clean leaf, the earth became extraordinarily beautiful, in spite of all the telegraph wires and their ugly posts. In spite of all the noise of the world, the earth was rich, abiding, enduring. And though there were earthquakes here and there, most destructive, the earth was still beautiful. One never appreciates the earth unless one really lives with it, works with it, puts one's hands in the dust, lifting big rocks and stones—one never knows the extraordinary sense of being with the earth, the flowers, the gigantic trees and the strong grass and the hedges along the road.

Everything was alive that morning. As we watched, there was a sense of great joy and the heavens were blue, the sun was slowly coming out of the hills and there was light. As we watched the mockingbird on the wire, it was doing its antics, jumping high, doing a somersault, then coming down on the same spot on the wire. As we watched the bird enjoying itself, jumping in the air and then coming down circling, with its shrill cries,

1983 年 4 月 20 日，星期三

在每片叶子的边缘，无论叶子宽大还是细小，都有一颗水珠在阳光下熠熠发亮，就像一件不可思议的珠宝一样。空气中有微风吹过，但那微风丝毫没有打扰或者破坏叶片上的水珠——那些叶子刚刚被雨水冲刷一新。这是一个非常静谧的清晨，充满了安宁的喜悦，空气中弥漫着一种至福。当我们凝视着每片明净的叶子上闪烁的光芒，大地变得惊人地美丽，尽管四处是电话线以及丑陋的电话线杆。尽管世俗扰攘喧嚣，但大地是丰饶、持久、永恒的。尽管各处都有极具破坏性的地震，大地依然美丽如故。你永远无法领略大地的美，除非你真的与它一起生活、一起劳作，把双手伸入泥土，掀起大大小小的石块——否则你永远都无法懂得与大地、与花朵、与巨树、与劲草、与路边树篱在一起的那种非凡的感受。

那天早上，万物生机勃发。当我们凝神观看，有一种巨大的喜悦汹涌而来，天空碧蓝，朝阳缓缓从山中升起，阳光四射而出。当我们凝望电话线上的那尾知更鸟，它正乐此不疲地做着各种古怪的动作，高高跳起，翻个跟斗，然后又飞落在电话线的同一个位置上。当我们看着那只自得其乐的小鸟，在空中转着圈地窜上跳下，高声尖叫着，

its enjoyment of life, only that bird existed, the watcher didn't exist. The watcher was no longer there, only the bird, grey and white, with a longish tail. That watching was without any movement of thought, watching the flurry of the bird that was enjoying itself.

We never watch for long. When we watch with great patience, watch without any sense of the watcher, watch those birds, those droplets on the quivering leaves, the bees and the flowers and the long trail of ants, then time ceases, time has a stop. One doesn't take time to watch or have the patience to watch. One learns a great deal through watching—watching people, the way they walk, their talk, their gestures. You can see through their vanity or their negligence of their own bodies. They are indifferent, they are callous.

There was an eagle flying high in the air, circling without the beat of the wings, carried away by the air current beyond the hills and was lost. Watching, learning: learning is time but watching has no time. Or when you listen, listen without any interpretation, without any reaction, listen without any bias. Listen to that thunder in the skies, the thunder rolling among the hills. One never listens completely, there is always interruption. Watching and listening are a great art—watching and listening without any reaction, without any sense of the listener or the see—er. By watching and listening we learn infinitely more than from any book. Books are necessary, but watching and listening sharpen your senses. For, after all, the brain is the centre of all the reactions, thoughts and remembrances. But if your senses are not highly awakened you cannot really watch and listen and learn, not only how to act but about learning, which is the very soil in which the seed of goodness can grow.

When there is this simple, clear watching and listening, then there is

唱出它生命的喜悦，此时只有那只鸟存在，观看者并不存在。观看者已不在那里，只有那只鸟，灰白相间，拖着一条长尾。这种观看没有丝毫的思想活动，只是看着那只自娱自乐的小鸟在欢腾喧闹。

我们从来没有长久地观察。当我们带着无限的耐心来观察，丝毫不带着观察者去观察，观察那些小鸟，观察颤动的树叶上的那些水珠，观察蜜蜂和花朵以及蚂蚁长长的队列，此刻时间止息了，时间停止了。我们不肯花时间去观察，也没有耐心去观察。通过观察——观察人们，他们走路、说话的方式，他们的姿态——你可以了解到很多东西。你可以看穿他们的虚荣或者他们对自己身体的漠视。他们漫不经心，他们冷酷无情。

高空中有一头鹰在盘旋，羽翼丝毫未动，被气流带到群山的另一边，然后消失不见了。至于观察和了解：了解就是时间，而观察是没有时间的。或者说，当你倾听时，丝毫不做解释，也没有任何反应，只是毫无偏见地倾听。聆听空中的那阵雷声，在群山中翻滚回荡。我们从来没有全然地聆听，我们总是被打断。观察与倾听是一门伟大的艺术——观察并倾听，不做任何反应，也没有一丝听者与看者的感觉。通过观察和倾听，我们所学到的远远胜过任何书本。书籍是必要的，但观察和倾听能够使你的感官敏锐。因为，归根结底，大脑就是所有反应、思想和记忆的中心。但是，如果你的感官不是高度清醒的，你就无法真正去看、去听、去了解，不只是了解如何行动，而且了解如何学习，而学习正是良善的种子得以成长的沃土。

当你有了这种简明、清晰的观察和倾听，那么你就有了觉知——

an awareness—awareness of the colour of those flowers, red, yellow, white, of the spring leaves, the stems, so tender, so delicate, awareness of the heavens, the earth and those people who are passing by. They have been chattering along that long road, never looking at the trees, at the flowers, at the skies and the marvellous hills. They are not even aware of what is going on around them. They talk a great deal about the environment, how we must protect nature and so on, but it seems they are not aware of the beauty and the silence of the hills and the dignity of a marvellous old tree. They are not even aware of their own thoughts, their own reactions, nor are they aware of the way they walk, of their clothes. It does not mean that they are to be self—centred in their watching, in their awareness, but just be aware.

When you are aware there is a choice of what to do, what not to do, like and dislike, your biases, your fears, your anxieties, the joys which you have remembered, the pleasures that you have pursued; in all this there is choice, and we think that choice gives us freedom. We like that freedom to choose; we think freedom is necessary to choose—or, rather, that choice gives us a sense of freedom—but there is no choice when you see things very, very clearly.

And that leads us to an awareness without choice—to be aware without any like or dislike. When there is this really simple, honest, choiceless awareness it leads to another factor, which is attention.The word itself means to stretch out, to grasp, to hold on, but that is still the activity of the brain, it is in the brain. Watching, awareness, attention, are within the area of the brain, and the brain is limited—conditioned by all the ways of past generations, the impressions, the traditions and all the folly and the goodness of man. So all action from this attention is still limited, and that

对那些花朵的缤纷色彩的觉知，红色、黄色、白色，对春天的新叶和嫩枝的觉知，它们是如此柔弱、如此精致，对天空、大地和匆匆走过的人们的觉知。他们沿路走来，一直在喋喋不休，从不去看树木、花朵、天空和不可思议的群山。他们甚至都没意识到自己周围都发生着什么。他们对环境高谈阔论，我们必须如何如何保护自然云云，但他们似乎完全没有发觉群山的美丽与静谧，还有一棵奇妙的古树的庄严。他们甚至都没有察觉自己的思想、自己的反应，也没有注意到他们走路和穿衣的方式。这并不是说他们要在观察中、在觉察中变得自我中心，而是仅仅清醒地觉察。

当你发觉自己心存该做什么、不该做什么的选择，心存好恶的选择，还有你的偏见、你的恐惧、你的焦虑、你铭记的喜悦和追逐的欢愉；其中都有选择，而我们以为选择给了我们自由。我们喜欢选择的自由，我们以为有了自由才能选择——或者不如说，是选择给了我们一种自由感——然而，当你非常非常清晰地看到了事实，就根本不存在选择的问题。

而这就把我们引向了一种毫无选择的觉察——觉察而不带有任何好恶。一旦有了这种真正简单、诚实、无选择的觉察，就会带来另一个因素，那就是关注。这个词本身的含义是伸出、抓住、抱持，但那依旧是大脑的活动，依旧处在大脑之中。观察、觉察、关注，都在大脑的疆域之内，而大脑是局限的——受制于以往世世代代的生活方式、印象、传统以及人类的愚蠢和善行。所以，来自这种关注的所有行动都依然是局限的，而局限的事物必定会导致失序。当一个人从早

which is limited must inevitably bring disorder. When one is thinking about oneself from morning until night—one's own worries, one's own desires, demands and fulfilments—this self—centredness, being very, very limited, must cause friction in its relationship with another, who is also limited; there must be friction, there must be strain and disturbances of many kinds, the perpetual violence of human beings.

When one is attentive to all this, choicelessly aware, then out of that comes insight. Insight is not an act of remembrance, the continuation of memory. Insight is like a flash of light. You see with absolute clarity, all the complications, the consequences, the intricacies. Then this very insight is action, complete. In that there are no regrets, no looking back, no sense of being weighed down, no discrimination. This is pure, clear insight— perception without any shadow of doubt.

Most of us begin with certainty and as we grow older the certainty changes to uncertainty and we die with uncertainty. But if one begins with uncertainty, doubting, questioning, asking, demanding, with real doubt about man's behaviour, about all the religious rituals and their images and their symbols, then out of that doubt comes the clarity of certainty. When there is clear insight into violence, for instance, that very insight banishes all violence. That insight is outside the brain, if one can so put it. It is not of time. It is not of remembrance or of knowledge, and so that insight and its action changes the very brain cells. That insight is complete and from that completeness there can be logical, sane, rational, action.

This whole movement from watching, listening, to the thunder of insight, is one movement; it is not coming to it step by step. It is like a swift arrow. And that insight alone can uncondition the brain, not the effort of thought, which is determination, seeing the necessity for something; none

到晚一直在想着自己——自己的忧虑，自己的欲望、要求和满足——这种以自我为中心，本身就是非常非常局限性的，它必然会导致与他人关系中的摩擦——他人同样也是局限的；因此必定会造成冲突，必定会造成各式各样的压力和困扰，以及人类永无止境的暴力。

当你关注这一切，无选择地觉察，从中就会产生洞察。洞察并非记忆的活动、记忆的延续。洞察就像一道闪电，你无比清晰地将事物所有的复杂微妙之处以及各种来龙去脉一览无遗。因而这种洞察本身就是行动，完满的行动。其中没有懊悔，没有回顾，没有忧虑，没有偏见。这就是纯粹而清晰的洞察——没有一丝疑虑的阴影的觉察。

我们大多数人都从确定开始，随着我们渐渐长大，确定变成了不确定，然后我们带着不确定死去。但是，如果我们从不确定开始，从怀疑、质疑、询问、探求开始，带着对人类行为的真正质疑，对所有的宗教仪式、形象和符号的真正质疑，那么从那种质疑中就会诞生笃定的清晰。比如说，一旦对暴力有了清晰的洞察，那洞察本身就消弭了所有暴力。那洞察存在于大脑之外，如果我们可以这样表达的话。它不属于时间，也不属于记忆或者知识，所以那种洞察以及它的行动就能够改变脑细胞本身。这份洞察是完满的，从那份完满中就会诞生逻辑的、理性的、清醒的行动。

从观察、倾听到电闪雷鸣般的洞察，这整个运动是一个活动，而不是一步步达到的。它就像是一支迅捷的利箭。这洞察本身就能解放大脑，而不是思想的努力——也就是决心——看到了事情的紧迫性；这些都无法带来从制约中的全然解脱。这就是时间以及时间的终结。

of that will bring about total freedom from conditioning.All this is time and the ending of time. Man is time—bound and that bondage to time is the movement of thought. So where there is an ending to thought and to time there is total insight. Only then can there be the flowering of the brain. Only then can you have a complete relationship with the mind.

人类被时间所束缚，而这种时间的束缚就是思想的运动。所以，只要思想和时间得以终结，就会有全然的洞察。只有此时头脑才能如鲜花般盛放，只有此时你才能与心灵拥有完满的关系。

Thursday, April 21, 1983

There is a cabin high among the hills, somewhat isolated although there are other cabins there. The cabin was among those gigantic marvellous old trees, the sequoias.*Some of them are said to have existed from the time of the ancient Egyptians, perhaps from Rameses the Second. They are really marvellous trees. Their bark is rose—coloured and bright in the morning sunlight. These trees cannot be burnt; their bark resists fire and you can see where the old Indians built a fire round the tree; the dark mark of fire is still there. They are really quite gigantic in size, their trunks are enormous and if you sit very still under them in the morning light, with the sun among the treetops, all the squirrels there will come up quite close to you. They are very inquisitive like the blue jays, for there are jays too, blue, blue birds, always ready to scold you, asking why you are there, telling you that you are disturbing their area and should go away as quickly as possible. But if you remain quiet, watching, looking at the beauty of the sunlight among the leaves in the still air, then they will leave you alone, accept you as the squirrels do.

It was not the season, so the cabins were empty and you were alone,

---

* In September 1942, Krishnamurti had stayed alone for three weeks in a cabin in the Sequoia National Park where he had been ecstatically happy. It is this experience that he is recalling in his dictation.

1983 年 4 月 21 日，星期四

高耸的群山之上有一座小木屋，虽然那里还有其他的木屋，它还是略显孤绝，栖身于那些高大而奇美的古树——红杉之间。① 据说这些红杉有的从古埃及时代就已经存在了，或许是拉美西斯二世时期。它们真是太美了，树皮泛着玫瑰色，在晨光中闪亮夺目。这些树不会被焚毁，它们的树皮可以防火，你可以发现古老的印第安人在树的周围生火的痕迹，火烧之后的黑色印记依然残留在那里。这些红杉身躯十分庞大，树干粗壮，如果你在晨曦中安静地坐在树下，阳光从树梢洒下来，所有的松鼠都会悄悄地靠近你。它们像蓝松鸦一样，充满了好奇心，因为那儿也有松鸦，一种湛蓝湛蓝的鸟儿，它们总是准备来责问你，问你为什么会在那儿，告诉你你侵扰了它们的领地，应该尽快离开。但是，如果你保持安静，观察着、注视着寂静空气中的树叶间闪耀的美丽阳光，那么它们就会任由你待着，像松鼠一样接纳你。

因为还没到季节，所以小木屋都是空的，只有你独自一人，到了夜晚，这里寂静无声。偶尔，会有熊光顾这里，你能听见它们笨重

---

① 1942 年 9 月，克里希那穆提独自一人在红杉国家公园待了三周的时间，在那里，他感受到了非同寻常的狂喜。他在口述中回忆的正是这次经历。

and at night it was so silent. And occasionally the bears would come and you could hear their heavy bodies against the cabin. It could have been quite a savage place, for modern civilization had not quite destroyed it. You have to climb from the planes, in and out, up and up and up, until you reach this sequoia forest. There were streams rushing down the slope. It was so extraordinarily beautiful to be alone among these vast, very tall great trees, ancient beyond the memory and so utterly unconcerned with what was going on in the world, silent in their ancient dignity and strength. And in this cabin, surrounded by these old ageless trees, you were alone day after day, watching, taking long walks, hardly meeting anyone. From such a height you could see the planes, sunlit, busy; you could see the cars like small insects chasing one another. And up here only the real insects were busy about their day.There were a great many ants. The red ones crawled over your legs but they never seemed to pay much attention to you.

From this cabin you fed the squirrels. There was one particular squirrel that would come every morning and you had a bag of peanuts and you would give them to it one by one: it would stuff it in its mouth, cross over the window—sill and come to the table with its bushy tail curled up, almost touching its head. It would take many of these shelled peanuts, or sometimes even the unshelled ones, and jump back across the window—sill down to the veranda and along the open space into a dead tree with a hollow in it which was its home. It would come perhaps for an hour or more wanting these peanuts, back and forth, back and forth. And it was quite tame by then, you could stroke it, it was so soft, so gentle, it looked with eyes of surprise and then friendship. It knew you wouldn't hurt it.

One day, closing all the windows when it was inside and the bag of peanuts was on the table, it took the usual mouthful and then went to the

的身躯靠在小木屋上。这里像是一片蛮荒之地，因为现代文明还没有怎么破坏它。你得从平地向上攀爬，进进出出，不断地向上、向上、向上，才能到达这片红杉树林。激流从山坡上奔涌而下。独自待在这片辽阔而高大的巨树中间，感觉真是美妙无比。它们的古老超越了记忆，丝毫不关心世间所发生的一切，只在它们古老的庄严和力量中静默无语。在这间被不朽的古树环绕的小木屋里，你日复一日地独处着，观察着，漫步着，几乎碰不到任何人。在这样的高度，你能看到阳光照耀下的忙碌平原，看到汽车像小昆虫一样彼此追逐。而在高高的这里，只有真正的昆虫在为生活忙碌。这里有非常多的蚂蚁，红蚂蚁爬到了你的腿上，但是它们似乎从没注意过你。

你会在这间小木屋给那些松鼠喂食。有一只很特别的松鼠每天早上都会过来，你拿着一袋花生，一颗一颗地喂它。它会把花生塞进嘴里，穿过窗台，来到桌边，毛茸茸的尾巴高高翘起，几乎能碰到它的头。它会塞进嘴里许多带壳的花生，有时甚至是不带壳的，然后从窗台上跳回去，爬下露台，沿着空地，钻进一棵空心的枯树中——那里就是它的家。一个多小时之后，它可能又会再来索要花生，来来回回的，一次又一次。那时它会非常乖顺，你可以抚摸它，它摸上去十分柔软，也很温和，它的眼神里先是惊讶，然后就变成了友善，它知道你不会伤害它。

有一天，在它进屋之后，你把窗户都关上了。桌上有一袋花生，它像往常一样塞了满嘴，然后跑到窗户和门边，可门窗都关上了，它意识到自己成了个囚犯。它一路跳过来，跳到了桌上，看着你，开始责问你。无论如何，你都不能把那个美丽鲜活的小生灵纳为囚徒，于

windows and the door, which were all closed, and realized it was a prisoner. It came hopping along to the table, jumped on to it, looked at one and began to scold. After all, you couldn't keep that lively beautiful thing as a prisoner, so you opened the windows. It jumped down to the floor, climbed over the window—sill, went back to the dead trunk and came right back asking for more. From then on we were really great friends. After it had stuffed that hole full of peanuts, probably for the winter, it would go along up the trunks of the trees chasing other squirrels and would always come back to its dead trunk. Then sometimes of an evening it would come to the window—sill and sit there and would chatter, looking at me, telling me something of the day's work, and as it grew darker it said goodnight and jumped back to its home in the hole in the dead old tree. And the next morning early it would be there on the window—sill calling, chattering, and the day would begin.

Every animal in that forest, every little thing, was doing the same— gathering food, chasing others in fun and in anger, and the big animals like the deer were curious and looked at you. And as you climbed to a moderate height and went along a rocky path, you turned and there was a big bear, black with four cubs, as large as large cats. It pushed them up a tree, the four of them, and they climbed up to safety, and then the mother turned round and looked at me. Strangely we weren't afraid. We looked at each other for perhaps two or three seconds or more and then you turned your back and went down the same path. Only then, when you were safe in your cabin, did you realize how dangerous had been this encounter with a mother bear with four cubs.

Life is an endless process of becoming and ending. This great country was still unsophisticated in those days; it was not so terribly advanced

是你打开了窗户。它跳下地板，爬上窗台，回到了枯树干那里，然后又径直回来索要更多的花生。从那以后，我们成了真正要好的朋友。在它把自己的窝装满了花生之后——那也许是为冬天储备的——它就会一路爬上其他的树干，去追逐其他的松鼠，但最后总是会返回它自己的枯树干。有时候在傍晚，它会来到窗台上，坐在那里，一边看着我，一边喋喋不休地告诉我一天的工作，天色渐晚的时候，它会道声晚安，然后跳回自己老枯树上的窝里。而第二天一大清早，它又会出现在窗台上打招呼，唠叨个不停，然后一天开始了。

那片森林里的每个动物、每个小生命，都在做着同样的事——收集食物，然后为了好玩儿或者因为生气而互相追逐。而像鹿那样的大动物非常好奇，它们会看着你。当你爬上半山，沿着一条石头路前行时，你忽然回过身来，那里有一头大黑熊，带着四头小熊仔，它们跟大猫一样大小。那头熊把四个孩子推到树上，它们爬到了安全的地方，然后母熊转过身来，看着我。奇怪的是，我们都不害怕。我们彼此对视了大约两三秒钟，或者更久，然后你转身沿着同一条路走下山去。当你安全地回到了自己的小木屋，只有此时你才意识到，与带着四头熊仔的母熊的这次遭遇是多么危险。

生命是一个无休止的成为和结束的过程。在那些日子里，这个伟大的国家尚未如此复杂，技术上的进步还没有如此可怕，也不像如今这般鄙陋粗俗。坐在小木屋的台阶上，你就这样看着，万物都生机勃勃——树木、蚂蚁、兔子、鹿、熊，还有松鼠。生命就是行动。生命是一系列连续的、无止境的行动，直到你死去。脱胎于欲望的行动是

technologically and there was not too much vulgarity, as there is now. Sitting on the steps of that cabin you watched and everything was active—the trees, the ants, the rabbits, the deer, the bear and the squirrel. Life is action. Life is a series of continuous, endless action until you die. Action born of desire is distorted, is limited, and this limited action must invariably, do what you will, bring about endless conflict.

Anything that is limited must in its very nature breed many problems, crises. It is like a man, like a human being, who is all the time thinking about himself, his problems, his experiences, his joys and pleasures, his business affairs—completely self—centred. The activity of such a person is naturally very limited. One never realizes the limitation of this self—centredness. They call it fulfilment, expressing oneself, achieving success, the pursuit of pleasure and becoming something inwardly, the urge, the desire to be. All such activity must not only be limited and distorted but its successive actions in whatever direction must inevitably breed fragmentation, as is seen in this world. Desire is very strong; the monks and the sannyasis of the world have tried to suppress it, tried to identify that burning flame with some noble symbols or some image—identifying the desire with something greater—but it is still desire. Whatever action comes out of desire, may it be called noble or ignoble, is still limited, distorted.

Now the blue jay has come back; it is there after its morning meal, scolding to be noticed. And you threw it a few peanuts. It scolded first, then hopped down to the ground, caught a few of them in its beak, flew back on to the branch, flew off, came back scolding. And it too, day by day, became gradually tame. It came quite close with bright eyes, its tail up, the blue shining with such brightness and clarity—a blue that no painter can catch. And it scolded other birds. Probably that was its domain and it didn't want any

扭曲的、局限的，而即使你使尽浑身解数，这种局限的行动都必定会导致无休止的冲突。

任何局限的事物都会滋生许多问题和危机，其本性即是如此。就像一个人，始终想着他自己，自己的问题，自己的经历，自己的喜悦和欢愉，自己的生意——完全地以自我为中心。这样一个人的行为自然是非常局限的。人从没意识到这种以自我为中心的局限。表达自己，获取成功，追逐快乐，内心努力成为什么人，这种成为的冲动和欲望，他们称之为自我实现。所有这类行为都必定是局限的、扭曲的，不仅如此，而且其后续的活动，无论在哪个方向上，都必然会导致分裂，就像你在这个世界上看到的那样。欲望非常强大，全世界的僧侣和苦行者都试图压抑它，试图把那团燃烧的火焰，与某些高尚的符号或者形象联系到一起——把欲望与某种更伟大的东西相等同——但那依然是欲望。无论从欲望中产生什么行动，不管称之为高尚还是卑鄙，都依然是局限的、扭曲的。

这会儿蓝松鸦回来了，它是为早餐而来的，它责怪着你，以引起你的注意。你扔给了它几颗花生。它先是责备，然后跳到地上，用喙啄起几颗，飞回到树枝上，然后又飞离了树枝，回来继续责备你。它也一样，一天天逐渐变得温顺起来。它离你很近，睁着明亮的眼睛，尾巴翘起，身上的蓝色闪烁着如此明亮而又清晰的光芒——那是一种任何一个画家都无法捕捉的蓝色。它也责备其他的鸟儿。也许那是它的领地，它不希望见到任何入侵者。但入侵者总是不断。其他的鸟儿很快就来了。它们看起来都喜欢葡萄干和花生。生命的全部活动都跃然于眼前。

intruders. But there are always intruders. Other birds soon came. They all seemed to like raisins and peanuts. The whole activity of existence was there.

The sun now was high in the heaven and there were very few shadows, but towards the evening there will be long shadows, shapely, sculptured, dark with a smile.

Is there an action not of desire? If we ask such a question, and we rarely do, one can probe, without any motive, to find an action which is of intelligence. The action of desire is not intelligent; it leads to all kinds of problems and issues. Is there an action of intelligence? One must always be somewhat sceptical in these matters; doubt is an extraordinary factor of purification of the brain, of the heart. Doubt, carefully measured out, brings great clarity, freedom. In the Eastern religions, to doubt, to question, is one of the necessities for finding truth, but in the religious culture of Western civilization, doubt is an abomination of the devil. But in freedom, in an action that is not of desire, there must be the sparkle of doubt.

When one actually sees, not theoretically nor verbally, that the action of desire is corrupt, distorted, the very perception is the beginning of that intelligence from which action is totally different. That is, to see the false as the false, the truth in the false, and truth as truth. Such perception is that quality of intelligence which is neither yours nor mine, which then acts. That action has no distortion, no remorse. It doesn't leave a mark, a footprint on the sands of time. That intelligence cannot be unless there is great compassion, love, if you will. There cannot be compassion if the activities of thought are anchored in any one particular ideology or faith, or attached to a symbol or to a person. There must be freedom to be compassionate. And where there is that flame, that very flame is the movement of intelligence.

此刻太阳高挂在天空，地上树影稀少，而接近傍晚的时候会有长长的树影，线条优美，有如精心刻画出的一般，带着一抹微笑，深深地印在地上。

有没有一种不属于欲望的行动？如果我们提出了这样一个问题——而我们很少这么做——我们就可以毫无动机地去探索，去发现一种智慧的行动。欲望的行动毫无智慧，它会导致各种各样的麻烦和问题。有没有一种智慧的行动？在这些问题上，你必须始终或多或少地保持一种质疑的态度，质疑是净化头脑和心灵的一个非同寻常的因素。质疑，细心地思量，会带来非凡的清晰和自由。在东方的宗教中，怀疑、质疑是发现真理必不可少的品质之一，而在西方文明的宗教文化中，质疑则是魔鬼的禁忌。但在自由中，在不属于欲望的行动中，必须存有质疑的火花。

当你真的看到——不是从理论上或者字面上——欲望的行动是腐败的、扭曲的，这份洞察本身就是智慧的开始，而从智慧发出的行动是截然不同的。也就是说，如实地看到虚假就是虚假、真理就是真理，从虚假中看到真理。这份洞察就是智慧的品质，它既不属于你也不属于我，但它会行动。那种行动没有扭曲，没有懊悔。它不会留下痕迹，不会在时间的沙滩上留下脚印。除非有浩瀚的慈悲与爱，否则那份智慧无法存在，你尽管一试。如果思想的活动驻足于任何一种特定的意识形态或信仰，或者依附于某个符号或某个人，慈悲就无法存在。若要慈悲，就必须有自由。而哪里有了那团火焰，那团火焰本身就是智慧的行动。

Friday, April 22, 1983

It is about 1, 400 feet up here among the orchards, the orange and avocado, with the hills behind the house. The highest hill around here is about 6, 500 feet. Probably it would be called a mountain and the old name is Topa Topa. The former Indians lived here: they must have been very odd and a rather nice race. They may have been cruel but the people who destroyed them were much more cruel. Up here, after a rainy day, nature is waiting breathlessly for another storm, and the world of flowers and the small bushes are rejoicing in this quiet morning, and even the leaves seem so bright, so sharply clear. There is a rose bush that is full of roses, bright red; the beauty of it, the perfume, the stillness of that flower is a marvel.

Going down in the old car which has been kept well polished, the engine running smoothly—going down to the village, through the village, past all those small buildings, schools, and then the open space filled with avocados—going down through the ravine, curving in and out on a smooth road, so well made; then going up and up and up, perhaps over5, 000 feet: there the car stopped and there we were high up, overlooking all the hills which were very green, with bushes, trees and deep ravines. It seemed that we were up among the gods.

Very few used that road, which went on through the desert to a big town miles away, far to your left. As you face the south you see the very

1983 年 4 月 22 日，星期五

　　这里的海拔有一千四百英尺高，四周环绕着橙树和鳄梨树的果园，房子后面是连绵的群山。这里最高的山峰大约有六千五百英尺高。也许应该称之为大山，它原来的名字叫作"托帕托帕"（Topa Topa）。以前印第安人生活在这里，他们肯定是一个非常古怪而又相当优秀的民族。他们也许有些残忍，但毁灭他们的人要残忍多了。在高高的这里，刚刚经历了一个雨天，大自然正在屏息等待另一场暴风雨，而这个布满了鲜花和小灌木的世界，正在这个静谧的清晨里欢欣雀跃，甚至连树叶看起来都是那么明亮，那么耀眼地清晰。那里有一丛玫瑰，开满了鲜红的花朵；其中的美，花朵的芬芳和宁静，真是一个奇迹。

　　坐上那辆被保养得光亮如新的老爷车——引擎也运转得十分顺畅——向山下的村庄驶去，然后穿过了那个村庄，经过了各种小房子和学校，以及栽满鳄梨树的开阔田地，接着又穿过峡谷，沿着修建得平顺、精良的马路蜿蜒而下；然后又不停地向上、向上、向上，到了大约五千多英尺的地方，车停了下来，我们来到了高高的山顶上，俯瞰着长满了灌木和树丛的苍翠群山，下面则是深深的峡谷。那感觉就

far distant sea—the Pacific. It is so very still here. Though man has made this road, fortunately there is no imprint of man. There have been fires up here but that was years ago. You can see some burnt out stumps, black, but round them it has now become green. There have been heavy rains and everything is now in flower, purple, blue and yellow, with here and there bright red spots.The glory of the earth has never been so deeply compassionate as up here.

We sat on the side of the road which was quite clean. It was the earth; earth is always clean. And there were little ants, little insects, crawling, running all over the place. But there are no wild animals up here, which is strange. There may be at night—deer, coyotes and perhaps a few rabbits and hares. Occasionally a car passed by, and that broke the silence, the dignity and the purity of silence. This is really an extraordinary place.

Words cannot measure the expanse, the rolling hills and the vast space, nor the blue sky and the distant desert. It was the whole earth. One hardly dared to talk, there was such compelling silence, not to be disturbed. And that silence cannot be measured by words. If you were a poet you would probably measure it with words, put it into a poem, but that which is written is not the actual. The word is not the thing. And here, sitting beside a rock which was becoming warm, man did not exist. The rolling hills, the higher mountains, the great sweeping valleys, deep in blue; there was no you, there was nothing but that.

From ancient times all civilizations have had this concept of measurement. All their marvellous buildings were based on mathematical measurement. When you look at the Acropolis and the glory of the Parthenon, and the hundred and ten floor buildings of New York, they have all had to have this measurement.

像是我们正置身于众神之中。

很少有人会走那条路，它从沙漠一直延伸到数英里外的一座大城市，远远的在你的左手方向。当你面朝南方，你能看到非常遥远的大海——太平洋。这里真是无比安静。尽管人类修建了这条公路，但幸运的是并没有留下人类的印记。这里曾经发生过火灾，但那是多年前的事了。你还能看到一些燃烧后残留的树桩，颜色黝黑，但如今它们四周又是郁郁葱葱了。刚刚下过几场豪雨，此刻万物都在盛放，满眼鲜艳的紫色、蓝色和黄色，偶尔有鲜红的花丛点缀其中。大地的壮丽辉煌从没有像这里这样，让人如此深深地感动。

我们在非常干净的马路边坐下，就坐在地上，大地永远是那么干净。那里有很多小蚂蚁、小昆虫在爬，奔忙在这一整片地方。但这里并没有野生动物，很是奇怪。也许晚上才会有——鹿、郊狼，也许还有几只兔子和野兔。偶尔会有一辆车经过，打破这里的宁静，打破这份庄严而又纯洁的宁静。这真是一个美丽非凡的地方。

言语无法度量那种广阔，那绵延的群山和广袤的空间，也无法度量蔚蓝的天空和遥远的沙漠。这就是整个地球。你几乎不敢呼吸，这里有一种如此强烈的寂静，不容打扰。那份寂静，也无法由言语衡量。如果你是个诗人，你也许会用文字来度量，把它诉诸诗篇，但写下来的并非真实。文字并非真实之物。而在这里，坐在一块逐渐变暖的岩石旁边，人类似乎并不存在。只有连绵的群山，高耸的山峰，还有激流直下的湛蓝的宽阔山谷；你并不存在，除了那些，一切都不存在。

Measurement is not only by the rule; measurement exists in the very brain: the tall and the short, the better, the more. This comparative process has existed for time beyond time. We are always comparing. The passing of examinations from school, college, university—our whole way of living has become a series of calculated measurements: the beautiful and the ugly, the noble and ignoble—one's whole set of values, the arguments that end in conclusions, the power of people, the power of nations. Measurement has been necessary to man. And the brain, being conditioned to measurement, to comparison, tries to measure the immeasurable—measuring with words that which cannot ever be measured. It has been a long process for centuries upon centuries—the greater gods and the lesser gods, measuring the vast expanse of the universe and measuring the speed of the athlete. This comparison has brought a great many fears and sorrows.

Now, on that rock, a lizard has come to warm itself quite close to us. You can see its black eyes, its scaly back and the long tail. It is so still, motionless. The sun has made that rock quite warm, and the lizard, coming out of its cold night and warming itself, is waiting for some fly or insect to come along—it will measure the distance and snap it up.

To live without comparison, to live without any kind of measurement inwardly, never to compare what you are with what you should be. The word "meditation" means not only to ponder, to think over, to probe, to look, to weigh; it also has a much deeper meaning in Sanskrit—to measure, which is "to become". In meditation there must be no measurement. This meditation must not be a conscious meditation in deliberately chosen postures. This meditation must be totally unconscious, never knowing that you are meditating. If you deliberately meditate it is another form of desire, as any other expression of desire. The objects may vary; your meditation

从远古时代开始，所有的文明就已经有了这个度量的概念。他们所有奇妙的建筑都奠基于数学的度量。当你看到雅典卫城和壮丽的帕特农神庙，还有纽约一百一十层的高楼大厦，它们都必须使用这种度量。

度量不仅仅依据标尺而存在，度量还存在于头脑当中：高与矮，更好，更多。这个比较过程的存在已经无限久远。我们总是在比较。从学校、学院、大学通过考试——我们的整个生活方式都变成了一系列精于计算的度量：美与丑，高尚与卑微——人一整套的价值观，终止于结论的争执，人们的权力、国家的权力。度量对于人类来说一直是不可或缺的。而大脑，受限于衡量和比较，试图衡量那不可估量的事物——用言语去度量那永远无法度量的事物。这是个漫长的过程，已经持续了千百年——更高级的神明和更低级的神明，度量宇宙广袤的范围，也度量运动员的速度。这种比较带来了无数的恐惧和悲伤。

此刻，在那块岩石上，一只蜥蜴爬到离你很近的地方，来温暖自己的身体。你可以看到它黑色的眼睛，它布满鳞片的背部和长长的尾巴。它是那么安静，一动不动。太阳把那块石头晒得很温暖，那只蜥蜴从寒冷的夜里爬出来，温暖着自己，等待着飞虫或者昆虫的出现——它会考量距离，然后将虫一口吞掉。

要毫无比较地活着，内心不做任何衡量地活着，绝不拿你实际的样子与你应当的样子比较。"冥想"这个词不仅仅意味着沉思、思索、探究、观察、权衡；在梵文中，它还有更为深刻的含义——衡量，也就是"成为什么"。冥想中决不能有任何衡量。这种冥想一定不能是以刻意选择的姿势进行的有意识的冥想。这种冥想必须是完全

may be to reach the highest, but the motive is the desire to achieve, as the businessman, as the builder of a great cathedral.

Meditation is a movement without any motive, without words and the activity of thought. It must be something that is not deliberately set about. Only then is meditation a movement in the infinite, measureless to man, without a goal, without an end and without a beginning. And that has a strange action in daily life, because all life is one and then becomes sacred. And that which is sacred can never be killed. To kill another is unholy. It cries to heaven as a bird kept in a cage. One never realizes how sacred life is, not only your little life but the lives of millions of others, from the things of nature to extraordinary human beings. And in meditation which is without measurement, there is the very action of that which is most noble, most sacred and holy.

The other day on the banks of a river*—how lovely are rivers; there isn't only one sacred river, all rivers throughout the world have their own divinity—the other day a man was sitting on the banks of a river wrapt in a fawn coloured cloth. His hands were hidden, his eyes were shut and his body was very still. He had beads in his hands and he was repeating some words and the hands were moving from bead to bead. He had done this for many years and he never missed a bead. And the river rolled along beside him. Its current was deep. It began among the great mountains, snow—clad and distant; it began as a small stream, and as it moved south it gathered all the small streams and rivers and became a great river. In that part of the world they worshipped it.

---

* This is a memory from when he was at Benares on the banks of the Ganges.

无意识的，绝不知道你在冥想。如果你刻意去冥想，那它就只是另一种形式的欲望罢了，就跟欲望的其他任何一种表达形式一样。对象也许各不相同；你的冥想也许是为了触及至高无上者，但动机就是达成的欲望，跟商人和大教堂的建造者没什么两样。

　　冥想是一种没有任何动机、没有言语、没有思想活动的运动。它必须是一件毫不刻意地做出的事。只有这样，冥想才是无限中的运动，对于人类来说才是不可估量的，没有目标，无始亦无终。而它会在日常生活中产生一种奇特的行动，因为所有的生命都是一个整体，进而是神圣的。而神圣者绝不能被杀害。杀害生命是邪恶的。它会像被囚禁在笼中的小鸟一样向天空发出哀嚎。人们从来没有意识到生命有多么神圣，不仅仅是你卑微的生命，而且还有千千万万其他的生命，从自然界的各种生灵到非同凡响的人类。而在没有衡量的冥想中，就有着最为高尚、神圣和圣洁的行动。

　　有一天，在一条河的岸边 ①——河流是那么美丽，不是只有一条圣河，全世界所有的河流都有自己的神圣之处——那天一个人坐在一条河的岸边，身上裹着一块黄褐色的布。他双手握起，双眼紧闭，身体一动不动。他的手中有串念珠，嘴里念念有词，手指一个接一个地捻着珠子。他这么做了很多年，从来没有错过一粒念珠。而大河就在他身边汹涌而过。水流很深。它发源于积雪覆盖的遥远的崇山峻岭之中，一开始只是一条小溪，在它流向南方的过程中，汇聚了所有的小溪、

---

① 　这些记忆来自他在恒河岸边的贝拿勒斯的经历。

One does not know for how many years this man had been repeating his mantra and rolling the beads. He was meditating—at least people thought he was meditating and probably he did too. So all the passers—by looked at him, became silent and then went on with their laughter and chatter. That almost motionless figure—one could see through the cloth only a slight action of the fingers—had sat there for a very long time, completely absorbed, for he heard no other sound than the sound of his own words and the rhythm of it, the music of it. And he would say that he was meditating. There are a thousand others like him, all over the world, in quiet deep monasteries among the hills and towns and beside the rivers.

Meditation is not words, a mantram, or self—hypnosis, the drug of illusions. It must happen without your volition. It must take place in the quiet stillness of the night, when you are suddenly awake and see that the brain is quiet and there is a peculiar quality of meditation going on. It must take place as silently as a snake among the tall grass, green in the fresh morning light. It must take place in the deep recesses of the brain. Meditation is not an achievement. There is no method, system or practice. Meditation begins with the ending of comparison, the ending of the becoming or not becoming. As the bee whispers among the leaves so the whispering of meditation is action.

小河，然后变成了一条大河。在世界的这片地方，人们对它顶礼膜拜。

你不知道这个人有多少年来一直在诵念咒语、转动念珠。他在冥想——至少人们以为他在冥想，或许他自己也这么以为。所以所有的路人经过的时候都要看看他，安静一会儿，然后又继续谈笑风生地向前走去。这个几乎一动不动的人——透过那块布，你可以看到只有手指有轻微的动作——他在那里坐了很久，完全沉浸在自己的世界中，因为除了他自己嘟哝的声音、节奏和韵律之外，他什么都听不到。而他会说他在冥想。全世界还有千千万万人像他一样，隐身于群山中、市镇中以及河岸边那些安静幽深的修道院之中。

冥想并非词句、咒语或者自我催眠，这些虚幻的麻醉剂。它只能在你不经意的时候发生。它必须发生在夜晚的安宁静谧之中，当你忽然醒来，发现头脑很安静，此时就有一种特别的冥想在进行。它的发生必须像穿过草丛的蛇一样静悄悄——高高的草丛在清新的晨曦中青翠欲滴。它必须发生在大脑的最深处。冥想不是一项成就，它没有方法、体系，也无法练习。冥想始于比较的终结、想成为或不成为什么的终结。就像蜜蜂在树叶间嗡鸣，冥想的低语即是行动。

Saturday, April 23, 1983

The clouds are still hanging over the hills, the valley and the mountains. Occasionally there is an opening in the sky and the sun comes through, bright, clear, but soon it disappears. One likes this kind of morning, cool, fresh, with the whole world green around you. As the summer comes on the sun will burn all the green grass, and the meadows across the valley will be parched, dry, and all the grass with the bright green will have gone. In the summer all the freshness has gone.

One likes these quiet mornings. The oranges are so bright and the leaves, dark green, are shining. And there is a perfume in the air from the orange blossom, strong, almost suffocating. There is a different kind of orange to be picked later on before the summer heat. Now there is the green leaf, the orange and the flower on the same tree at the same time. It is a beautiful world and man is so indifferent to it, spoiling the earth, the rivers and the bays and the fresh—water lakes.

But let's leave all that behind and walk along a narrow path, up the hill where there is a little stream which in a few weeks will be dry. You and a friend are walking along the path, talking now and then, looking at all the various colours of green. What a variety there is, from the lightest green, the Nile green, and perhaps even lighter, bluer, to the dark greens, luscious, full of their own richness. And as you go along up the path,

层云依然笼罩在丘陵、山谷和群山之上。空中的云朵偶尔会闪出一道缝来，阳光直射下来，明亮而耀眼，但很快又消失了。你喜欢这样的早晨，凉爽，清新，围绕着你的整个世界一片翠绿。当夏天来临的时候，艳阳会烤焦所有的绿草，山谷里的草地会变得焦干，翠绿的青草都会消失不见。到了夏天，所有的清新都将不复存在。

你喜欢这些静谧的早晨。树上的橙子是如此明亮，深绿色的叶子也在闪闪发光。空气中有一股来自橙花的香气，浓烈得几乎令人窒息。还有另一种橙子，要在炎热的夏季来临之前才采摘。此刻在同一棵橙树上，同时存在着绿叶、果实和花朵。这是一个美丽的世界，而人类对此无动于衷，破坏着土地、河流、海湾和淡水湖。

但是让我们把那些都抛在身后，沿着一条小路向山上走去，那里有一条小溪，几周之后它就会干涸。你和一位朋友正沿着小路散步，一边时不时交谈几句，一边望着各种深浅不同的绿色。这绿色可真是丰富啊，从最浅淡的绿色，尼罗河绿——也许还有更浅的、更接近蓝色的——到深绿色，青翠欲滴，充满了浓烈的色彩。当你们沿路而上，那条小路刚刚够两个人并肩而行，你突然拾起了一样瑰丽无比、

just managing to walk along together side by side, you happen to pick up something ravishingly beautiful, sparkling, a jewel of extraordinary antiquity and beauty. You are so astonished to find it on this path of so many animals which only a few people have trodden. You look at it with great astonishment. It is so subtly made, so intricate that no jeweller's hand can ever have made it. You hold it for some time, amazed and silent. Then you put it very carefully in your inside pocket, button it, and are almost frightened that you might lose it or that it might lose its sparkling, shining beauty. And you put your hand outside the pocket that holds it. The other sees you doing this and sees that your face and your eyes have undergone a remarkable change. There is a kind of ecstasy, a speechless wonder, a breathless excitement.

When the man asks: "What is it that you have found and are so extraordinarily elated by?" you reply in a very soft, gentle voice (it seems so strange to you to hear your own voice) that you picked up truth. You don't want to talk about it, you are rather shy; the very talking might destroy it. And the man who is walking beside you is slightly annoyed that you are not communicating with him freely, and he says that if you have found the truth, then let's go down into the valley and organize it so that others will understand it, so that others will grasp it and perhaps it will help them. You don't reply, you are sorry that you ever told him about it.

The trees are full of bloom. Even up here on the slight breeze coming up the valley you smell the orange blossom and look down the valley and see the many orange trees and feel the quiet, still, breathless air. But you have come upon something that is most precious, that can never be told to another. They may find it, but you have it, grasp it and adore it.

Institutions and organizations throughout the world have not

光彩熠熠的东西，那是一件极其古老而又美丽的珠宝。在这条动物出没、人迹罕至的小路上找到了它，你感觉极其讶异。你带着无比惊奇的眼神看着它。它制作得如此精美、如此细致，乃至没有哪个能工巧匠的手能够造出它。你捧着它，看了一会儿，惊讶而又安静。然后你非常小心地把它装入里面的口袋，扣上扣子，生怕会把它丢失，或者怕它失去那光彩熠熠的美。然后你把手放在了装着它的口袋外面。旁边的人看到了你的这些动作，也看到了你的脸和你的眼睛发生了一种显著的变化。有一种狂喜，一种无法言喻的惊奇，一种令人屏息的兴奋。

当那个人问道："你发现了什么？又是对什么感到无比欢欣？"你用一种非常轻柔的声音回答说（听到你自己的声音，真是一件奇怪的事）你捡到了真理。你不想谈论它，你非常害羞；谈论本身就可能毁了它。而与你并肩而行的那个人，对你没有直截了当地跟他交流，感到有些恼火，于是他说，如果你找到了真理，那就让我们走下山谷把它组织起来，这样其他人就能了解它、领会它了，那也许会帮到他们。你没有回答，你很遗憾竟把这些告诉了他。

树木绽满了鲜花。即使在高高的这里，循着从山谷里吹上来的微风，你也能嗅到橙花的香气，俯瞰山谷，你能看到成片的橙树，感受到那安宁、寂静、令人屏息的空气。你偶遇了某种极为珍贵的东西，但你无法把它传达给别人。他们也许会找到它，但你已经拥有了它，领会了它，也钟爱着它。

全世界的机构和组织都没有帮到人类。世界上有各种满足人类

helped man. There are all the physical organizations for one's needs; the institutions of war, of democracy, the institutions of tyranny and the institutions of religion—they have had their day and they continue, and man looks up to them, longing to be helped, not only physically but inside the skin, inside the throbbing ache, the shadow of time and the far reaching thoughts. There have been institutions of many, many kinds from the most ancient of days, and they have not inwardly changed man. Institutions can never change man psychologically, deeply. And one wonders why man created them, for all the institutions in the world are put together by man, hoping that they might help him, that they might give him some kind of lasting security. And strangely they have not. We never seem to realize this fact. We are creating more and more institutions, more and more organizations—one organization opposing another.

Thought is inventing all these, not only the democratic organizations or the totalitarian organizations; thought is also perceiving, realizing, that what it has created has not basically changed the structure, the nature of one's own self. The institutions, the organizations and all religions are put together by thought, by cunning, clever, erudite thought. What thought has created, brought about, shapes its own thinking. And one asks oneself, if one is serious, earnest in one's enquiry: why has not thought realized its own activity? Can thought be aware of its own movement? Can thought see itself, see what it is doing, both in the outer and the inner?

There is really no outer and inner: the inner creates the outer, and the outer then shapes the inner. This ebb and flow of action and reaction is the movement of thought, and thought is always trying to overcome the outer, and succeeds, bringing about many problems; in solving one problem other problems arise. Thought has also shaped the inner, moulded it according to

需求的物质方面的组织；有战争机构、民主机构、专制机构和宗教机构——它们已经盛行于世，并且会继续存在，而人类仰视它们，渴望得到帮助，不仅仅从物质层面，而且在体肤之下，在悸动的痛苦中，在时间与影响深远的思想的阴影之下，渴望得到它们的帮助。自远古时代开始，就有了各种各样的机构，但它们从未改变人类的内心。机构永远无法从心理上深刻地改变人类。你会纳闷人类为什么建立了它们，因为世界上的所有机构都是人类造就的，希望它们能帮助自己，能带给自己某种持久的安全。但奇怪的是它们没有。我们似乎从未意识到这个事实。我们还在建立越来越多的机构，越来越多的组织——互相对立的组织。

是思想发明了这些，不只是民主主义的组织或者极权主义的组织，而且思想也开始洞察到、意识到，它所建造的一切并没有从根本上改变人类自我的结构和本质。各种机构、组织和所有的宗教都由思想，由狡猾、聪明、博学的思想所造。思想所建造的一切，又反过来塑造了它自身的思维。于是你问自己，如果你在探询中足够认真、足够热切的话：思想为什么没有意识到自己的行为？思想能觉察到自己的活动吗？思想能够看清自己，看到自己在外在和内在世界的所作所为吗？

实际上并不存在什么内外之分：内在创造了外在，然后外在又来塑造内在。行动和反应的这种起起落落是思想的运动，而思想总是企图战胜外在，战胜之后却招来了更多的问题；在解决一个问题的过程中，另外的问题又产生了。思想也塑造了内在，根据外在的需求把

the outer demands. This seemingly endless process has created this society, ugly, cruel, immoral and violent. And having created it, the inner becomes a slave to it. The outer shapes the inner and the inner shapes the outer. This process has been going on for thousands upon thousands of years and thought seems not to realize its own activity.

So one asks: can thought ever be aware of itself—aware of what it is doing? There is no thinker apart from thought; thought has made the thinker, the experiencer, the analyser. The thinker, the one who is watching, the one who acts, is the past, with all the inheritance of man, genetically, biologically—the traditions, the habits and all accumulated knowledge. After all, the past is knowledge, and the thinker is not separate from the past. Thought has created the past, thought is the past; then thought divides the thinker and the thought, which the thinker must shape, control. But that is a fallacy; there is only thought. The self is the "me", the past. Imagination may project the future but it is still the activity of thought.

So thought, which is the outcome of knowledge, has not changed man and will never change him because knowledge is always limited and will always be limited. So again one asks: can thought become aware of itself, thought which has put together all our consciousness—action and reaction, the sensory response, the sensuality, the fears, the aspirations, the pursuit of pleasure, all the agony of loneliness and the suffering which man has brought upon himself through wars, through his irresponsibility, through callous self—centredness? All that is the activity of thought, which has invented the limitless and the god who lives in the limitless. All that is the activity of time and thought.

When one comes to this point one asks the old instrument, which is worn out, whether it can bring about a radical mutation in man, which

它装入模子。这个看起来永无休止的过程造就了这个社会，这个丑陋、残忍、堕落和暴力的社会。建立起社会之后，内在又变成了社会的奴隶。外在塑造着内在，内在也塑造着外在。这个过程已经上演了千千万万年，而思想似乎并没有意识到它自己的行为。

于是你问道：思想究竟能不能觉察到自己——觉察到自己的所作所为？并不存在一个脱离思想存在的思想者；是思想造就了思想者、经验者、分析者。思想者，那个在观察、在行动的人，就是过去，包含了人类所有的遗产，基因上的、生物学上的，还有传统、习惯和积累的所有知识。归根结底，过去就是知识，而思想者与过去是分不开的。思想制造了过去，思想就是过去；然后思想划分出了思想者和思想，说思想者必须塑造和控制思想。但这是个谬论，存在的只有思想而已。自己就是"我"，就是过去。想象力可以投射出未来，但那依然是思想的活动。

所以思想，也就是知识的产物，并没有改变人类，也永远不会改变人类，因为知识始终是局限的，也将永远都是局限的。所以我们再来问一问：思想能不能觉察到它自身，认识到是思想造就我们所有的意识——行动和反应，感官反应，感官享受，恐惧，渴望，对快乐的追逐，各种孤独的痛苦，还有人类通过战争、自己的不负责任和冷漠自私为自己带来的苦难？这一切都是思想的作为，思想也发明了无限，以及生活在无限中的神明。这些都是时间和思想的活动。

当你意识到了这一点，你就会问，这个破败不堪的旧工具，它能否为人类——归根结底，也就是大脑——带来彻底的转变？当思想

is, after all, the brain. When thought realizes itself, sees where knowledge is necessary in the physical world and realizes its own limitation, it then becomes quiet, silent. Only then is there a new instrument which is not put together by time or thought, totally unrelated to knowledge. It is this instrument—perhaps the word instrument may be wrong—it is this perception which is always fresh, because it has no past, no remembrance; it is intelligence born of compassion. That perception brings a deep mutation in the very brain cells themselves, and its action is always the right action, clear, precise, without the shadow of the past and time.

认清了自己，明白物质世界中有知识的用武之地，同时也意识到了它自身的局限，此时它就会安静下来。只有此时才会出现一个崭新的工具，它并非由时间或思想所拼凑，与知识也毫不相干。正是这个工具——也许"工具"这个词是错的——这份洞察是永远新鲜的，因为它没有过去，也没有记忆；它就是诞生于慈悲的智慧。这份洞察会在脑细胞本身之中带来一种深刻的突变，因而它的行动永远是正确的行动、清晰、精准，没有过去和时间的丝毫阴影。

Sunday, April 24, 1983

It is a spring morning, a morning that has never been before and never will be again.

It is a spring morning. Every little blade of grass, the camellias, the roses, all are blooming and there is perfume in the air.

It is a spring morning and the earth is so alive, and up in this valley all the mountains are green and the tallest of them so extraordinarily vital, immovable and majestic. It is a morning that as you go along the path and look around at the beauty and the ground squirrels, every tender leaf of the spring is shining in the sun. Those leaves have been waiting for this the whole winter and have just come out, tender, vulnerable. And without being romantic, imaginative, there is a feeling of great love and compassion, for there is so much beauty, incorruptible. There have been a thousand spring mornings but never such a morning as this, so still, so quiet, breathless— perhaps it is with adoration. And the squirrels are out and so are the lizards.

It is a spring morning and the air is festive; there are festivals all over the world because it is spring. The festivals are expressed in so many different ways but that which is can never be expressed in words. Everywhere, with the song and the dance, there is a deep feeling of spring.

Why is it that we seem to be losing the highly vulnerable quality of sensitivity—sensitivity to all the things about us, not only to our own

1983 年 4 月 24 日，星期日

这是一个春日的早晨，一个空前绝后的清晨。

这是一个春日的早晨。每一片小小的青草叶片，数不清的山茶花和玫瑰花，都在盛放，空气中弥漫着香气。

这是一个春日的早晨，大地是如此生机勃勃，在这座山谷内，所有的山峦都郁郁葱葱，它们中最高的山峰有着如此非凡的活力，又是那么岿然不动、肃穆庄严。在这个早晨，当你沿着小路漫步，望着四周的美景和地松鼠，春天的每片嫩叶都在阳光下熠熠生辉。那些新叶为此已经等待了整个冬天，刚刚钻出枝头，新鲜，柔嫩。你心中涌现出一股强大的爱和慈悲感，因为天地间充盈着如此浩瀚的不朽的美，但这与浪漫或者想象毫不相干。尽管曾经有过一千个春日的早晨，但从没有过这样的一个清晨，如此安宁，如此静谧，令人屏息凝视——也许还带着敬慕之情。然后松鼠们出来了，蜥蜴也出来了。

这是一个春日的早晨，空气中有一股节日般的喜庆；全世界都在欢度节日，因为春天来了。人们用如此之多的方式庆祝着节日，但此刻的存在，绝无言语可以表达。伴随着无处不在的歌声和舞蹈，飘来一股浓浓的春天的气息。

problems and turmoils? To be actually sensitive, not about something but just to be sensitive, to be vulnerable, like that new leaf, which was born a few days ago to face storms, rain, darkness and light. When we are vulnerable we seem to get hurt; being hurt we withdraw into ourselves, build a wall around ourselves, become hard, cruel. But when we are vulnerable without any ugly, brutal reactions, vulnerable to all the movements of one's own being, vulnerable to the world, so sensitive that there is no regret, no wounds, no self—imposed discipline, then there is the quality of measureless existence.

We lose all this vulnerability in the world of noise and brutality, vulgarity and the bustle of everyday life. To have one's senses sharpened, not any one particular sense but to have all the senses fully awake, which does not necessarily mean to indulge—to be sensitive to all the movements of thought, the feelings, the pains, the loneliness, the anxiety—with those senses fully awakened, there is a different kind of sensation that goes beyond all the sensory or sensual responses. Have you ever looked at the sea, or at those vast mountains, the Himalayas, which stretch from horizon to horizon—have you ever watched a flower, with all your senses? When there is such observation there is no centre from which you are observing, there is no "me". The "me", the limited observation of one or two senses, breeds the egotistic movement. After all, we live by the senses, by sensation, and it is only when thought creates the image out of the sensations that all the complexities of desire arise.

On this morning, you look down into the valley, seeing the extraordinary spread of green and the distant town, feeling the pure air, watching all the crawling things of the earth, watching without the interference of the images thought has built. Now the breeze is blowing

我们似乎正在失去那份高度敏感的品质——不仅仅是对我们自己的问题和混乱敏感，而是对我们周围万事万物的敏感性——这是为什么？真正的敏感，不是对什么敏感，而只是敏感而已，就像那片刚刚绽出几天的嫩叶，它已然可以迎接暴风骤雨，迎接光明和黑暗。当我们敏感时，我们似乎就容易受伤；受伤后我们就退缩回自己的内心，在自己四周建起围墙，变得冷漠、残忍。但是，当我们敏感却没有任何丑陋和残忍的反应，对自己生活中的所有活动都敏感，对整个世界敏感，如此敏感以至于悔恨、伤害和自我强加的戒律都不复存在，此时就会有那种不可估量的事物存在。

在这个喧嚣而残忍的世界上，在粗俗、忙乱的日常生活中，我们丧失了所有的敏感性。让你的感官敏锐起来，不是某一个特定的感官，而是让所有的感官都充分觉醒——而这并不意味着沉溺——对思想的所有活动，对感情，对痛苦、孤独和焦虑都敏感起来，让所有的感官都充分觉醒，就会出现一种截然不同的感受，它超越了所有的感官享受或者欲乐的反应。你可曾望着大海，或者那广袤的群山，铺满地平线的喜马拉雅山脉——你可曾凝视一朵花，用你所有的感官？若有这样一种观察，就不会有一个你的观察所发源的中心，就不会有一个"我"。"我"，一两个感官的有限观察，催生了自我中心的活动。毕竟，我们仰赖感官和感觉生活，而只有当思想从感觉中建立起意象时，纷繁复杂的欲望才会产生。

今天早上，你俯瞰山谷，看着一望无垠的绿色和远处的城镇，感受着纯净的空气，注视着大地上蠕动着的所有生命，就那样观看，

from the valley up the canyon and you turn as the path turns. Going down, there is a bobcat right in front of you, about ten feet away. You can hear it purring, rubbing itself against a rock, the hair sticking out of its ears, its short tail and extraordinary, graceful movement. It is a spring morning for it too. We walked together down the path and it was hardly making any noise except for its purring, highly enjoying itself, delighted to be out in the spring sunshine; it was so clean that its hair was sparkling. And as you watch it, the whole wild nature is in that animal. You tread on a dead branch which makes a noise, and it is off, not even looking behind it; that noise indicated man, the most dangerous of all animals. It is gone in a second among bushes and rocks and all the joy has gone out of it. It knows how cruel man is and it doesn't want to wait; it wants to be away, as far away as possible.

It is a spring morning and it is peaceful. Aware that a man was behind it, a few feet away, that cat must have instinctively responded to the image of what man is—the man who has killed so many things, destroyed so many cities, destroyed culture after culture, ever pursuing his desires, always seeking some kind of security and pleasure.

Desire, which has been the driving force in man, has created a great many pleasant and useful things; desire also, in man's relationships, has created a great many problems and turmoils and misery—the desire for pleasure. The monks and the sannyasis of the world have tried to go beyond it, have forced themselves to worship an ideal, an image, a symbol. But desire is always there like a flame, burning. And to find out, to probe into the nature of desire, the complexity of desire, its activities, its demands, its fulfilments—ever more and more desire for power, position, prestige, status, the desire for the unnameable, that which is beyond all our

而不被思想构建的意象所干扰。此刻微风从山谷吹送上来，在小路转弯的地方，你转身开始下山。下山途中，一只山猫出现你面前大约十英尺远的地方。你听到了它发出的咕噜声，它在一块石头上蹭着自己的身体，耳朵上、短尾巴上的毛发竖立起来，它的动作是那么奇妙，那么优雅。对它来说，这也是一个春日的早晨。我们一起沿着小路往下走，它几乎没有发出任何声音，除了咕噜声，它尽情地享受着，很高兴沐浴在春天的阳光下。它非常干净，连毛发都闪着光。当你凝望它，你能从那个小动物身上看到所有的野性。你踩到了一根枯枝，弄出了一些声音，然后它就走掉了，都没有回头看一眼；那个声音表明了人的存在——那是所有动物中最危险的动物。瞬息之间它就消失在了灌木丛和山石之间，所有的喜悦也随之而去。它知道人类有多残忍，它不想等待，它想立刻离开，越远越好。

这是一个春日的早晨，十分安宁。那只猫发觉自己后面有个人，有几英尺远，然后它肯定是本能地对人的形象做出了反应——人类屠杀了如此多的生灵，摧毁了多少座城市，摧毁了一个又一个文化，永远在追逐自己的欲望，永远在寻求某种安全和快乐。

欲望，一直是人类身上的驱动力，它制造了大量令人愉悦和有用的东西；而在人与人的关系中，欲望也造成了无数的问题、混乱和不幸——追求快乐的欲望。全世界的僧侣与苦行者都试图超越它，强迫自己膜拜某个理想、形象或者符号。但欲望始终在那里，就像一团熊熊燃烧的火焰。要探究、发现欲望的本质，欲望的复杂性，它的诸多活动、需求和满足——对权力、地位、名望、身份愈演愈烈的欲望，

daily life—has made man do all kinds of ugly and brutal things. Desire is the outcome of sensation—the outcome with all the images that thought has built.

And this desire not only breeds discontent but a sense of hopelessness. Never suppress it, never discipline it but probe into the nature of it—what is the origin, the purpose, the intricacies of it? To delve deep into it is not another desire, for it has no motive; it is like understanding the beauty of a flower, to sit down beside it and look at it. And as you look it begins to reveal itself as it actually is—the extraordinarily delicate colour, the perfume, the petals, the stem and the earth out of which it has grown. So look at this desire and its nature without thought which is always shaping sensations, pleasure and pain, reward and punishment. Then one understands, not verbally, nor intellectually, the whole causation of desire, the root of desire. The very perception of it, the subtle perception of it, that in itself is intelligence. And that intelligence will always act sanely and rationally in dealing with desire.

So without too much talk this morning, without too much thinking, to be entirely enveloped by this spring morning, to live with it, to walk in it, is a joy that is beyond all measure. It cannot be repeated. It will be there until there is a knock on the door.

还有对那不可命名者、对超越我们日常生活的事物的欲望，让人类做出了各种各样丑陋和残忍的事情。欲望是感受的产物——是思想构建的所有意象的产物。

　　而这种欲望不仅仅会滋生不满，还会招来一种绝望感。绝不要压抑它，也不要约束它，而是探究它的本质——它的起源、目的和复杂性何在？深入探究，这并非另一种欲望，因为这里没有动机；那就像是了解一朵花的美，坐在它旁边看着它。当你看着它，它就会开始如实地展露自己——它无比微妙的色彩，它的芬芳，它的花瓣，它的茎叶，还有它赖以生长的泥土。就这样看着欲望和它的特性，没有任何思想——是思想一直在塑造感受，塑造快乐和痛苦、奖赏与惩罚。然后你就会懂得——但不是从字面上、道理上——欲望的整个起因和根源。对此的洞察，那份微妙的洞察，本身就是智慧。然后那份智慧在应对欲望时，就会始终清醒地、理智地行动。

　　今天早上没有太多的交谈，也没有太多的思考，而是被这个春日的早晨全然包裹，与它共处，在其中漫步，真是一种无法估量的巨大喜悦。它无法被人为地复制。它会一直在那里，直到敲门声响起。

Tuesday, April 26, 1983

One saw a bird dying, shot by a man. It was flying with rhythmic beat and beautifully, with such freedom and lack of fear. And the gun shattered it; it fell to the earth and all the life had gone out of it. A dog fetched it, and the man collected other dead birds. He was chattering with his friend and seemed so utterly indifferent. All that he was concerned with was bringing down so many birds, and it was over as far as he was concerned. They are killing all over the world. Those marvellous, great animals of the sea, the whales, are killed by the million, and the tiger and so many other animals are now becoming endangered species. Man is the only animal that is to be dreaded.

Some time ago, staying with a friend high in the hills, a man came and told the host that a tiger had killed a cow last night, and would we like to see the tiger that evening? He could arrange it by building a platform in a tree and tying up a goat, and the bleat of the goat, of the small animal, would attract the tiger and we could see it. We both refused to satisfy our curiosity so cruelly. But later that day the host suggested that we get the car and go into the forest to see the tiger if we could. So towards evening we got into an open car with a chauffeur driving us and went deep into the forest for several miles. Of course we saw nothing. It was getting quite dark and the headlights were on, and as we turned round, there it was

1983 年 4 月 26 日，星期二

你看到一只鸟在垂死挣扎，一个人把它打了下来。它本在韵律十足地挥动翅膀，在优美地飞翔，自由自在，无所畏惧。子弹突然击中了它，它摔落地面，所有的生命力就那样从它身体里流逝了。一条狗把它叼走了，那个人也捡走了另一些死鸟。他正跟朋友聊着天，看起来完全无动于衷。他唯一关心的就是打下了那么多只鸟，在他看来这些已经足够了。他们在全世界大肆杀戮。大海里那些美妙的、大型的动物，那些鲸鱼，遭到了大规模的屠杀，而老虎和很多其他的动物现在也变成了濒危物种。人类才是唯一可怕的动物。

一段时间之前，跟一位朋友待在高山上的时候，有个人过来告诉主人说，昨晚一只老虎杀死了一头奶牛，问我们今天晚上愿不愿意去看看那只老虎。他可以给安排一下，在树上搭一个平台，然后绑一只山羊在上面，那头小山羊的叫声会吸引老虎过来，这样我们就能看到它了。我们都拒绝了用如此残忍的方式来满足我们的好奇心。但是那天稍晚的时候，主人建议我们坐上车，进入森林去探访老虎，如果可以的话。所以天色将晚的时候，我们坐上了一辆敞篷车，由一位司机开车，我们进入了森林深处数英里的地方。当然我们什么也没有看

sitting right in the middle of the road waiting to receive us. It was a very large animal, beautifully marked, and its eyes, caught by the headlights, were bright, scintillating. It came growling towards the car, and as it passed just a few inches from the hand that was stretched out, the host said, "Don't touch it, it is too dangerous, be quick for it is faster than your hand." But you could feel the energy of that animal, its vitality; it was a great dynamo of energy. And as it passed by one felt an enormous attraction towards it. And it disappeared into the Woods.*

Apparently the friend had seen many tigers and had helped long ago in his youth to kill one, and ever since he had been regretting the terrible act. Cruelty in every form is now spreading in the world. Man has probably never been so cruel as he is now, so violent. The churches and the priests of the world have talked about peace on earth; from the highest Christian hierarchy to the poor village priest there has been talk about living a good life, not hurting, not killing a thing; especially the Buddhists and Hindus of former years have said, "Don't kill the fly, don't kill anything, for next life you will pay for it." That was rather crudely put but some of them maintained this spirit, this intention not to kill and not to hurt another human being. But killing with wars is going on and on. The dog so quickly kills the rabbit. Or the man shoots another with his marvellous machines, and he himself is perhaps shot by another. And this killing has been going on for millennia upon millennia. Some treat it as a sport, others kill out of hatred, anger, jealousy, and organized murder by the various nations with their armaments goes on. One wonders if man will ever live on this beautiful

---

* Krishnamurti tells of this meeting with a tiger more fully in his *Journal*.

到。夜色渐浓，汽车头灯已经打开，而就在我们调头返回的时候，就在马路的中央，它坐在那里，等着迎接我们。那真是一头非常庞大的动物，浑身布满美丽的条纹，而它的眼睛在头灯的照射下闪闪放光，显得异常明亮。它低吼着向车走来，当它经过的时候，离你伸出的手只有几英寸，这时主人说道："别碰它，太危险了，快走，因为它可比你的手快多了。"但你依然能感受到那个动物的能量，它的活力；它真像一个巨大的发电机。当它经过的时候，你感受到一股庞大的吸引力。然后它就消失在了丛林中。①

那位朋友显然见过很多老虎，很久之前，在他还年轻的时候也曾协助杀死过一只老虎，从那以后就一直懊悔自己做过这样糟糕的一件事。各种形式的残忍如今正在这个世界上蔓延。人类可能从来没有像现在这样冷酷，这样暴力。全世界的教会和牧师都对世界和平高谈阔论，从最高等级的基督教徒，到贫穷的乡村牧师，都说要过一种善良的生活，不伤害，不杀生；特别是早年间的佛教徒和印度教徒说过："不要杀死苍蝇，不要杀死任何生灵，因为来世你会为之付出代价。"这种说法非常粗糙，但他们中的一些人一直恪守着这种精神、这个宗旨，不杀生，也不伤害别人。但战争带来的杀戮却一直从未间断。狗飞快地就可以杀死一只兔子。或者人用他精密的器械射杀他人，而他自己也可能被他人所射杀。这种杀戮已经上演了千千万万年。有人把杀戮当作一种运动来取乐，另一些人则出于仇恨、愤怒和

---

① 克里希那穆提在他的《日记》中更详细地记述了与老虎的这次遭遇。

earth peacefully, never killing a little thing, or being killed, or killing another, but live peacefully with some divinity and love in his heart.

In this part of the world, which we call the West, the Christians have perhaps killed more than anyone else. They are always talking about peace on this earth. But to have peace one must live peacefully, and that seems so utterly impossible. There are arguments for and against war, the arguments that man has always been a killer and will always remain so, and those who maintain that he can bring about a change in himself and not kill. This is a very old story. The endless butchering has become a habit, an accepted formula, in spite of all the religions.

One was watching the other day a red—tailed hawk, high in the heavens, circling effortlessly, without a beat of the wing, just for the fun of flying, just to be sustained by the air—currents. Then it was joined by another, and they were flying together for quite a while. They were marvellous creatures in that blue sky, and to hurt them in any way is a crime against heaven. Of course there is no heaven; man has invented heaven out of hope, for his life has become a hell, an endless conflict from birth to death, coming and going, making money, working endlessly. This life has become a turmoil, a travail of endless striving. One wonders if man, a human being, will ever live on this earth peacefully. Conflict has been the way of his life—within the skin and outside the skin, in the area of the psyche and in the society which that psyche has created.

Probably love has totally disappeared from this world. Love implies generosity, care, not to hurt another, not to make another feel guilty, to be generous, courteous, and behave in such a manner that your words and thoughts are born out of compassion. Of course you cannot be compassionate if you belong to organized religious institutions—large,

嫉妒而杀人，同时，握有武器装备的各个国家，也在进行着有组织的谋杀。你想知道人类究竟能不能和平地生活在这个美丽的星球上，不再荼毒生灵，不再被杀，也不再杀害别人，而是心中带着些许神圣和爱，和平地活着。

在世界的这个部分，也就是我们所谓的"西方"，基督教徒杀害的人或许比任何人都要多。他们总是谈论世界和平。但是，若要拥有和平，人就必须和平地活着，而这似乎是完全不可能的。有各种支持和反对战争的言论，有人认为人类历来嗜杀成性，并且会一直如此，另一些人则坚持说人类可以改变自身，不再杀戮。这些都是老调重弹了。尽管有各派宗教的存在，无休止的屠戮已经成为一种习惯、一种公认的模式。

有一天你看到了一头红尾山鹰，在高高的天空中毫不费力地盘旋，丝毫没有挥动羽翼，单靠气流即可支撑，只是为了飞翔的乐趣而飞翔。然后另一头鹰加入了它，它们一起飞了好一会儿。它们是蓝天上神奇的生灵，以任何方式伤害它们，都是对上天犯下的罪过。当然了，天堂并不存在，人类出于自己的希望而发明了天堂，因为他的生活变成了地狱，从生到死是一场无尽的冲突，来来去去，赚钱谋生，没完没了地工作。这种生活变成了一场无尽的混乱而又艰辛的奋争。你想知道人类，一个人，究竟能不能和平地生活在这个地球上。冲突已经成了他的生活方式——无论是在体肤之内还是体肤之外，无论在心智的领域内，还是在心智所建立的社会之中。

也许爱已经从这个世界上彻底消失了。爱意味着慷慨、关怀，不

powerful, traditional, dogmatic, that insist on faith. There must be freedom to love. That love is not pleasure, desire, a remembrance of things that have gone. Love is not the opposite of jealousy, hate and anger.

All this may sound rather Utopian, idealistic, something that man can only aspire to. But if you believe that then you will go on killing. Love is as real, as strong, as death. It has nothing to do with imagination, or sentiment, or romanticism; and naturally it has nothing to do with power, position, prestige. It is as still as the waters of the sea and as powerful as the sea;it is like the running waters of a rich river flowing endlessly, without a beginning or an end. But the man who kills the baby seals, or the great whales, is concerned with his livelihood. He would say, "I live by that, that is my trade." He is totally unconcerned with that something which we call love. He probably loves his family—or he thinks he loves his family—and he is not very much concerned with how he gains his livelihood.

Perhaps that is one of the reasons why man lives a fragmentary life; he never seems to love what he is doing—though perhaps a few people do. If one lived by the work one loves, it would be very different—one would understand the wholeness of life. We have broken up life into fragments: the business world, the artistic world, the scientific world, the political world and the religious world. We seem to think that they are all separate and should be kept separate. So we become hypocritical, doing something ugly, corrupt, in the business world and then coming home to live peacefully with our family; this breeds hypocrisy, a double standard of life.

It is really a marvellous earth. That bird sitting on the tallest tree has been sitting there every morning, looking over the world, watching for a greater bird, a bird that might kill it, watching the clouds, the passing shadow, and the great spread of this rich earth, these rivers, forests and

伤害他人，不让别人觉得愧疚，意味着大度有礼，一言一行、一思一想都诞生于慈悲。但毫无疑问，假如你隶属于有组织的宗教机构——庞大、有力、传统、教条、固守信仰不放的机构——你就不可能是慈悲的。要爱，就必须有自由。那份爱不是欢愉、欲望，也不是对过去事物的回忆。爱并非嫉妒、仇恨和愤怒的反面。

这一切也许听起来都非常理想化，像个乌托邦，是人类可望而不可即的事。然而，假如你那样认为，你就会继续杀戮。爱就像死亡一样真实、一样强大。它与想象、伤感、浪漫都毫不相干，当然与权力、地位和威望也没有半点关系。它就像海水一样宁静，又像大海一样强大；它像奔腾不息的大河中的流水一样，无始无终。但猎杀小海豹或者巨大的鲸鱼的那些人，关心的是自己的生计。他会说："我以此为生，那是我的生意。"他完全不关心我们称为"爱"的那件事。他也许爱着自己的家人——或者他以为自己是爱着家人的——但他并不太关心自己是如何谋生的。

或许这就是人类活得支离破碎的原因之一；他似乎从来不爱自己所做的事——尽管也许有那么几个人是例外。如果你以自己热爱的事为生，情形就会很不同——你会懂得生命的完整。我们把生活拆成了碎片：商界、艺术界、科学界、政界和宗教界。我们似乎认为它们都是分开的，而且也应该维持这种分离。所以我们变得虚伪，在生意场上做着丑陋、腐败的事，然后回到家里和家人平和地生活在一起；这滋生了虚伪，一种双重标准的生活。

这真是一个神奇的地球。坐在最高枝头的那只鸟，每天早上都在

all the men who work from morning until night. If one thinks at all, in the psychological world, it is to be full of sorrow. One wonders too if man will ever change, or only the few, the very, very few. Then what is the relationship of the few to the many? Or, what is the relationship of the many to the few? The many have no relationship to the few. The few do have a relationship.

Sitting on that rock, looking down into the valley, with a lizard beside you, you daren't move in case the lizard should be disturbed or frightened. And the lizard too is watching. And so the world goes on: inventing gods, following the hierarchy of god's representatives; and all the sham and the shame of illusions will probably go on, the thousand problems getting more and more complex and intricate. Only the intelligence of love and compassion can solve all problems of life. That intelligence is the only instrument that can never become dull, useless.

那里俯瞰着世界，警惕着更大的鸟——那只鸟可能会杀死它——看着流云，看着飘移的树影，看着这片广阔、富饶的土地，看着那些河流、森林，还有从早到晚不停劳作的所有人类。如果你真的思考过，会发现人的内心世界充满了悲伤。你也想知道人类究竟能不能改变，还是只有少数人，极少极少的人能改变。那样的话，那几个人与大多数人会有怎样的关系？或者说，大多数人与那几个人之间又是怎样的关系？大多数人与那几个人没有关系，而那几个人的确有一份关系存在。

坐在那块岩石上俯瞰山谷，你身旁有只蜥蜴，你不敢动，生怕惊扰或者吓到它。而那只蜥蜴也在观察。世界就这样延续着：发明各路神明，遵循神的代表人设下的层级体系；然后也许所有的虚假和可耻的幻觉就那样延续了下去，不计其数的问题变得越来越错综复杂。只有爱和慈悲的智慧才能解决生活的所有问题。那份智慧是唯一不会变得迟钝和无用的工具。

Wednesday, May 4, * 1983

It is a foggy morning, you can hardly see the orange trees which are about ten feet away. It is cold and all the hills and the mountains are hidden, and there is dew on the leaves. It will clear up later. It is early morning yet and the beautiful Californian sun and cool breeze will come a little later on.

One wonders why human beings have always been so cruel, so ugly in their responses to any statement they don't like, aggressive, ready to attack. This has been going on for thousands of years. One hardly ever meets nowadays a gentle person who is ready to yield, totally generous and happy in his relationships.

Last night there was the hooting of the owl; it was a great horned owl, it must be very large. And it waited for its mate to reply, and the mate replied from a distance and the hoot went down into the valley and you could hardly hear it. It was such a perfectly still night, dark, and strangely quiet.

Everything seems to live in order, in its own order—the sea with its tides, the new moon and the setting of the full moon, the lovely spring and the warmth of summer. Even the earthquake of yesterday has its own order. Order is the very essence of the universe—the order of birth

---

*　Between April 26 and May 1 Krishnamurti had been to San Francisco and given two talks in the Masonic Hall and a radio interview.

1983 年 5 月 4 日，[①] 星期三

这是一个雾蒙蒙的早晨，你几乎看不到十英尺之外的橙树。天气很冷，所有的丘陵和山峦都隐没了，树叶上缀满露珠。稍后就会晴朗起来。时间尚早，美丽的加州阳光和清凉的微风晚些时候才会到来。

你会好奇，人类对自己不喜欢的言论所做的回应，为何总是那么残忍，那么丑陋，那么有攻击性，并且时刻准备反击。这一幕已经上演了数千年。现如今，你几乎从未遇到这样温和的一个人，他在关系中随时准备让步，并且完全是大度的、喜悦的。

昨夜你听到了一只猫头鹰的呼叫，那是一只巨大的角鸮，它的身形肯定非常庞大。它等待自己的伴侣回应，而它的伴侣从遥远的地方发出一声应答，那声呼叫钻入了山谷深处，你几乎听不到它。那是一个如此静谧的夜晚，漆黑一片，安静得出奇。

万物似乎都生活在秩序中，它自身的秩序中——大海与它的潮汐，新月与落下的满月，怡人的春日与炎热的夏日。即使昨天的地震也有它自身的秩序。秩序正是宇宙的核心——诞生与死亡等的秩序。似乎只有人类生活在如此不堪的失序和混乱之中。他一直如此生活，

① 4 月 26 日至 5 月 1 日期间，克里希那穆提在旧金山的共济会大厅做了两场讲话和一次电台采访。

and death and so on. It is only man that seems to live in such disorder, confusion. He has lived that way since the owl began.

Talking to the visitor sitting on the veranda, with the red climbing rose and a young wisteria and the smell of the earth and the trees, it seemed such a pity to discuss disorder. When you look around at those dark hills and the rocky mountain and hear the whisper of a stream which will soon be dry in summer, it all has such curious order that to discuss human disorder, human confusion and misery, seems so utterly out of place. But there he is, friendly, knowledgeable and probably given to thought.

The mockingbird is on the telephone wire; it is doing what it generally does—flying into the air, circling and landing on the wire and then mocking at the world. This it does so often and the world apparently doesn't care. But the bird still mocks on.

The fog is clearing, there is that spring sunshine and the lizard is coming out, warming itself on the rock, and all the little things of the earth are busy. They have their order, they have their pleasure, amusement. They all seem to be so happy, enjoying the sunshine, no man near to hurt them, to spoil their day. "If one may ask, " the visitor began, "what to you is the most important thing in life? What to you is the most essential quality that man must cultivate?"

"If you cultivate, as you cultivate the fields of the earth, then it is not the most essential thing. It must happen naturally—whatever happens— naturally, easily, without any self—centred motives. The most important thing for each human being, surely, is to live in order, in harmony with all the things around him—even with the noise of the great towns, even with something that is ugly, vulgar, without letting it affect or alter the course of his life, alter or distort the order in which he is living. Surely, sir, order is the

就如同猫头鹰的存在一样久远。

坐在露台上，与来访者交谈着，身旁是蔓生的红蔷薇和新发的紫藤，空气中弥漫着泥土和树木的清香，此时谈论失序，真是一件憾事。当你环顾四周，望见那些黝黯的丘陵和嶙峋的山峦，听着夏日里很快就会干涸的小溪的呢喃，那一切都有着如此神奇的秩序，以至于探讨人类的失序、混乱和苦难，看起来是那么不合时宜。但是他来了，态度友好，知识渊博，或许还惯于思考。

一只知更鸟停在电话线上，做着它惯常做的事情——飞上天空，盘旋一周，然后又落在电话线上，嘲弄着这个世界。这些事它经常做，而世界显然不以为意。但那只鸟继续嘲笑着。

晨雾正在散去，春日的阳光洒下，蜥蜴从洞里出来，在岩石上温暖着自己的身子，大地上所有的小生灵都在忙碌。它们有自己的秩序，有自己的乐事和消遣。它们看起来都是那么开心，享受着阳光，没人走过来伤害它们，破坏它们美好的一天。"如果可以，我想问一问，"来访者开口说道，"对你来说，生命中最重要的事是什么？在你看来，人必须培养的最重要的品质是什么？"

"如果你培养什么，就像你培育田地一样，那么那就不是最重要的事了。事情必须自然地发生——无论发生什么——必须是自然的、轻松的，没有丝毫以自我为中心的动机。对于每个人来说，最重要的无疑是活在秩序当中，与他周围的一切都和谐共处——甚至与大城市的喧嚣，与丑陋、粗俗的事物和谐相处，不让它们影响或者改变他自己的生活进程，也不改变或者扭曲他所处的秩序。毫无疑问，先生，

most important thing in life, or, rather, one of the most important."

"Why, " he asks, "should order be a quality of a brain that can act correctly, happily, precisely?"

"Order isn't created by thought. Order isn't something that you follow day after day, practise, conform to. As the streams join the sea, so the stream of order, the river of order, is endless. But that order cannot be if there is any kind of effort, any kind of struggle to achieve, or to put aside disorder and slip into a routine, into various well defined habits. All that is not order. Conflict is the very source of disorder, is the very cause."

"Everything struggles, doesn't it? Those trees, they have struggled to exist, struggled to grow. The marvellous oak there behind this house, it has withstood storms, years of rain and hot sunshine, it has struggled to exist. Life is conflict, it is a turmoil, a storm. And you are saying, are you not, that order is a state in which there is no conflict? It seems almost impossible, like talking in a strange language, something utterly foreign to one's own life, one's own way of thinking. Do you, if I am not impudent, live in order in which there is no conflict whatsoever?"

"Is it very important, sir, to find out if another is living without effort, without conflict? Or would you rather ask if you, as a human being, who live in disorder, can find out for yourself the many causes—or perhaps there is only one cause—of this disorder? Those flowers know neither order nor disorder, they just exist. Of course, if they were not watered, looked after, they would die, and dying also is their order. The bright, hot sun will destroy them next month, and to them that is order."

The lizard has warmed itself on the rock and is waiting for the flies to come. And surely they will come. And the lizard with its quick tongue will swallow them. It seems to be the nature of the world: the big things live

秩序是生命中最重要的事，或者说是最重要的事情之一。"

他问道："为什么秩序是一颗能够正确、快乐、准确地行动的头脑所应具备的品质？"

"秩序并非由思想所造。秩序不是某种你日复一日遵守、练习和照搬的东西。如同溪流汇入大海，秩序的溪流与秩序的江河，也是无始无终的。但是，只要有任何一种想要达成的努力和挣扎，或者摒弃了失序却落入例行公事，落入各种根深蒂固的习惯，那种秩序就不会到来。那些都不是秩序。冲突正是失序的源头、失序的根源。"

"万物都需要努力，不是吗？那些树木，它们都要努力活下去，努力地成长。这栋房子后面的那棵美丽非凡的橡树，它挺过了暴风雨，历经了多年的豪雨和艳阳，它经过一番努力才活了下来。生命就是冲突，就是混乱，就是暴风雨。而你说，秩序是一种没有冲突的状态，不是吗？这看起来几乎是不可能的，就像你说的是一种奇怪的语言，对我自己的生活和思维方式来说，是如此陌生。恕我冒昧发问，你是活在这种毫无冲突的状态中的吗？"

"搞清楚别人是不是活得毫不费力、毫无冲突，有那么重要吗？还是说你应该问问自己，你，作为一个人，生活在失序中，能不能自己去发现这种失序的众多根源——又或许只有一个根源？那些花朵对秩序和失序都一无所知，它们只是存在着。当然，如果得不到灌溉和照料，它们也会枯萎，但枯萎也属于它们的秩序。耀眼、炎热的太阳下个月就会把它们烤干，但对它们来说，那也是秩序。"

蜥蜴在岩石上温暖了身体，正等待着飞虫出现。毫无疑问它们会

on little things, and the bigger live on the big. This is the cycle in the world of nature. And in that there is neither order nor disorder. But we know for ourselves from time to time the sense of total harmony and also the pain, the anxiety, the sorrow, the conflict. The cause of disorder is the everlasting becoming—to become, to seek identity, the struggle to be. As long as the brain, which is so heavily conditioned, is measuring, "the more", "the better", moving psychologically from this to that, it must inevitably bring about a sense of conflict, and this is disorder. Not only the words "more", "better", but the feeling, the reaction of achieving, gaining—as long as there is this division, duality, there must be conflict. And out of conflict is disorder.

Perhaps one is aware of all this, but being negligent of this awareness, one carries on in the same way day after day all the days of one's life. This duality is not only verbal but has the deeper division as the thinker and the thought, as the thinker separate from himself. The thinker is put together by thought, the thinker is the past, the thinker is knowledge, and thought too is born out of knowledge. Actually there is no division between the thinker and the thought, they are one inseparable unit; but thought plays a clever trick upon itself, it divides itself. Perhaps this constant division of itself, its own fragmentation, is the cause of disorder. Just to see, to realize, the truth of this, that the perceiver is the perceived, ends disorder.

The mockingbird has gone and the mourning dove is there with its plaintive cry. And soon its mate joins it. They sit together on that wire, silent, motionless, but their eyes are moving, looking, watching for danger. The red—tailed hawk and the predatory birds who were there an hour or two ago have gone. Perhaps they will come back tomorrow. And so the morning ends and the sun now is bright and there are a thousand shadows. The earth is quiet and man is lost and confused.

出现的。然后那只蜥蜴会用它迅捷的舌头把它们吞掉。这个世界的本质似乎就是如此：弱肉强食，然后强者被更强者掠食。这是自然界的循环，其中无所谓秩序和失序。但我们自己知道，偶尔会有那种全然的和谐感，也会有痛苦、焦虑、悲伤和冲突。失序的根源即是无休止的成为活动——成为什么，寻求身份，努力成就。只要严重受限的大脑还在衡量——"更多""更好"，内心希望由此及彼——它就必然会招来冲突，而这就是失序。不只是"更多""更好"这些词，还有成就、获取的感受和反应——只要存在这种分裂和二元性，冲突就必然会存在。而从冲突之中就会产生失序。

也许你察觉到了这些，但是你忽略了这些发现，在余生中日复一日地延续着旧有的生活方式。这种二元性不仅仅是字面上的，而且有着更为深层的分裂——思想者与思想的分裂，思想者把自己分离了出来。思想者是思想拼凑而成的，思想者就是过去，思想者就是知识，而思想也脱胎于知识。实际上思想者和思想之间并无分别，它们是不可分割的一个整体；但思想对自己玩了一个狡猾的把戏，分裂了自己。也许这种对自己的不停分裂，自身的这种支离破碎，正是失序的根源。只要看到、意识到这个真相——观者即被观之物——就会终结失序。

知更鸟飞走了，哀鸠在那里唱着悲伤的歌曲。它的配偶不久就飞来陪伴它了。它们一起坐在那条电话线上，很安静，一动不动，但它们的眼睛在转动，在四处查看，警惕着危险。红尾山鹰和猛禽们已经离开了，一两个小时之前它们还在那里。或许明天它们还会再回来。清晨已远，此刻阳光明媚，地上树影婆娑。大地寂静无声，但人类却困惑而又迷茫。

Friday, May 6, 1983

It was a pleasant morning, cloudy, a slight nip in the air, and the hills were covered and quiet. There was a scent of orange blossom, not very strong but it was there. It is a peculiar, penetrating smell and it came into the room. And all the flowers this morning were ready for the sun to come out. The clouds would soon pass away and there would be bright sunshine later on. The car went through the little village, past the many small hamlets, the oil derricks, oil tanks, and all the activity around those oil fields, and at last you came to the sea. You passed again through a big town, not too big, past the various lemon and orange groves, and you came upon, not patches of strawberries, not small cabbage fields, but acres of them, miles of them—strawberries, celery, spinach, lettuce and other vegetables—miles of flat rich soil between the hills and the sea. Here everything is done on a grand scale, almost too extravagant—miles of lemons and oranges, walnuts and so on. It is a rich land, beautiful. And the hills were so friendly that morning.

At last you came to the blue Pacific. It was like a pond this morning, so quiet, so extraordinarily still, and the morning light was on it. One should really meditate on that light, not directly on the sun but on the reflection of the sun on the glittering water. But the sea is not always like that; a month or two ago it rolled in fury, smashing the pier, destroying

1983 年 5 月 6 日，星期五

这是一个令人愉快的多云的早晨，空气中有些微寒意，群山被层云覆盖，寂然无声。空气中有一股橙花的香气，不是很浓烈，但的确存在。那是一种奇特而又穿透力极强的味道，悄然飘进了房间。今天早上所有的花朵都已整装待发，期盼太阳露面。云层很快就会散去，明亮的阳光稍后就会现身。汽车穿过了那座小村庄，经过很多小村落、油井架和大油箱，还有油田周围的各种活动，然后你终于见到了大海。你又穿过了一座大市镇，也不是太大，经过了各种柠檬和橙树林，然后忽然映入眼帘的，不是小片的草莓园，也不是小块的甘蓝地，而是多达数英亩、连绵数英里的——草莓、芹菜、菠菜、莴苣及各色蔬菜——位于群山和大海之间的连绵数英里的平坦而又肥沃的田地。这里的一切都采用大规模的耕种方式，几乎可以说是叹为观止——数英里的柠檬、橙树、核桃等。这是一片富饶、美丽的土地。而那天早上的群山也显得如此友好。

最后，你终于来到了蓝色的太平洋边。今天早上它就像一湾池塘，如此平静，安宁得不可思议，而晨曦就洒在海面上。你真的应该就那片光芒展开冥想，不是直接对太阳，而是对着金光闪闪的水面上

the houses around the beach, bringing havoc, even to the high road along it. Now they were repairing the smashed pier with all the lumber washed ashore, great quantities of it. Today, though, like a tamed animal, you could stroke it, you could feel the depth and the width and the beauty of this vast sea, so blue. Nearer the shore it was a Nile green. To go along that road beside the sea in the salty air was a most pleasant thing, just to see the hills, the waving grass and the vast sea of water. All this disappeared into the huge ugly town, a city that has spread for miles upon miles upon miles. It was not a very pleasant city, but people lived there and seemed to like it.

I don't know if, sitting on the beach, you have ever watched the sea, watched the waves come and go. The seventh wave seems to be the largest, thundering towards the land. There is very little tide in the Pacific—at least not here, not like those tides that pull out many miles and come in so rapidly. Here there is always a little ebb and flow, coming in and going out, repeated for centuries upon centuries. If you can look at that sea, the sparkle of the dazzling light, and the clear water, with all your senses highly awakened to their excellence, in that observation there is not the centre, as you, watching. It is a beautiful thing to watch that sea, and the sand, clean, washed every day. No footprint can remain there, even the little birds of the sea never leave their mark, the sea washes them away.

The houses along the beach are small, tidy; probably very rich people live along there. But all that doesn't count for anything—their riches, their vulgarity, their smart cars. One saw a very old Mercedes with exhaust pipes outside the bonnet, three on each side. The owners seemed to be very proud of it, they had polished it, washed it, taken such great care of it. Probably they had bought that machine rather than many other things. You could still do a great many miles in it; it was well put together to last.

朝阳的倒影冥想。但大海可不是一直那样；一两个月前，它怒吼着翻滚，粉碎了码头，摧毁了海滩四周的房屋，甚至给高处的海滨公路也带来了巨大的破坏。此刻人们正用冲到岸边的大量木材修理着破碎的码头。而今天，尽管它就像一只驯服的动物，你可以抚摸它，但你依然可以感受到这片广袤无际的蔚蓝大海的深度、宽阔和美丽。而靠近岸边的海水则呈现出一种尼罗河的绿色。在咸咸的空气中，沿着海滨公路兜风，真是一件极为惬意的事，可以看到群山、摇曳的绿草以及无边的海水。而这一切消失在了巨大而丑陋的城镇里，一座城市漫无边际地延伸着。这不是一座令人愉快的城市，可人们就住在那里，而且似乎很喜欢它。

我不知道你可曾坐在海边凝望大海，凝望着海浪来来去去。七层浪似乎是最高的海浪，呼啸着扑向大地。而太平洋的潮水很少——至少这里没有，不像那些可以退去数英里然后又迅速涌来的潮汐。这里的海水始终只有一点点涨落，来来去去，重复了无数个世纪。倘若你可以看着大海，凝望令人眼花缭乱的波光和清澈的海水，让你所有的感官都高度觉醒、卓越地运转，那么那份观察中便不存在中心，也就是没有一个你在观看。看着大海和每天被洗刷干净的沙滩，真是一件美好的事。没有脚印可以留存在那里，即使那些小海鸟也无法留下自己的印记，大海会把它们全部冲刷殆尽。

沿海滩而建的那些房子小小的，很整洁；也许住在那里的人都非常富有。但那些根本无足轻重——他们的富有，他们的粗俗，以及他们的豪车。你看到一辆非常古老的梅赛德斯汽车，引擎盖外面的两侧

Sitting on the shore watching the birds, the sky, and hearing the distant sound of passing cars, it was a most beautiful morning. You went out with the ebb and came in with the tide. You went out far and came back again—this endless movement of in and out and out and in. You could see as far as the horizon where the sky met the waters. It was a big bay with blue and white water and tiny little houses all around it. And behind you were the mountains, range after range. Watching without a single thought, watching without any reaction, watching without identity, only endlessly watching, you really are not awake, you are absent minded, not all there; you are not you but watching. Watching the thoughts that arise and then fade away, thought after thought, thought itself is becoming aware of itself. There is no thinker watching the thought, the thinker is the thought.

Sitting on the beach watching the people pass by, two or three couples and a single woman, it seems that all nature, everything around you, from the deep blue sea to those high rocky mountains, was also watching. We are watching, not waiting, not expecting anything to happen but watching without end. In that watching there is learning, not the accumulation of knowledge through learning that is almost mechanical, but watching closely, never superficially but deeply, with a swiftness and a tenderness; then there is no watcher. When there is a watcher it is merely the past watching, and that is not watching, that is just remembering and it is rather dead stuff. Watching is tremendously alive, every moment a vacancy. Those little crabs and those seagulls and all those birds flying by are watching. They are watching for prey, for fish, watching for something to eat; they too are watching. Somebody passes close by you and wonders what you are watching. You are watching nothing, and in that nothingness everything is.

The other day a man who had travelled a great deal, seen a great deal,

各有三根排气管。它的主人似乎对此非常自豪，他们给它抛光，清洗它，小心翼翼地照顾它。也许他们更愿意购买那台机器，而不是很多其他的东西。你还可以坐在里面行驶无数里程，它建造出来就是为了能够长久地使用。

坐在岸边，望着鸟儿和天空，听着远处疾驰而过的汽车声，真是一件极为美好的事。你随着潮水退去，又随着涨潮回来。你远远地退下去，然后又涨回来——这种进进退退、涨涨落落的运动无休无止。最远你能看到海平线，海天在那里相接。这是一个大港湾，有着蔚蓝和洁白的海水，还有四周环绕的小房子。你身后则是连绵的山峦。就那样看着，没有任何思绪，不做任何反应，也没有任何身份，只是无止境地看下去，你其实并不清醒，你有些心不在焉，并没有全然在那里；你不再是你，只是那样凝望着。看着思绪浮现随后又消失，一念接着一念，思想开始对自身觉察起来。并没有一个思想者在看着思想，思想者就是思想。

坐在海滩上，看着人们走过——有两三对夫妇和一个女人经过——似乎大自然以及你周围的一切，从深深的蓝色大海，到那些高耸的山峦，也都在观察着。我们在观察，不是在等待或者期待任何事情发生，而是没有尽头地看着。那份观察之中就有学习，并非通过近乎机械的学习来积累知识，而是密切地观察，不是肤浅地而是深入地观察，带着一种敏捷和一种柔软；此时观察者已不复存在。如若有观察者，那就只是过去在观察，那其实并不是观察，而只是记忆，是相当陈腐的东西。观察有着惊人的活力，每一刻都是空无的。那些小螃

written something or other, came—an oldish man with a beard, which was well kept; he was dressed decently without the sloppiness of vulgarity. He took care of his shoes, of his clothes. He spoke excellent English, though he was a foreigner. And to the man who was sitting on the beach watching, he said he had talked to a great many people, discussed with some professors and scholars, and while he was in India he had talked to some of the pundits. And most of them, it seemed, according to him, were not concerned with society, not deeply committed to any social reform or to the present crisis of war. He was deeply concerned about the society in which we were living, though he was not a social reformer. He was not quite sure whether society could be changed, whether you could do something about it. But he saw what it was; the vast corruption, the absurdity of the politicians, the pettiness, the vanity, and the brutality that is rampant in the world.

He said, 'What can we do about this society?—not petty little reforms here and there, changing one President for another, or one Prime Minister for another—they are all of the same breed more or less; they can't do much because they represent the mediocrity, or even less than that, the vulgarity; they want to show off, they will never do anything. They will bring about potty little reforms here and there but society will go on in spite of them." He had watched the various societies, cultures. They are not so very different fundamentally. He appeared to be a very serious man with a smile and he talked about the beauty of this country, the vastness, the variety, from the hot deserts to the high Rockies with their splendour. One listened to him as one would listen to and watch the sea.

Society cannot be changed unless man changes. Man, you and others, have created these societies for generations upon generations; we have

蟹、飞过的那些海鸥和鸟儿也在观察。它们为了猎食和捕鱼而观察，看看有没有什么东西可以下肚；它们也在观察。有人从你身边经过，好奇你在看什么。你什么都没有看，而一切就在那份空无之中。

几天前，来了一位游历广泛、见识广博、有所著述的人——那是一个蓄着整洁胡须的老式男人，衣着体面，丝毫没有不修边幅的粗俗。他把自己的鞋子和衣服打理得很好。他说一口流利的英语，尽管他是个外国人。他对那个坐在海边观看的人说，他跟很多人交谈过，与一些教授和学者探讨过，他在印度也跟一些有学问的人交流过。而他们之中的大多数人，在他看来，似乎都不关心社会，没有深度地投入任何社会改革，也不真正关心如今的战争危机。他深切地关注我们所处的社会，尽管他并非一个社会改革者。他不太确定社会能否改变，你能否对它有所作为。但是他看到了社会的现状：大范围的腐败，政客的荒唐行径，以及世界上猖獗的狭隘、虚荣和残忍。

他说："我们能对这个社会做些什么呢？——不是零星地做些微不足道的改革，把一个总统或一个首相换成另一个——他们或多或少都是一丘之貉；他们起不了多大作用，因为他们是平庸的代表，甚至是粗俗的代表；他们想要炫耀，他们永远都做不了什么。他们会在各处做些琐碎不堪的改革，但完全扭转不了社会的进程。"他观察过各种各样的社会和文化，它们在本质上没有多少不同。他面带微笑，看起来是一个非常认真的人，他也谈到了这个国家的美丽、广博和丰富，从炎热的沙漠到壮丽高耸的落基山脉，应有尽有。你倾听了他的话，就像倾听和观察大海一样。

all created these societies out of our pettiness, narrowness, out of our limitation, out of our greed, envy, brutality, violence, competition, and so on. We are responsible for the mediocrity, the stupidity, the vulgarity, for all the tribal nonsense and religious sectarianism. Unless each one of us changes radically, society will never change. It is there, we have made it, and then it makes us. It shapes us, as we have shaped it. It puts us in a mould and the mould puts it into a framework which is the society.

So this action is going on endlessly, like the sea with a tide that goes far out and then comes in, sometimes very, very slowly, at other times rapidly, dangerously. In and out; action, reaction, action. This seems to be the nature of this movement, unless there is deep order in oneself. That very order will bring about order in society, not through legislation, governments and all that business —though as long as there is disorder, confusion, the law, the authority, which is created by our disorder, will go on. Law is the making of man, as the society is—the product of man is law.

So the inner, the psyche, creates the outer according to its limitation; and the outer then controls and moulds the inner. The Communists have thought, and probably still do, that by controlling the outer, bringing about certain laws, regulations, institutions, certain forms of tyranny, they can change man. But so far they have not succeeded, and they never will succeed. This is also the activity of the Socialists. The Capitalists do it in a different way, but it is the same thing. The inner always overcomes the outer, for the inner is far more strong, far more vital, than the outer.

Can this movement ever stop—the inner creating the outer environment psychologically, and the outer, the law, the institutions, the organizations, trying to shape man, the brain, to act in a certain way, and the brain, the inner, the psyche, then changing, circumventing the outer?

社会无法改变，除非人类改变。人类，也就是你与他人，一代代地造就了这个社会；我们都出于自己的琐碎、狭隘、局限、贪婪、嫉妒、残忍、暴力、竞争等，而造就了这个社会。我们对于平庸、愚蠢、粗俗负有责任，对于所有部落主义的无稽之谈和宗教的派系之争也要负责。除非我们每个人都彻底转变，否则社会永远无法改变。它就在那里，是我们一手造就的，然后它又造就了我们。它塑造着我们，就像我们塑造了它一样。它把我们放进了模子里，而那个模子把它纳入了一个框架，那就是社会。

所以说这种活动永无休止地进行着，就像潮汐落下去又涨上来的大海一样，有时非常非常平缓，另一些时候则迅猛而又危险。涨涨落落，行动，反应，再行动——这似乎就是这种运动的本质，除非人的内心建立起深刻的秩序。这秩序本身就会让社会井井有条，而并非借助立法、政府以及那一套把戏——因为只要存在失序和混乱，我们的失序所催生的法律、权威就必然会继续存在。法律是人类的产物，就像社会一样——人类的产物就是法律。

所以说，是内心、心智出于自己的局限而建造了外在的世界；随后外在控制和塑造了内在。共产主义者曾经以为，也许依然以为，通过控制外在，建立某些法律、规定、机构和某种形式的专制，他们就可以改变人类。但是迄今为止，他们还没有成功，也永远不会成功。这也是社会主义者的做法。资本主义者采用另外的做法，但实际上都是一回事。内在总是会战胜外在，因为内在比外在要更为强大，更为关键。

这种运动究竟能否停止——内在从心理上建造了外在的环境，然

This movement has been going on as long as man has been on this earth, crudely, superficially, sometimes brilliantly—it is always the inner overcoming the outer, like the sea with its tides going out and coming in. One should really ask whether this movement can ever stop—action and reaction, hatred and more hatred, violence and more violence. It has an end when there is only watching, without motive, without response, without direction. Direction comes into being when there is accumulation. But watching, in which there is attention, awareness, and a great sense of compassion, has its own intelligence. This watching and intelligence act. And that action is not the ebb and flow. But this requires great alertness, to see things without the word, without the name, without any reaction; in that watching there is a great vitality, passion.

后外在，法律、机构、组织，试图塑造人类和大脑以某种方式行动，然后大脑、内在、心智再去改变和规避外在？这种运动自人类有史以来就一直在上演着，原始而又肤浅，偶尔显得精彩绝伦——内在总是会战胜外在，就像潮汐涨涨落落的大海一样。你真的应该问一问，这种运动究竟能否停止——行动和反应，仇恨与更多的仇恨，暴力与更多的暴力。只有当存在没有动机、没有反应、没有方向的观察时，它才能终止。当存在积累时，方向就会产生。但是观察——其中有着关注、觉知和一种伟大的慈悲感——它有着自身的智慧。这份观察和智慧自会行动，而那种行动不再是涨涨落落。但这需要非凡的警觉，需要不着一词、不加命名、不做反应地去看清事物；在这份观察中，就有着浩瀚的生命力与激情。

You were already fairly high up, looking down into the valley, and if you climb a mile or more up and up the winding path, passing all kinds of vegetation—live oaks, sage, poison oak—and past a stream which is always dry in the summer, you can see the blue sea far away in the distance, across range after range. Up here it is absolutely quiet. It is so still there isn't a breath of air. You look down and the mountains look down on you. You can go on climbing up the mountain for many hours, down into another valley and up again. You have done it several times before, twice reaching the very top of those rocky mountains. Beyond them to the north is a vast plain of desert. Down there it is very hot, here it is quite cold; you have to put something on in spite of the hot sun.

And as you come down, looking at the various trees, plants and little insects, suddenly you hear the rattle of a rattlesnake. And you jump, fortunately away from the rattler. You are only about ten feet away from it. It is still rattling. You look at each other and watch. Snakes have no eyelids. This one was not very long but quite thick, as thick as your arm. You keep your distance and you watch it very carefully, its pattern, its triangular head and its black tongue flickering in and out. You watch each other. It doesn't move and you don't move. But presently, its head and its tail towards you, it slithers back and you step forward. Again it coils up and rattles and you

1983 年 5 月 9 日，星期一

你已经爬得很高了，俯瞰着山谷，要是沿着蜿蜒的山路再往上爬个一英里，经过各种植被——槲树、鼠尾草和毒栎——再经过一条夏季经常干涸的小溪，你就能望见蔚蓝的大海了——铺展在层层山峦的背后，是那么遥远。而在高高的这里，有着绝对的寂静。一切都是如此安宁，没有一丝空气的流动。你向下俯瞰，而群山则俯视着你。你可以继续往山上爬几个小时，下到另一条山谷，然后再爬上去。你以前这么做过几次，有两次到达了那些遍布岩石的群山的顶峰。越过它们去往北方，则是广袤无垠的沙漠。那里非常炎热，而这里相当凉爽；尽管艳阳高照，可你还是得披件衣服。

当你走下山来，一路浏览种类繁多的树木、植物和小昆虫，你突然听到了一阵响尾蛇发出的沙沙声。幸运的是，你随即就跳离了那条蛇。你离它也就大约十英尺远。它还在把尾巴摇得沙沙作响。你们就那样看着对方，互相凝视着。你保持着自己的距离，非常小心地望着它，看着它的外形、它三角形的头，还有它黑色的舌头在飞快地进进出出。你们互相对视着。它没有动，你也没有动。但是顷刻间，它的头尾朝着你，身子向后滑去，你则往前进了一步。然后它又盘了起

watch each other. And again, with its head and tail towards you, it begins to go back and again you move forward; and again it coils and rattles. You do this for several minutes, perhaps ten minutes or more; then it gets tired. You see that it is motionless, waiting, but as you approach it, it doesn't rattle. It has temporarily lost its energy. You are quite close to it. Unlike the cobra which stands up to strike, this snake strikes lunging forward. But there was no movement. It was too exhausted, so you leave it. It was really quite a poisonous, dangerous thing. Probably you could touch it but you are disinclined to, though not frightened. You feel that you would rather not touch it and you leave it alone.

And as you come further down you almost step on a quail with about a dozen or more babies. They scatter into the nearby bushes, and the mother too disappears into a bush and they all call to each other. You go down and wait, and if you have the patience to watch, you presently see them all come together under the mother's wing. It is cool up there and they are waiting for the sun to warm the air and the earth.

You come down across the little stream, past a meadow which is almost losing its green, and return to your room rather tired but exhilarated by the walk and by the morning sun. You see the orange trees with their bright yellow oranges, the rose bushes and the myrtle, and the tall eucalyptus trees. It is all very peaceful in the house.

It was a pleasant morning, full of strange activities on the earth. All those little things alive, rushing about, seeking their morning food— the squirrel, the gopher. They eat the tender roots of plants and are quite destructive. A dog can kill them so quickly with a snap. It is very dry, the rains are over and gone, to return again perhaps in four months or more. All the valley below is still glistening. It is strange how there is a brooding

来，摇动尾巴，你们继续对视着。又一次，它的头尾朝向了你，开始后退，于是你又向前挪动了一步；然后它又盘了起来，摇动尾巴。你们这么做了几分钟，也许有十分钟或者更久，然后它觉得累了。你发现它一动不动，在等待着，但是当你趋近它，它并没有摇动尾巴。它暂时失去了自己的活力。你离它已经很近了。这种蛇不像眼镜蛇那样竖立起来出击，而是会猛扑过来攻击。但是此刻它一动不动。它已经精疲力尽了，于是你离开了它。它真是一个毒性很大、非常危险的东西。或许你还能摸摸它，但是你不愿意这么做，尽管你并不害怕。你觉得自己不愿意碰它，所以也就随它去了。

在继续下山的途中，你差点儿踩到了一只带着十几个孩子的鹌鹑。它们四散着逃入近旁的灌木丛，鹌鹑母亲也消失在了一丛灌木中，它们于是纷纷呼唤着对方。你蹲下身来等待，如果有足够的耐心观察，你很快就会看到它们都躲到了母亲的翅膀底下。那里很高，很阴凉，它们在等待太阳来温暖空气和大地。

你继续往下走去，跨过小溪，经过一片几乎失去了所有绿色的草地，然后回到了自己的房间，很疲惫，但因散步和朝阳而兴奋不已。你看到橙树上挂满了明黄的橙子，窗外还有玫瑰花丛、桃金娘和高大的桉树。房子里的一切都非常宁和。

这是一个怡人的早晨，大地上到处是各种奇特的活动。所有的小生灵都生机勃勃，四处奔忙，寻觅着自己的早餐。松鼠和囊地鼠，在啃噬植物的嫩根，它们的破坏性非常巨大。一条狗就可以轻轻松松地迅速把它们了结。天气非常干燥，雨季已经结束，也许四个月或者更

silence over the whole earth. In spite of the noise of towns and the traffic, there is something almost palpable, something holy. If you are in harmony with nature, with all the things around you, then you are in harmony with all human beings. If you have lost your relationship with nature you will inevitably lose your relationship with human beings.

A whole group of us sitting at table towards the end of the meal began a serious conversation as has happened several times before. It was about the meaning of words, the weight of the word, the content of the word, not merely the superficial meaning of the word but the depth of it, the quality of it, the feeling of it. Of course the word is never the actual thing. The description, the explanation, is not that which is described, nor that about which there is an explanation. The word, the phrase, the explanation are not the actuality. But the word is used as a communication of one's thought, one's feeling, and the word, though it is not communicated to another, holds the feeling inside oneself. The actual never conditions the brain, but the theory, the conclusion, the description, the abstraction, do condition it.The table never conditions the brain but god does, whether it is the god of the Hindus, Christians or Muslims. The concept, the image, conditions the brain, not that which is actually happening, taking place. To the Christian, the word Jesus or Christ has great significance, great meaning, it evokes a deep sentiment, a sensation. Those words have no meaning to the Hindu, to the Buddhist, or to the Muslim. Those words are not the actual. So those words, which have been used for two thousand years, have conditioned the brain. The Hindu has his own gods, his own divinities. Those divinities, as the Christians'', are the projections of thought, out of fear, out of pleasure and so on.

It seems that language really doesn't condition the brain; what does

久才会回来。低处的山谷依然熠熠发光。奇妙的是，整片大地之上有着怎样一种令人沉思的寂静。尽管市镇和交通的喧嚣不断，这里还是有一种几乎触手可及的、神圣的东西。如果你与自然和谐相处，与你四周的一切和谐相处，你就能与所有人类和谐共处。倘若你失去了与自然的连接，你便必然会失去与人类的连接。

用餐快结束的时候，我们一群人围坐在桌子四周，开始了一场严肃的谈话，就像之前发生过的几次对话一样。谈话的主题是语言的意义，以及文字的分量和内容，不仅仅是文字表面的意思，还包括它深层的含义，它的品质，它的感受。毫无疑问，文字绝不是那真实的事物本身。描述、解释并非所描述之物，也并非解释的对象。文字、词语和解释，并非事实本身。但文字被人用作交流思想、感情的工具，而文字，即使没有传达给他人，也会把感受留在一个人的内心之中。真实的事物从不会局限大脑，而理论、结论、描述和抽象的概念，确实会局限大脑。桌子绝不会局限大脑，但神明会，无论是印度教、基督教还是穆斯林的神明。概念和意象会局限大脑，而不是实际发生的事情。对于基督教徒来说，"耶稣"或者"基督"这些词具有重大的内涵和意义，能唤起一种深切的感情和感受。而对于印度教徒、佛教徒或者穆斯林来说，这些词就毫无意义了。它们没有真实性。所以说那些被使用了两千年的词语，局限了大脑。印度教徒有他们自己的神明、自己的各方神圣。那些神明，就像基督教徒的一样，是思想出于恐惧、欢愉等的投射之物。

似乎语言并不会真的局限大脑，局限大脑的是语言组成的理论，

is the theory of the language, the abstraction of a certain feeling and the abstraction taking the form of an idea, a symbol, a person—not the actual person but a person imagined, or hoped for, or projected by thought. All those abstractions, those ideas, conclusions, however strong, condition the brain. But the actual, like the table, never does.

Take a word like "suffering". That word has a different meaning for the Hindu and the Christian. But suffering, however described by words, is shared by all of us. Suffering is the fact, the actual. But when we try to escape from it through some theory, or through some idealized person, or through a symbol, those forms of escape mould the brain. Suffering as a fact doesn't and this is important to realize.

Like the word "attachment"; to see the word, to hold it as if in your hand and watch it, feel the depth of it, the whole content of it, the consequences of it, the fact that we are attached—the fact, not the word; that feeling doesn't shape the brain, put it into a mould, but the moment one moves away from it, that is, when thought moves away from the fact, that very movement away, movement of escape, is not only a time factor, but the beginning of shaping the brain in a certain mould.

To the Buddhist the word Buddha, the impression, the image, creates great reverence, great feeling, devotion; he seeks refuge in the image which thought has created. And as the thought is limited, because all knowledge is always limited, that very image brings about conflict—the feeling of reverence to a person, or to a symbol, or to a certain long—established tradition—but the feeling of reverence itself, divorced from all the external images, symbols and so on, is not a factor of conditioning the brain.

There, sitting in the next chair, was a modified Christian. And when across the table one mentioned Christ one could immediately feel the

是对感受的抽象，以及化身为一个观念、一个符号和一个人的抽象概念——并不是一个真实的人，而是想象中、希望中的，或者思想投射出来的一个人。所有这些抽象的概念、想法和结论，无论多么强大，都会局限大脑。但事实，比如这张桌子，绝不会如此。

以"痛苦"一词为例。对于印度教徒和基督教徒来说，这个词有着不同的含义。但痛苦，无论词语如何描述它，都由我们所有人所共有。痛苦是事实，是真实的。但是，当我们试图通过某套理论，通过某个理想化的人，或者通过一个符号来逃避它，这些逃避的形式就会框定大脑。痛苦作为一个事实，并不会框定大脑，而认识到这一点，非常重要。

再比如"依附"这个词。看看这个词，就好像把它捧在你的手心然后看着它，感受它的深度，它的全部内容，它的各种后果，看着我们有所依附这个事实——事实，而不是词语。这种感受并不会塑造大脑、把它装入模板；但是，一旦你逃避它，也就是，当思想逃离事实，那种离开、逃离的活动本身，就并非仅是一个时间因素而已，而且也在依照某个模式开始了对大脑的塑造。

对佛教徒来说，"佛陀"一词，那种印象、那个形象，会引发一份无上的崇敬和仰慕之情。他们在思想制造的那个意象中寻求庇护。然而，由于思想是局限的，因为所有的知识都是局限的，所以那个形象本身——对于某个人、某个符号或者某种根深蒂固的传统的尊崇感——就会造成冲突，但尊崇感本身，如若脱离了外在所有的形象、符号等，并不是一个局限大脑的因素。

restrictive, reverential reserve. That word has conditioned the brain. It is quite extraordinary to watch this whole phenomenon of communication with words, each race giving different significance and meaning to the word and thereby creating a division, a limitation, to the feeling which mankind suffers. The suffering of mankind is common, is shared by all human beings. The Russian may express it in one way, the Hindu, the Christian in another and so on, but the fact of suffering, the actual feeling of pain, grief, loneliness, that feeling never shapes or conditions the brain. So one becomes very attentive to, aware of, the subtleties of the word, the meaning, the weight of it.

The universal, the global feeling of all human beings and their interrelationship, can only come into being when the words "nation", "tribe", "religion", have all disappeared. Either the word has depth, significance, or none at all. For most of us words have very little depth, they have lost their weight. A river is not a particular river. The rivers of America or England or Europe or India are all rivers, but the moment there is identification through a word, there is division. And this division is an abstraction of the river, the quality of water, the depth of the water, the volume, the flow, the beauty of the river.

坐在旁边椅子上的，是一位改良的基督教徒。而当桌对面有人提到了基督，你立刻就能感受到那种克制的、有所保留的尊重之情。那个词局限了大脑。观察这整个言语交流的现象，真是一件奇妙非凡的事，每个种族都为词语赋予了不同的意义和内涵，进而为人类遭受的痛苦感受带来了分裂和局限。人类的痛苦是共通的，为全人类所共有。俄罗斯人也许会用一种方式来表达，而印度教徒、基督教徒会用另外的方式，如此等等，但受苦的事实，痛苦、悲伤、孤独这些真实的感受，绝不会塑造或者局限大脑。因此你对于词语的各种微妙之处，它的含义和分量，变得非常敏感、非常警觉。

只有当"国家""部落""宗教"这些词语统统消失不见，对于全人类以及人与人之间关系的那种放眼宇宙的、全球化的感受才会产生。词语要么拥有深度和意义，要么毫无意义。对我们大多数人来说，词语的意义甚微，它们失去了自己的分量。一条河不只是一条特定的河而已。美国、英国、欧洲、印度的所有河流都是河流，然而，一旦通过词语产生了身份的认同，分裂就产生了。而这种分裂是对河流，对水的品质和深度，对河流的水量和水流，以及对河流之美进行的一种抽象。

Thursday, May 12,*1983

It is dawn in these northern latitudes. In these latitudes dawn begins very early and lasts a long time. It is one of the most beautiful things on earth, the beginning of a dawn and the beginning of a day.

After a stormy night, the trees battered about, the leaves shaken and dry branches broken, the long pursuing winds have cleansed the air, which is dry. The dawn was so slowly creeping over the earth; it had an extraordinary quality this morning, especially this morning—it is probably after the winds of yesterday. But this dawn on this particular day was something more than the dawn of other days. It was so utterly quiet. You hardly dared to breathe for fear of disturbing anything. The leaves were still, even the most tender leaves. It was as though the whole earth were holding its breath, probably in great adoration. And slowly the sun touched the top of the mountains, orange, yellow, and there were specks of light on other hills. And still there was great silence. Then the noises began—the song of birds, the red—tailed hawk hovering in the sky, and the dove began its mourning song—but the silence of the dawn was in the morning, in the whole earth.

---

*   Krishnamurti's 88th birthday.

1983 年 5 月 12 日，^① 星期四

这是一个北半球的黎明。在这样的纬度上，黎明早早地就到来了，并且会持续很久。这是地球上最为美丽的事情之一——黎明的来临和一天的开始。

一个风雨交加的夜晚之后，树木备受摧残，树叶凌乱不堪，干枯的枝条纷纷折断，持久的劲风涤荡了干燥的空气。黎明慢慢爬满整个大地；这个早上有一种与众不同的品质，尤其是今天早上——也许是因为昨天经过了大风的洗礼。但是这个特殊日子的黎明似乎超越了其他所有的日子。一切都格外安静，你甚至都不敢呼吸，害怕惊扰到什么。树叶静止不动，甚至最为柔嫩的树叶也是如此。就好像整个地球出于极度的尊崇之情而屏住了自己的呼吸。然后朝阳慢慢地触碰山顶，发出橙色、黄色的光芒，周围的群山也染上了斑驳的光影。四周依然是一片深沉的寂静。然后各色扰攘便开始了——鸟儿在鸣唱，红尾的山鹰盘旋在天空，鸽子也唱起了哀曲——但黎明的寂静依然布满了整个清晨，铺展在整个大地之上。

---

① 克里希那穆提 88 岁的生日。

If you walk down below the hill, high across the valley, past the orange groves and some green lawns, past the tall slender eucalyptus, you come to a hill on which there are many buildings. It is an institute for something or other, and across the valley there is a long golf course, beautifully kept; we have played on it long ago. One has forgotten the course, the bunkers, but there it still is, very carefully maintained. One sees quite a lot of people with heavy bags playing on it. In the old days one had a bag of only six clubs but now there are about a dozen. It is getting too professional, too expensive.

You come over to another hill, and there too there are several institutions, foundations, organizations of almost every kind. All over the world there are dozens of institutions, forums, inner and outer directive groups. Everywhere you go in the so—called free world there is every kind of institution, organization, forum, to do this and to do that, to bring peace to man, to preserve the wilderness, to save the various animals and so on. It is quite bewildering and quite common now—groups of this and groups of that, each group with its own leaders, its own presidents and secretaries, the man who started it and the others who followed him. It is quite extraordinary, all these little organizations and institutions. And slowly they begin to deteriorate; probably it is inherent in all institutions, including the institutions that help man outwardly, like the institutions for greater knowledge. Those are probably necessary, but one is rather startled that there are also these inner directed groups of various types which do different kinds of meditation. They are rather curious those two words "inner directed"—who is the director and what is the direction? Is the director different from the direction? We never seem to ask fundamental questions.

There are organizations to help man in the physical world, controlled

如果你沿着高耸于山谷之上的山峦走下，穿过橙树林和葱绿的草地，经过瘦高的桉树，你就来到了一座盖满了建筑物的小山。那是一家不知为何而建的机构，而山谷的另一边是一片长长的高尔夫球场，打理得很漂亮；我们很久以前在那里打过球。你已经忘记了那座球场，那些沙坑，但它依然在那里，被精心地维护着。你看到有很多人背着沉重的球包在上面打球。过去你也曾有一个球包，里面只有六支球杆，而现在有了十二支。这项运动已经变得太专业、太昂贵了。

你来到了另一座山上，那里也有几家机构、基金会和各种组织。遍及全世界，到处都是数不清的各种机构、论坛，以及各种内在和外在的指导性团体。在所谓的自由世界，无论你走到哪里，都有各种各样的机构、论坛和组织，要做这个、做那个，要为人类带来和平，要保护野生环境，要挽救各种动物，等等。这相当令人不解，但如今已经相当普遍了——这种群体、那种群体，每个群体都有自己的领袖、主席和秘书，有创建人和其他的追随者。这真的非同寻常——所有这些小小的组织和机构。然后渐渐地，它们开始腐败，但所有的机构本质就是如此，包括从外在帮助人类的机构，比如为了获取更多知识而存在的那些机构。那些也许是必要的，但你非常惊讶，竟然还有进行各式冥想的各种各样的指导内心的团体。这两个词——"指导内心"，真的相当古怪——谁是指导者，指导又是什么？指导者有别于所谓的指导吗？我们似乎从不提出根本性的问题。

世界上有各种从物质方面帮助人类的组织，它们被自身有着各种问题、野心和成就，并且膜拜成功的人所控制，但这似乎是不可避免

by men who in themselves have their problems and their ambitions and achievements, worshipping success, but that seems to be almost inevitable and that kind of thing has been going on for thousands and thousands of years. But are there institutions to study man or bring peace to man? Do various systems, based on some conclusion, actually help man? Apparently all the organizers in the world feel they do, but have they actually helped man to be free from his sorrow, pain, anxiety and all the travail of life? Can an outside agency, however exalted, however established in some kind of mystical ideational tradition, in any way change man?

What will fundamentally bring about a radical change in man's brutality, end the wars he has been through and the constant conflict in which he lives? Will knowledge help him? If you like to use that word, evolution—man has evolved through knowledge. From ancient day she has gathered a great deal of information, knowledge about the world around him, above him, from the bullock cart to the jet, from the jet to going to the moon, and so on. There is tremendous advancement in all this. But has this knowledge in any way put an end to his selfishness, to his aggressive, competitive recklessness? Knowledge, after all, is to be aware of and to know all the things of the world, how the world was created, the achievements of man from the beginning to the present day.

We are all well informed, some more, some less, but inwardly we are very primitive, almost barbarous, however cultured we may be outwardly, however well informed about many, many things, able to argue, to convince, to come to some decisions and conclusions. This can go on endlessly outwardly. There are dozens and dozens of specialists of every kind, but one asks seriously: can any kind of outside agency, including god, help man to end his grief, his utter loneliness, confusion,

的，这样的事情也已经发生了千千万万年。但是，有没有什么组织可以了解人类，或者为人类带来和平？建立在结论之上的各种体系，真的能帮助人类吗？显然世界上的所有组织者都认为他们可以，但他们真的帮助人类摆脱自己的悲伤、痛苦、焦虑，以及生活的所有艰辛了吗？一个外在的机构，无论被鼓吹得多么完美，无论依某种神秘的传统观念构建得多么严密，可曾改变过人类一丝一毫？

什么能从根本上为人类的残忍带来彻底的转变，结束他所经历的战争以及他所处的无尽冲突？知识能帮到他吗？如果你喜欢用这个词——进化——人类借助知识得到了进化。从远古时代开始，关于自己周围和自己之上的世界，人类就积累了大量的信息和知识，从牛车到喷气机，从喷气机再到登月，诸如此类。这些方面都取得了巨大的进步。然而，这些知识对于终结人类的自私、颇具攻击性和争强好胜的鲁莽，可曾有丝毫帮助？知识，归根结底，就是意识到和了解世上的万事万物，世界是如何产生的，以及人类从古至今的所有成就。

我们或多或少都见多识广，但内心深处，我们依然十分原始，几乎是野蛮不化的，无论从外在看来我们多么有文化，我们掌握了多少事物的信息、能够争辩、说服、做出某些决定和结论。从外在来讲，这个过程可以永无休止地进行下去。每个领域都有不计其数的专家，但我们认真地问一问：任何一种外在的代理，包括上帝，能够帮助人类结束他的悲伤，他无边的孤寂、困惑和焦虑吗？还是说，他只能永远地忍受这些、习惯这些，然后说这就是生活的一部分？全世界人类

anxiety and so on? Or must he always live with that, put up with it, get used to it and say that it is part of life? The vast majority of mankind throughout the world tolerate it, accept it. Or they have institutions to pray to something outside—pray for peace, hold demonstrations for peace, but there is no peace in the heart of man.

What will change man? He has suffered endlessly, caught in the network of fear, ever pursuing pleasure. This has been the course of his life, and nothing seems to change it. Instead of being cynical about it all, or bitter, or angry, it is like that, life is that, and we ask, how can all that be changed? Certainly not by an outside agency. Man has to face it, not avoid it, and examine it without asking for any aid; he is master of himself. He has made this society, he is responsible for it, and this very responsibility demands that he bring about a change in himself. But very few pay attention to all this. For the vast mass of people, their thinking is so utterly indifferent, irresponsible, seeking to fulfil their own selfish life, sublimating their desires but still remaining selfish.

To look at all this is not being a pessimist or trying to be an optimist. One has to look at all this. And you are the only one who can change yourself and the society in which you live. That is a fact, and you can't escape from it. If you do escape from it then you are never going to have peace on this earth, never an abiding sense of joy, a sense of bliss.

The dawn is over and a new day has begun. It is really a new day, a new morning. And when one looks around, one wonders at the beauty of the land and the trees and the richness of it. It is really a new day and the wonder of it is, it is there.

的绝大部分都在忍受这些，也接受了这些。或者他们有各种组织，可以向某种外在的东西祈祷——祈祷和平，为和平示威游行，但人类的内心深处依然没有和平。

什么能改变人类？人类遭受了无尽的苦难，深陷恐惧的罗网，无休止地追逐着快乐。这就是人一生的历程，似乎没什么能改变。对此，我们完全不必愤世嫉俗、牢骚满腹或者满心愤怒，而是事实就是如此，生活就是如此，于是我们问：这一切如何才能改变？当然不能假借外在的代理。人必须面对它，不回避，审视它，而不寻求任何帮助；他是自己的主人。是他建造了这个社会，他对此负有责任，而这种责任就要求他为自身带来一场转变。但极少数人注意到了这一切。对于绝大多数人来说，他们的思想是如此冷漠和不负责任，只寻求满足自己自私的生活，升华自己的欲望，但依然自私如故。

审视这一切，并不是要做一个悲观主义者，也不是努力去做一个乐观主义者。你必须仔细观察这一切。而你是唯一能够改变你自己和你所处社会的人。这是一个事实，对它你无可逃避。如果你逃避它，那么你就永远无法在地球上拥有和平，永远无法拥有持久的喜悦和幸福。

黎明消失了，新的一天开始了。这真是崭新的一天，一个崭新的早晨。而当你环顾四周，你讶异于大地和树木的美丽与丰饶。这真是崭新的一天，它的到来非常神奇，而它就在那里。

第二部分
英国汉普郡，布洛克伍德公园 ①

BROCKWOOD
PARK，HAMPSHIRE②

① 5 月 14—22 日欧亥有一场集会，此间克里希那穆提做了四场讲话，并
举行了问答会。5 月 27 日，他飞往英国，然后在他布洛克伍德公园的学校逗
留了一段时间。

② From May 14–22 there was a gathering at Ojai during which Krishnamurti gave
four talks and held Question and Answer meetings. On May 27 he flew to England and
went to stay at his school at Brockwood Park.

Monday, May 30, 1983

It has been raining here for over a month every day. When you come from a climate like California where the rains stopped over a month ago, where the green fields were drying up and turning brown and the sun was very hot (it was over 90° and would get hotter still, though they say it is going to be a mild summer)—when you come from that climate it is rather startling and surprising to see the green grass, the marvellous green trees and the copper beeches, which are a spreading, light brown, becoming gradually darker and darker. To see them now among the green trees is a delight. They are going to be very dark as the summer comes on. And this earth is very beautiful. Earth, whether it is desert or filled with orchards and green, bright fields, is always beautiful.

To go for a walk in the fields with the cattle and the young lambs, and in the woods with the song of birds, without a single thought in your mind, only watching the earth, the trees, the sheep and hearing the cuckoo calling and the wood pigeons; to walk without any emotion, any sentiment, to watch the trees and all the earth: when you so watch, you learn your own thinking, are aware of your own reactions and do not allow a single thought to escape you without understanding why it came, what was the cause of it. If you are watchful, never letting a thought go by, then the brain becomes very quiet. Then you watch in great silence and that silence has immense

1983 年 5 月 30 日，星期一

一个多月以来，这里每天都在下雨。当你从加利福尼亚那样的气候来到这里——那里一个多月之前就不再下雨了，绿色的田地开始干涸，颜色转黄，而太阳依然炙热（气温超过了九十华氏度，而且还会更热，尽管有人说今年将有一个温和的夏天）——当你从那样的气候来到这里，你会无比讶异于映入眼帘的茵茵绿草和成荫的绿树，还有那些紫叶山毛榉，大片大片浅棕色的树冠，正渐渐染上更浓的色彩。看到它们如今出现在绿树丛中，真是一件赏心乐事。盛夏来临的时候，它们的色彩会变得非常浓烈。这个地球真的非常美丽。地球，无论是沙漠，还是铺满了果园和翠绿明亮的田野，都始终美丽如一。

漫步在点缀着牛群和小绵羊的田野上，漫步在鸟儿啁啾的林中，你脑中没有任何思绪，只是凝望着大地、树木和绵羊，聆听布谷鸟和斑鸠的鸣唱；不带丝毫情绪、丝毫感伤地漫步，凝望着树林和整片大地。当你就这样看着，你能明了自己的思维，觉察自己的反应，若有念头出现，在未曾了解其为何出现的缘由之前，决不让它溜走。如果你足够警觉，从不放过一个念头，那么大脑就会变得非常安静。此时你就可以在广袤的寂静中观察，而那寂静有着无限的深度，有着持久

depth, a lasting incorruptible beauty.

The boy was good at games, really quite good. He was also good at his studies; he was serious. So one day he came to his teacher and said, "Sir, could I have a talk with you?" The educator said, "Yes, we can have a talk; let us go out for a walk." So they had a dialogue. It was a conversation between the teacher and the taught, a conversation in which there was some respect on both sides, and as the educator was also serious, the conversation was pleasant, friendly, and they had forgotten that he was a teacher with a student; the rank was forgotten, the importance of one who knows, the authority, and the other who is curious.

"Sir, I wonder if you know what all this is about, why I am getting an education, what part will it play when I grow up, what role have I in this world, why do I have to study, why do I have to marry and what is my future? Of course I realize I have to study and pass some sort of exams and I hope I will be able to pass them. I will probably live for some years, perhaps fifty, sixty or more, and in all those years to come what will be my life and the life of those people around me? What am I going to be and what is the point of these long hours over books and hearing the teachers? There might be a devastating war; we might all be killed. If death is all that lies ahead, then what is the point of all this education? Please, I am asking these questions quite seriously because I have heard the other teachers and you too pointing out many of these things."

"I would like to take one question at a time. You have asked many questions, you have put several problems before me, so first let us look at perhaps the most important question: what is the future of mankind and of yourself? As you know, your parents are fairly well off and of course they want to help you in any way they can. Perhaps if you get married they

而不朽的美。

那男孩擅长体育运动，真的非常拿手。他的学业也很优秀，而且他很认真。于是有一天他来到老师面前，问道："先生，我可以和你谈谈吗？"老师答道："好的，我们可以谈谈；我们出去散个步吧。"然后他们就有了一次谈话。这是一场师生之间的对话，一场双方都相互尊重的谈话。同时，因为老师也很认真，所以这场对话是愉快的、友好的，他们甚至忘了是一个老师和一个学生在一起，身份——一个人是重要的知道者、权威，另一人则是好奇的讨教者——这些都被淡忘了。

"先生，我好奇你是不是知道这一切都是怎么回事，我为什么要受教育，在我长大之后，教育会起到什么作用，我在这个世界上会有什么角色，我为什么必须上学，我为什么必须结婚，还有我的未来会怎样。当然，我明白我必须学习然后通过一些考试，我也希望我能通过。我也许能活上一些年头，比如五十年、六十年或者更久，而在未来的这些年岁中，我的生活，以及我周围那些人的生活将会如何？我将会成为怎样的人？而花在书本上和听老师讲的这些漫长的时间，其意义何在？也许会爆发毁灭性的战争，我们也许都会被杀死。如果死亡就是我们的归宿，那么受这些教育的意义何在？请你明白，我是在很认真地提出这些问题，因为我听其他的老师讲过，你也指出了很多类似的事情。"

"我希望一次只探讨一个问题。你问了很多问题，你把好几个问题抛给了我，所以我们或许可以先来看看最重要的一个问题：人类以及你自己的未来将会如何？如你所知，你的父母也许非常富有，而且毫无疑问，他们也希望尽自己所能地帮助你。也许你结婚的时候他

might give you a house, buy a house with all the things necessary in it, and you might have a nice wife—might. So what is it you are going to be? The usual mediocre person? Get a job, settle down with all the problems around you and in you—is that your future? Of course a war may come, but it may not happen; let us hope it does not happen. Let us hope man may come to realize that wars of any kind will never solve any human problem.

Men may improve, they may invent better aeroplanes and so on but wars have never solved human problems and they never will. So let us forget for the moment that all of us might be destroyed through the craziness of super powers, through the craziness of terrorists or some demagogue in some country wanting to destroy his invented enemies. Let us forget all that for the moment. Let us consider what is your future, knowing that you are part of the rest of the world. What is your future? As I asked, to be a mediocre person? Mediocrity means to go half way up the hill, half way in anything, never going to the very top of the mountain or demanding all your energy, your capacity, never demanding excellence.

"Of course you must realize also that there will be all the pressures from outside—pressures to do this, all the various narrow religious sectarian pressures and propaganda. Propaganda can never tell the truth; truth can never be propagated. So I hope you realize the pressure on you—pressure from your parents, from your society, from the tradition to be a scientist, to be a philosopher, to be a physicist, a man who undertakes research in any field; or to be a businessman. Realizing all this, which you must do at your age, what way will you go? We have been talking about all these things for many terms, and probably, if one may point out, you have applied your mind to all this.

们会送你一栋房子，买一栋里面应有尽有的房子，你也许会有个漂亮的妻子——也许会的。那么你会成为怎样的人？普普通通的平庸之辈吗？找份工作，然后带着你周围和自己内心的一堆问题安定下来——这就是你的未来吗？当然，也许会爆发战争，但也有可能不会；我们祈望它不会发生。我们也希望人类能明白一点：任何形式的战争都无法解决人类的任何问题。

"人类可以改进或者发明更好的飞机等之类的东西，但战争从未解决人类的问题，而且永远也解决不了。所以，让我们暂时忘掉我们都有可能被那些超级大国、恐怖分子或者某些国家的煽动家的疯狂行为所毁灭——他们都想消灭自己假想出来的敌人。让我们暂时忘掉那一切，来思考一下你的未来究竟会怎样，既然你知道自己就是整个世界的一部分。你的未来是什么？就像我问过的那样，做一个平庸的人吗？平庸意味着只爬到半山腰，做事半途而废，从未到达山顶，或者从不付出你所有的能量和能力，从不对卓越孜孜以求。

"当然，你也必须意识到存在来自外界的各种压力——敦促你这么做的压力，还有各式各样狭隘的宗教派别的压力和宣传。宣传永远无法揭示真理，真理绝不能被鼓吹宣扬。所以我希望你能意识到你所受的压力——来自你的父母、社会和传统的压力——要成为一名科学家、哲学家、物理学家或者任一领域的研究者，要么就做一名商人。认识到了这一切——这是在你的年纪就必须认识到的——你会朝哪个方向走？关于这些问题，我们已经探讨了很多个学期，而且如果我可以冒昧指出的话，也许你已经用心思考过了这一切。

So as we have some time together to go around the hill and come back, I am asking you, not as a teacher but with affection as a friend genuinely concerned, what is your future? Even if you have already made up your mind to pass some exams and have a career, a good profession, you still have to ask, is that all? Even if you do have a good profession, perhaps a life that is fairly pleasant, you will have a lot of troubles, problems. If you have a family, what will be the future of your children? This is a question that you have to answer yourself and perhaps we can talk about it. You have to consider the future of your children, not just your own future, and you have to consider the future of humanity, forgetting that you are German, French, English or Indian.

Let us talk about it, but please realize I am not telling you what you should do. Only fools advise, so I am not entering into that category. I am just questioning in a friendly manner, which I hope you realize; I am not pushing you, directing you, persuading you. What is your future? Will you mature rapidly or slowly, gracefully, sensitively? Will you be mediocre, though you may be first class in your profession? You may excel, you may be very, very good at whatever you do, but I am talking of mediocrity of the mind, of the heart, mediocrity of your entire being."

"Sir, I don't really know how to answer these questions. I have not given too much thought to it, but when you ask this question, whether I am to become like the rest of the world, mediocre, I certainly don't want to be that. I also realize the attraction of the world. I also see that part of me wants all that. I want to have some fun, some happy times, but the other side of me also sees the danger of all that, the difficulties, the urges, the temptations. So I really don't know where I will end up. And also, as you pointed out on several occasions, I don't know myself what I am. One

"所以，既然我们有些时间，可以一起绕着小山转一转然后再回来，那么我来问你一个问题——不是作为一个老师，而是作为一个抱有真诚关怀的朋友——你的未来会如何？即使你已经下定决心通过一些考试，然后找份工作，找份好差事，你还是得问一问，那就是全部了吗？即使你谋到了一份好职业，或许生活也相当愉快，你还是会有很多烦恼和问题。如果你成了家，你的孩子们会有怎样的未来？这是一个你必须自己来回答的问题，我们或许可以就此谈一谈。你得考虑自己孩子的未来，而不仅仅是你自己的未来，而且你也必须考虑人类的未来，忘掉你是一个德国人、法国人、英国人或者印度人。

"我们来探讨一下这个问题，但是请明白，我并不是在告诉你该怎么办。只有蠢人才会给出建议，所以我不会让自己归入那类人。我只是在以一种非常友好的方式提出问题，这一点我希望你能明白；我并不是在催促你、指导你、说服你。你的未来是什么？你会很快就成熟起来，还是会优雅地、敏感地慢慢成熟？你会不会变得平庸，尽管你也许是自己行业中的翘楚？你也许非常优秀，也许十分擅长自己做的任何事，但我谈的是头脑和心灵的平庸，你的整个存在的平庸。"

"先生，我真的不知道该如何回答这些问题。我没有太多地思考过这些，但是当你提出这个问题——我是否会变得像世上的其他人一样平庸——我当然不想变成那样。我也意识到了这世界的那份吸引力，我也发现自己的一部分还是想得到那些的。我希望得到快乐、愉快的时光，但我的另一面也看到了那些——各种难题、渴望和诱惑的危险之处。所以我真的不知道我将终于何处。同时，就像你在有些场

thing is definite, I really don't want to be a mediocre person with a small mind and heart, though with a brain that may be extraordinarily clever. I may study books and acquire a great deal of knowledge, but I may still be a very limited, narrow person.

Mediocrity, sir, is a very good word which you have used and when I look at it I am getting frightened—not of the word but of the whole implications of what you have shown. I really don't know, and perhaps in talking it over with you it may clear things up. I can't so easily talk with my parents. They probably have had the same problems as I have; they may be more mature physically but they may be in the same position as I am. So if I may ask, sir, may I take another occasion, if you are willing, to talk with you? I really feel rather frightened, nervous, apprehensive of my capacity to meet all this, face it, go through it and not become a mediocre person.

It was one of those mornings that has never been before: the near meadow, the still beeches and the lane that goes into the deeper wood—all was silence. There wasn't a bird chirping and the nearby horses were standing still. A morning like this, fresh, tender, is a rare thing. There is peace in this part of the land and everything was very quiet. There was that feeling, that sense of absolute silence. It was not a romantic sentimentalism, not poetic imagination. It was and is. A simple thing is all this is. The copper beeches this morning were full of splendour against the green fields stretching to the distance, and a cloud full of that morning light was floating lazily by.

The sun was just coming up, there was great peace and a sense of adoration. Not the adoration of some god or imaginative deity but a reverence that is born of great beauty. This morning one could let go all the things one has gathered and be silent with the woods and the trees and the

合指出的那样，我并不知道自己是什么。有件事情很明确，那就是我真的不想成为一个头脑和内心都十分狭隘的庸人，尽管那颗头脑也许极其聪明。我可以研读书本然后获得一大堆知识，但我依然可能是一个非常局限和狭隘的人。

"平庸，先生，是你用过的一个非常恰当的词，而当我仔细审视它时，我被吓坏了——不是被这个词吓坏，而是被你所指出的整个含义吓坏了。我真的不知道，但也许和你详谈之后，事情就会明了起来。和我的父母就没那么容易沟通了。他们也许有着和我同样的问题，他们或许只是身体上更成熟一些，但与我的处境是一样的。所以，恕我冒昧请求，先生，如果你愿意，我可以改天再来和你探讨吗？我真的感觉很害怕、很紧张，担忧我应对这一切的能力——面对它，经历它，而不会变成庸人的能力。"

那是多日来从未出现过的一个清晨：草地近在咫尺，山毛榉寂然不动，一条小径伸入林中——四周一片静谧。小鸟没有歌唱，邻近的马匹也站立着一动不动。这样的一个早晨，清新而又温存，是非常稀有的事。这片土地上有一种宁和感，一切都非常安静。有那样一种感觉，一种绝对的寂静。这不是浪漫的多愁善感，也不是诗意的想象。那寂静曾经存在，如今也依然在那里，那是一件至简的事，仅此而已。今天早上，紫色山毛榉充盈着光辉，映衬着延伸到远方的绿色田野，天空中有片满载着晨曦的云朵，正懒洋洋地飘过。

朝阳刚刚升起，四周有一片广袤的祥和，以及一种尊崇感。并非对某个上帝或者虚幻的神明的敬拜，而是一种诞生于大美的尊崇。这

quiet lawn. The sky was a pale and tender blue and far away across the fields a cuckoo was calling, the wood pigeons were cooing and the blackbirds began their morning song. In the distance you could hear a car going by. Probably when the heavens are so quiet with loveliness it will rain later on. It always does when the early morning is very clear. But this morning it was all very special, something that has never been before and could never be again.

"I am glad you have come of your own accord, without being invited, and perhaps if you are prepared, we can continue with our conversation about mediocrity and the future of your life. One can be excellent in one's career; we aren't saying that there is mediocrity in all professions; a good carpenter may not be mediocre in his work but in his daily, inward life, his life with his family, he may be. We both understand the meaning of that word now and we should investigate together the depth of that word. We are talking about inward mediocrity, psychological conflicts, problems and travail. There can be great scientists who yet inwardly lead a mediocre life. So what is going to be your life?

In some ways you are a clever student, but for what will you use your brain? We are not talking about your career, that will come later; what we should be concerned about is the way you are going to live. Of course you are not going to be a criminal in the ordinary sense of that word. You are not, if you are wise, going to be a bully; they are too aggressive. You will probably get an excellent job, do excellent work in whatever you choose to do. So let us put that aside for a moment; but inside, what is your life? Inwardly, what is the future? Are you going to be like the rest of the world, always hunting pleasure, always troubled with a dozen psychological problems?"

天早上，你可以抛开自己所积攒的一切，与丛林、绿树和安然的草地静静地待在一起。天空呈现出一种浅淡柔和的蓝色，越过田野的远处，有一只布谷鸟在呼唤，斑鸠们在咕咕作响，青鸟也唱起了它们的晨曲。你能听到远处有辆汽车驶过。也许当天空如此宁静、如此怡人的时候，雨水不久后就要降临了。通常会是这样的，尤其当清晨非常晴朗的时候。但这个早晨真的非常特别，像是有某种空前绝后的东西存在。

　　"我很高兴你能顺应自己的内心，未经邀约就再次来到这里。如果你准备好了，或许我们可以继续我们之前关于平庸和你未来生活的谈话。你可以在自己的职业中非常优秀，我们并不是说所有的职业都难免平庸；一名出色的木匠，也许在自己的工作中并不平庸，但在日常生活中，在内心世界中，在与家人的生活中，他也许就是平庸的。现在我们都理解了这个词的意思，接下来我们应该一起来探究一下它更深层的含义了。我们谈的是内在的平庸，心理上的冲突、问题和痛苦。世上也许会有伟大的科学家，但他们内心依然过着平庸的生活。那么，你未来的生活将会怎样？

　　"从某些方面看，你是个聪明的学生，但你会用你的大脑做什么？我们谈的不是你的职业，那是后面的事情了；我们关心的应当是你未来的生活方式。当然，你不会成为一个通常意义上的罪犯。假如你是明智的，你不会成为一个恃强凌弱者；他们的攻击性太强了。你很可能会找到一份很棒的工作，无论你选择从事什么职业，都会做得很出色。所以让我们暂且把那些放在一边，然后从内在来看，你的生活将会怎样？从内在来看，你的未来会如何？你会不会像世上的其他

"At present, sir, I have no problems, except the problems of passing examinations and the weariness of all that. Otherwise I seem to have no problems. There is a certain freedom. I feel happy, young. When I see all these old people I ask myself, am I going to end up like that? They seem to have had good careers or to have done something they wanted to do but in spite of that they become dreary, dull, and they seem never to have excelled in the deeper qualities of the brain. I certainly don't want to be like that. It is not vanity but I want to have something different. It is not an ambition. I want to have a good career and all that business but I certainly in no way want to be like these old people who seem to have lost everything they like."

"You may not want to be like them but life is a very demanding and cruel thing. It won't let you alone. You will have great pressure from society whether you live here or in America or in any other part of the world. You will be constantly urged to become like the rest, to become something of a hypocrite, say things you don't really mean, and if you do marry that may raise problems too. You must understand that life is a very complex affair— not just pursuing what you want to do and being pigheaded about it. These young people want to become something—lawyers, engineers, politicians and so on; there is the urge, drive of ambition for power, money.

That is what those old people whom you talk about have been through. They are worn out by constant conflict, by their desires. Look at it, look at the people around you. They are all in the same boat. Some leave the boat and wander endlessly and die. Some seek some peaceful corner of the earth and retire; some join a monastery, become monks of various kinds, taking desperate vows. The vast majority, millions and millions, lead a very small life, their horizon is very limited. They have their sorrows, their

人那样，一直在寻求快乐，总是被数不清的心理问题所困扰？"

"从目前来看，先生，我没什么问题，除了通过考试这个问题，以及随之而来的各种枯燥乏味。否则我看起来没有任何问题。我感受到某种自由，我觉得很开心，很年轻。当我看到那些老人，我问我自己，我会像他们那样终老吗？他们似乎有着优秀的职业生涯，或者做过一些他们想做的事，但尽管如此，他们还是变得乏味、迟钝，在大脑更深层的品质上，他们似乎从未表现出足够的卓越。我当然不想变成那样。这不是虚荣，而是我想拥有某种不同的东西。这也不是野心。我希望获得一份好职业诸如此类，但我绝不希望像那些老人一样——他们似乎失去了他们所热爱的一切。"

"你也许不想变成他们那样，但生活是一件非常艰苦而残酷的事。它不会随你去的。你会受到来自社会的巨大压力，无论你生活在这里，在美国，还是在世界的其他任何地方。你会时常受到督促：要像其他人一样，变成一个伪君子，说些言不由衷的话，而如果你确实结了婚，那也可能会带来问题。你必须了解，生活是一件非常复杂的事——并非只是从事你想做的事，然后故步自封。这些年轻人希望成为某某人物——律师、工程师、政客等；对权力和金钱的渴望和野心的驱动确实存在。

"这就是你所说的那些老年人所经历的。他们被持续不断的冲突和他们的欲望所消耗。看看这个事实，看看你周围的那些人，他们都在同一条船上。有些人离开了那条船，然后在无尽的迷茫中终老。有些人在地球上找到了一个安静的角落，然后就此隐退；有些人则加入

joys and they seem never to escape from them or understand them and go beyond.

So again we ask each other, what is our future, specifically what is your future? Of course you are much too young to go into this question very deeply, for youth has nothing to do with the total comprehension of this question. You may be an agnostic; the young do not believe in anything, but as you grow older then you turn to some form of religious superstition, religious dogma, religious conviction. Religion is not an opiate, but man has made religion in his own image, blind comfort and therefore security. He has made religion into something totally unintelligent and impracticable, not something that you can live with. How old are you?"

"I'm going to be nineteen, sir. My grandmother has left me something when I am twenty—one and perhaps before I go to the university I can travel and look around. But I will always carry this question with me wherever I am, whatever my future. I may marry, probably I will, and have children, and so the great question arises—what is their future? I am somewhat aware of what the politicians are doing right throughout the world. It is an ugly business as far as I am concerned, so I think I won't be a politician. I'm pretty sure of that but I want a good job. I'd like to work with my hands and with my brain but the question will be how not to become a mediocre person like ninety—nine percent of the world. So, sir, what am I to do? Oh, yes I am aware of churches and temples and all that; I am not attracted to them. I rather revolt against all that—the priests and the hierarchy of authority, but how am I going to prevent myself becoming an ordinary, average, mediocre person?"

"If I may suggest, never under any circumstances ask "how". When you use the word "how" you really want someone to tell you what to do,

修道院，成为各式各样的僧侣，立下孤注一掷的誓言。而大多数人，数以百万计的人，过着一种非常狭隘的生活，他们的视野非常局限。他们有着自己的悲伤、自己的喜悦，他们似乎从来没有从中逃离出来，也没能了解它们进而得以超越。

"所以，我们再来问问彼此：我们的未来会如何，特别是你的未来会如何？当然，你太年轻了，还没法十分深入地探究这个问题，因为年轻与全面地领会这个问题毫不相关。你也许是个不可知论者；年轻人不相信任何事情，但是随着你长大成人，你就会转投某些宗教迷信、教条或者信仰。宗教并不是一种鸦片，但人类根据他自己的意象，把宗教变成了盲目的安慰剂，进而变成了盲目的安全感。人类把宗教变成了一种毫无智慧而又不切实际的东西，而不是一种可以与你相生相伴的东西。你多大了？"

"我就要十九岁了，先生。我的祖母留给了我一些财产，当我到了二十一岁，或者在我上大学之前，我可以去旅行，然后四处看看。但是无论到了哪里，我始终会带着这个问题：我的未来究竟会如何？我也许会结婚，很可能会，然后生儿育女，然后这个大问题就会出现——他们的未来会如何？我或多或少知道全世界的政客都在做些什么。在我看来，那是一件丑陋的勾当，所以我想我不会成为一个政客。这一点我很清楚，但我想得到一份好工作。我想用我的双手和头脑去工作，但问题是，如何才能不像世上百分之九十九的人那样成为一个庸人。所以，先生，我该怎么办？噢，是的，我明白教堂和寺庙的那一套；它们对我没有吸引力。我相当反感那一切——教士和权威的等

some guide, some system, somebody to lead you by the hand so that you lose your freedom, your capacity to observe, your own activities, your own thoughts, your own way of life. When you ask "how" you really become a second—hand human being; you lose integrity and also the innate honesty to look at yourself, to be what you are and to go beyond and above what you are. Never, never ask the question "how". We are talking psychologically, of course. You have to ask "how" when you want to put a motor together or build a computer. You have to learn something about it from somebody. But to be psychologically free and original can only come about when you are aware of your own inward activities, watch what you are thinking and never let one thought escape without observing the nature of it, the source of it. Observing, watching. One learns about oneself much more by watching than from books or from some psychologist or complicated, clever, erudite scholar or professor.

"It is going to be very difficult, my friend. It can tear you in many directions. There are a great many so—called temptations—biological, social, and you can be torn apart by the cruelty of society. Of course you are going to have to stand alone but that can come about not through force, determination or desire but when you begin to see the false things around you and in yourself: the emotions, the hopes. When you begin to see that which is false, then there is the beginning of awareness, of intelligence. You have to be a light to yourself and it is one of the most difficult things in life."

"Sir, you have made it all seem so very difficult, so very complex, so very awesome, frightening."

"I am just pointing all this out to you. It doesn't mean that facts need frighten you. Facts are there to observe. If you observe them they never

级体系，但我要如何才能防止自己成为一个普通的、寻常的、平庸的人呢？"

"如果我可以提议的话，请无论怎样都不要问'如何'。当你使用'如何'一词，你实际上是想让别人来告诉你该怎么办，让某个向导、某套体系或某个人手把手地引领你，那样的话，你就失去了观察的自由和能力，失去了你自己的行动、思想和生活之道。当你问'如何'，你就变成了二手的人类，你就丧失了完整性，也失去了本有的诚实，无法诚实地看待自己、做真实的自己，也无法超越你实际的样子。所以，永远不要问'如何'这个问题。当然，我们现在讨论的是心理上的问题。当你要组装一辆汽车或制造一台电脑时，你需要问'如何'。这时你不得不向别人学习有关的知识。然而，只有当你觉知自己内心的各种活动，观察自己的所思所想，在观察到一个念头的本质和源头之前，决不让它逃走，这样你才能从心理上获得自由和创造性。要观察、要去看。通过观察，你对自己获得的了解，远远超过了从书本、从某些心理学家，或者从复杂、聪明、渊博的学者或者教授那里的所得。

"但这会很难，我的朋友，它可能会把你往各个方向撕扯。会有大量所谓的诱惑——身体上的、社会上的，你或许会被残忍的社会撕成碎片。毫无疑问，你必须孑然独立，但是，这无法借助强力、决心或者欲望来实现，而是当你开始看到自己周围和自己身上那些虚妄的东西——各种情绪和希望时，那份独立才会到来。当你开始看到何为虚假，那就是觉察和智慧的开端。你必须做自己的明灯，而这是生命中最难做到的事情之一。"

frighten you. Facts are not frightening. But if you want to avoid them, turn your back and run, then that is frightening. To stand, to see that what you have done may not have been totally correct, to live with the fact and not interpret the fact according to your pleasure or form of reaction, that is not frightening. Life isn't very simple. One can live simply but life itself is vast, complex. It extends from horizon to horizon. You can live with few clothes or with one meal a day, but that is not simplicity. So be simple, don't live in a complicated way, contradictory and so on, just be simple inwardly... You played tennis this morning. I was watching and you seem to be quite good at it. Perhaps we will meet again. That is up to you."

"Thank you, sir."

"先生，你把这些说得太难了，太复杂了，太恐怖、太可怕了。"

"我只是在向你指出所有的事实。这并不意味着事实会吓坏你。事实就在那里，等你去观察。如果你观察它们，它们绝不会吓到你。事实并不可怕。但是，如果你想避开它们，转身逃离它们，那才会可怕。你所做的也许并不完全正确，看到这一点，身处事实之中，与这个事实共存，而不根据你的好恶或者反应模式来诠释它，这并不可怕。生活没那么简单。你可以活得很简单，但生活本身是广阔的、复杂的。它的范围无边无际。你可以只靠很少几件衣服或者一日一餐而活，然而这并不是简单。所以，简单地活着，不要过一种复杂的、矛盾重重的生活，而只是保持内心的简单……你今天早上打网球了，我看到了，你看起来很擅长这项运动。也许我们还会再见面，那取决于你。"

"谢谢你，先生。"

第三部分

加利福尼亚，欧亥 ①

OJAI, CALIFORNIA ②

① 1983 年 6 月 6 日，布洛克伍德公园学校的校长多萝西·西蒙斯突发心脏病，此后克里希那穆提一直忙于学校的事务，无暇再做更多的口述。7 月 1 日，他前往瑞士萨能参加一年一度的国际大会。8 月 15 日，他回到布洛克伍德参加那里的会议，并于 10 月 22 日飞往德里。直到 1984 年 2 月 22 日，他才回到欧亥，但不幸的是，他仅多做了三篇口述。

② On June 6, 1983, Dorothy Simmons, the Principal of Brockwood Park School, had a heart attack. Thereafter Krishnamurti was too busy with school affairs for any more dictations. On July 1 he went to Saanen, Switzerland, for the international annual gathering. On August 15 he returned to Brockwood for a gathering there, and on October 22 he flew to Delhi. He did not go back to Ojai until February 22, 1984. Unfortunately he dictated only three more pieces.

Tuesday, March 27, 1984

On that drive from the airport through the vulgarity of large towns spreading out for many, many miles, with glaring lights and so much noise, then taking the freeway and going through a small tunnel, you suddenly came upon the Pacific. It was a clear day without a breath of wind but as it was early morning there was a freshness before the pollution of the monoxide gas filled the air. The sea was so calm, almost like an immense lake. And the sun was just coming over the hill, and the deep waters of the Pacific were the colour of the Nile, but at the edges they were light blue, gently lapping the shores. And there were many birds and you saw in the distance a whale.

Following the coast road, there were very few cars that morning, but houses everywhere; probably very rich people lived there. And you saw the pleasant hills on the left when you arrived at the Pacific. There were houses right up among the hills and the road wound in and out, following the sea, and again came upon another town, but fortunately the highway didn't go through it. There was a naval centre there with its modern means of killing humanity.

And you went along and turned to the right, leaving the sea behind, and after the oil wells, you drove further away from the sea, through orange groves, past a golf course, to a small village, the road winding through

1984 年 3 月 27 日，星期二

汽车从机场驶出，一路穿过绵延数英里的丑陋的大都市——那里有耀眼的灯光和无尽的喧嚣——然后驶入高速公路，穿过了一条小隧道，你突然就遭遇了太平洋。这是晴朗的一天，没有一丝微风，但因为是清晨，尚有一股在一氧化物污染充满空气之前的清新。大海是如此平静，像极了一面无边的湖水。太阳刚刚爬上山坡，太平洋深处的海水就像是尼罗河的颜色，而边缘的海水则呈现出浅蓝色，轻拍着海岸。那里有很多鸟儿，远处你还看到有一头鲸鱼的身影。

那天早上，沿着海滨公路驶去，路上的车子很少，但到处都是房子，也许有一些非常富有的人住在那里。当你来到了太平洋边，你看到左手边有怡人的群山。山上有数座房子，而公路沿着海岸线，蜿蜒着进进出出，然后又再次遇到另一座城镇，但幸运的是，公路并没有从中穿过。那里有一座海军基地，有着各类现代化的杀人工具。

你继续往前驶去，然后向右转弯，把大海留在了身后。经过了几座油井，你离大海越来越远，随后穿过橙树林，经过一座高尔夫球场，来到了一个小村庄。公路蜿蜒穿过橙树园，空气中弥漫着橙花的香气。所有的树叶都闪着光。这座山谷看起来是如此平和，如此宁

orange orchards, and the air was filled with the perfume of orange blossom. And all the leaves of the trees were shining. There seemed to be such peace in this valley, so quiet, away from all crowds and noise and vulgarity. This country is beautiful, so vast—with deserts, snow—capped mountains, villages, great towns and still greater rivers. The land is marvellously beautiful, vast, all inclusive.

And we came to this house which was still more quiet and beautiful, recently built and with the cleanliness that houses in towns don't have. There were lots of flowers, roses and so on. A place in which to be quiet, not just vegetate, but to be really deeply, inwardly, quiet.Silence is a great benediction, it cleanses the brain, gives vitality to it, and this silence builds up great energy, not the energy of thought or the energy of machines but that unpolluted energy, untouched by thought. It is the energy that has incalculable capacity, skills. And this is a place where the brain, being very active, can be silent. That very intense activity of the brain has the quality and the depth and the beauty of silence.

Though one has repeated this often, education is the cultivation of the whole brain, not one part of it; it is a holistic cultivation of the human being. A High school or Secondary school should teach both science and religion. Science really means the cultivation of knowledge, doesn't it? Science is what has brought about the present state of tension in the world for it has put together through knowledge the most destructive instrument that man has ever found. It can wipe out whole cities at one blow, millions can be destroyed in a second. A million human beings can be vaporized.

And science has also given us a great many beneficial things—communication, medicine, surgery and innumerable small things for the comfort of man, for an easy way of life in which human beings need not

静，远离了所有的人群、喧嚣和粗俗。这里的乡村是如此美丽，如此广袤——既有沙漠，也有白雪覆盖的群山，有村庄、大都市，还有更大的河流。这片土地无与伦比地美丽、辽阔，以及包罗万象。

然后我们来到了这座还要安静和美丽很多的房子，房子新建不久，有着城市里的房子所没有的干净整洁。那里有很多花，很多玫瑰等。这是一个可以静处的地方，并非只是无所事事，而是内心深处拥有真正的宁静。寂静是一种至福，它能涤净大脑，赋予它生命力，这种寂静会积聚巨大的能量，并非思想的能量或者机器的能量，而是那未受污染的能量，未被思想所沾染的能量。正是这种能量具有无法计数的能力和技巧。而这里恰是一个可以让非常活跃的大脑安静下来的地方。大脑那非常剧烈的活动于是具有了寂静的品质、深度和美。

尽管我经常重复这些话，但教育确是对整个大脑的培育，而不只是它的一部分；教育是对一个人整体的培养。中学应当既教科学，也教宗教。科学实际上就意味着对知识的培养，不是吗？而科学正是当今世界的紧张局势的始作俑者，因为通过运用知识，它造出了人类前所未见的最具破坏力的工具。它可以一举摧毁整座整座的城市，使数百万人瞬间殒命。一百万人顷刻之间就可以从人间全部蒸发。

而科学也给了我们很多有益的东西——通信、医药、外科手术和不计其数的小东西，可以让人类生活得更舒适、更轻松，而不必再费尽气力去寻找食物和烹调等。它也给我们带来了现代的神明——计算机。你可以列举出科技带给人类的很多很多帮助，同时也包括足以

struggle endlessly to gather food, cook and so on. And it has given us the modern deity, the computer. One can enumerate the many, many things that science has brought about to help man and also to destroy man, destroy the entire world of humanity and the vast beauty of nature. Governments are using the scientists, and scientists like to be used by governments for then they have a position, money, recognition and so on. Human beings also look to science to bring about peace in the world, but it has failed, just as politics and the politicians have failed to give them total security, peace to live and cultivate not only the fields but their brain, their heart, their way of living, which is the highest art.

And religions—the accepted, traditional, superficial religions, creeds and dogmas—have brought about great damage in the world. They have been responsible for wars in history dividing man against man—one whole continent with very strong beliefs, rituals, dogmas against another continent which does not believe the same things, does not have the same symbols, the same rituals. This is not religion, it is just repetition of a tradition, of endless rituals that have lost meaning except that they give some kind of stimulus; it has become a vast entertainment. Religion is something entirely different. We have often spoken about religion. The essence of religion is freedom, not to do what you like, that is too childish, too immature and too contradictory, bringing great conflict, misery and confusion. Freedom again is something entirely different. Freedom means to have no conflict, psychologically, inwardly. And with freedom the brain becomes holistic, not fragmented in itself. Freedom also means love, compassion, and there is no freedom if there is not intelligence. Intelligence is inherent in compassion and love. We can go into this endlessly, not verbally or intellectually, but inwardly live a life of such a nature.

摧毁人类、摧毁整个人类世界和美丽的大自然的无数手段。政府在利用科学家，而科学家们也乐于被政府利用，因为那样他们就会拥有地位、金钱、名气之类。人类也寄希望于科学能够带来世界和平，但它失败了，就像政治和政客无法带给人类赖以生存的彻底的安全与和平，也无法培育包括他们的大脑、心灵和生活方式在内的整片领域——而这才是最高的艺术。

而各派宗教——公认的、传统的、肤浅的宗教、信条和教义——给世界带来了巨大的破坏。它们对历史上分裂人类的各次战争都负有责任——抱守着强烈的信仰、仪式和教条的一整个大洲，对抗不相信同样的东西、不持有同样的符号和仪式的另一个大洲。这根本不是宗教，而只是对某种传统和无尽仪式的重复——除了能提供某种刺激以外，它们早已失去了意义，变成了一种庞大的消遣。宗教是某种截然不同的东西。我们经常谈到宗教。宗教的核心是自由，但并非为所欲为，那就太幼稚、太不成熟、太自相矛盾了，那会带来巨大的冲突、苦难和混乱。自由也是某种截然不同的东西。自由意味着内在、心理上毫无冲突。而有了那种自由，大脑本身就会变得完整，不再支离破碎。自由也意味着爱、慈悲，而如果没有智慧，自由就不会存在。智慧就蕴含在慈悲和爱之中。我们可以不停地深入下去，并非从字面上或者智力上，而是从内心深处过一种拥有如此品质的生活。

而在中学或者高中，科学就意味着知识。知识可以无限扩展，但知识永远是有限的，因为知识是基于经验的，而经验也许是理论和假设的产物。知识是必要的，然而，只要科学是一个分离的群体或者一

And in a Secondary school or a High school, science is knowledge. Knowledge can expand endlessly, but that knowledge is always limited because knowledge is based on experience and that experience may be a theoretical, hypothetical result. Knowledge is necessary but as long as science is the activity of a separate group, or a separate nation, which is tribal activity, such knowledge can only bring about greater conflict, greater havoc in the world, which is what is happening now. Science with its knowledge is not for destroying human beings because scientists after all are human beings first, not just specialists; they are ambitious, greedy, seeking their own personal security like all the other human beings in the world. They are like you and another. But their specialization is bringing great destruction as well as some benefit. The last two great wars have shown this. Humanity seems to be in a perpetual movement of destruction and building up again—destroy and build; destroy human beings and give birth to a greater population. But if all the scientists in the world put their tools down and said, "We will not contribute to war, to destroying humanity", they could turn their attention, their skill, their commitment to bringing about a better relationship between nature, environment and human beings.

If there is some peace among a few people, then those few, not necessarily the élite, will employ all their skill to bring about a different world, then religion and science can go together.

Religion is a form of science. That is, to know and to go beyond all knowledge, to comprehend the nature and immensity of the universe, not through a telescope, but the immensity of the mind and the heart. And this immensity has nothing whatsoever to do with any organized religion. How easily man becomes a tool of his own belief, his own fanaticism,

个分离的国家的行为——那其实是一种部落行为——那样的知识就只会给世界造成更大的冲突、更大的动荡，而这就是世界上正在发生的事。科学以及相关的知识，本不是用来毁灭人类的，因为科学家毕竟首先是人类，而不只是专家；他们野心勃勃、贪婪，追求着自己的个人安全，就像世界上其他的所有人一样。他们就跟你和别的人一样。但是他们的专业技能在带来某些益处的同时，也带来了巨大的灾难。上两次世界大战证明了这一点。人类似乎始终处在一个破坏然后重建的进程之中——破坏之后再建设，摧毁人类然后再催生更多的人口。但是，如果世界上所有的科学家都把自己的工具放下，然后说，"我们不会再为战争和毁灭人类贡献力量"，那么他们就可以把他们的注意力、他们的技术、他们的责任心，投到建立自然、环境与人类之间更良好的关系上来。

如果在少数几个人当中能有和平，那么那几个人——未必是精英——就会运用他们所有的技巧来造就一个不同的世界，进而宗教和科学就可以并驾齐驱。

宗教是一种科学。那就是，要去了解并超越所有的知识，领会宇宙的本质与无限，不是透过望远镜，而是了解头脑与心灵的无限。而这种无限，与任何组织化的宗教都没有丝毫干系。人类是多么轻易地就成了他自身信仰和幻想的工具，去信奉某种毫无真实性的教条。没有什么庙宇、清真寺、教堂能握有真理。它们或许只是符号，但符号并非真实。膜拜符号，你就会错失真相和真理。但不幸的是，符号被赋予的重要性远远超过了真理。人们膜拜符号。所

committed to some kind of dogma which has no reality. No temple, no mosque, no church, holds truth. They are symbols perhaps but symbols are not the actual. In worshipping a symbol you will lose the real, the truth. But unfortunately the symbol has been given far greater importance than truth. One worships the symbol. All religions are based on some conclusions and beliefs, and all beliefs are divisive, whether political beliefs or religious.

Where there is division there must be conflict. And a High school is not a place for conflict. It is a place for learning the art of living. This art is the greatest, it surpasses all other arts, for this art touches the entire human being, not one part of him, however pleasant that may be. And in a school of this kind, if the educator is committed to this, not as an ideal, but as an actuality of daily life—committed, let's repeat again, not to some ideal, some Utopia, some noble conclusion, he can actually try to find out in the human brain a way of living that is not caught in problems, strife, conflict and pain.

Love is not a movement of pain, anxiety, loneliness; it is timeless. And the educator, if he would stick at it, could instil in the students" acquisition of knowledge this true religious spirit which goes far beyond all knowledge, which is perhaps the very end of knowledge—not perhaps—it is the end of knowledge. For there must be freedom from knowledge to understand that which is eternal, which is timeless. Knowledge is of time, and religion is free from the bondage of time.

It seems so urgent and important that we bring about a new generation, even half a dozen people in the world would make a vast difference. But the educator needs education. It is the greatest vocation in the world.

有的宗教都基于某些结论和信仰，而所有的信仰都具有分裂性，无论是政治还是宗教信仰。

哪里有划分，哪里就必然会有冲突。而中学并不是一个为冲突而存在的地方，而是一个学习生活的艺术的地方。这种艺术是最伟大的，它超越了其他所有的艺术，因为这门艺术影响的是人的整体，而非他的一部分，无论那个部分多么令人愉快。在这样的一所学校里，如果教育者致力于此，不是作为一个理想，而是作为日常生活中的一个事实——投身于此，我们重申一次，不是投身于某个理想、某种乌托邦、某个高尚的结论，而是他真的试着在人类的大脑中找到一条生活之道——没有困在问题、挣扎、冲突和痛苦中的生活之道。

爱并不是一种痛苦、焦虑和孤独的运动，它是永恒的。而教育者，如果他愿意坚守爱，那么他就可以在向学生传授知识的同时，把这份真正的宗教精神注入，这种精神远远超越了所有知识，也许恰恰是知识的终结——不是也许——它就是知识的终结。因为若要了解那永恒的、超越时间的事物，就必须从知识中解脱出来。知识是属于时间的，而宗教摆脱了时间的束缚。

我们要造就新的一代，这看起来是如此紧迫、如此重要，哪怕世上只有几个这样的人，也会带来巨大的不同。但教育者本身需要教育，而这是世界上最伟大的职业。

Wednesday, March 28, 1984

The Pacific does not seem to have great tides, at least not on this side of the Pacific along the coast of California. It is a very small tide, it goes in and goes out, unlike those vast tides that go out several hundred yards and come rushing in. There is quite a different sound when the tide is going out, when the flow of water is withdrawing, from when it is coming in with a certain sense of fury, a quality of sound totally different from the sound of the wind among the leaves.

Everything seems to have a sound. That tree in the field, in its solitude, has that peculiar sound of being separate from all other trees. The great sequoias have their own deep lasting ancient sound. Silence has its own peculiar sound. And of course the endless daily chatter of human beings about their business, their politics and their technological advancements and so on, has its own sound. A really good book has its peculiar vibrations of sound.The vast emptiness also has its throbbing sound.

The ebb and flow of the tide is like human action and reaction. Our actions and reactions are so quick. There isn't a pause before the reaction takes place. A question is put and immediately, instantly, one tries to seek an answer, a solution to a problem. There is not a pause between the question and the answer. After all, we are the ebb and flow of life—the outward and the inward. We try to establish a relationship with the outward, thinking that the inward is

1984 年 3 月 28 日，星期三

此刻的太平洋，看起来没有太大的潮汐，至少加利福尼亚沿岸这边的太平洋是这样。潮水很小，涨涨落落，不像那些巨大的潮水，会退去数百码，然后再一拥而上。潮水回落时，水流退去的声音，与带着狂怒涌上来的声音大不相同，那种声音与树叶间的风声也迥然不同。

万物似乎都有自己的声音。田间的那棵树，傲然独立，有一种远离其他所有树木的奇特声响。巨大的红杉有它们自己深沉持久的古老声音。寂静也有自己独特的声音。当然，人类对自己的生意、政治和科技进步等，每天都在喋喋不休，这也有它自身的声音。一本真正的好书有自己颤动的独特声响，浩瀚的空无也有着自己嗡嗡的轰鸣。

潮水的涨落就像是人类的行动和反应。我们的行动和反应如此迅速，反应发生之前甚至没有一丝停顿。一个问题在提出之后，我们立刻、马上就试图找到一个答案，找到问题的解决办法。问题和回答之间没有停顿。毕竟，我们就是生命的涨涨落落——也就是外在和内在。我们试图与外在世界建立关系，以为内在与外在是分开的、脱离的。但毫无疑问，外在的运动就是内在的流淌。它们两者是一回事，

something separate, something that is unconnected with the outer. But surely the movement of the outer is the flow of the inward. They are both the same, like the waters of the sea, this constant restless movement of the outer and the inner, the response to the challenge. This is our life.

When we first put together from the inward, then the inner becomes the slave of the outer. The society we have created is the outer, then to that society the inner becomes the slave. And the revolt against the outer is the same as the revolt of the inner. This constant ebb and flow, restless, anxious, fearful: can this movement ever stop? Of course the ebb and flow of the waters of the sea are entirely free from this ebb and flow of the outer and the inner—the inner becoming the outer, then the outer trying to control the inner because the external has become all important; then the reaction to that importance from the inner. This has been the way of life, a life of constant pain and pleasure.

We never seem to learn about this movement, that it is one movement. The outer and the inner are not two separate movements. The waters of the sea withdraw from the shore, then the same water comes in, lashing the shores, the cliffs. Because we have separated the external and the inner, contradiction begins, the contradiction that breeds conflict and pain. This division between the outer and the inner is so unreal, so illusory, but we keep the external totally separate from the inner. Perhaps this may be one of the major causes of conflict, yet we never seem to learn—learn not memorize, learn, which is a form of movement all the time—learn to live without this contradiction. The outer and the inner are one, a unitary movement, not separate, but whole.

One may perhaps intellectually comprehend it, accept it as a theoretical statement or intellectual concept, but when one lives with concepts one

外在和内在的这种焦躁不安的恒常运动，这种对挑战的回应，就像海水一样。这就是我们的生活。

当我们最初从内在构建起自我，内在就成为外在的奴隶。我们所建立的社会就是外在世界，然后内在世界就成了那个社会的奴隶。对外在的反抗与内在的反抗其实是一回事。这种不断的涨潮、落潮，充满了不安、焦虑和恐惧，这种运动究竟能否停止？当然，海水的涨落完全不受制于内在和外在的这种起起落落——内在变成了外在，然后外在又试图控制内在，因为外在变得无比重要；然后从内在就产生了对那种重要性的反抗。这是人类一直以来的生活方式，一种充满了无尽的痛苦和快乐的生活。

我们似乎从未了解这种运动，不了解这其实是同一种运动。外在和内在并非截然分开的两种运动。海水退下海岸，然后同一些海水又涨上来，拍打着岸边和悬崖。因为我们把内外分离了开来，矛盾于是产生，而矛盾滋生了冲突和痛苦。这种内外的划分是如此不真实，如此虚幻，但我们却保持着内外之间泾渭分明的分割。或许这就是冲突产生的首要根源之一，然而我们却从未学会——学习不是记忆，而是了解，是一种无始无终的运动——学会没有矛盾地活着。内外是一体的，是统一的运动，不是分离的，而是整体的。

你也许从道理上理解了这一点，把它作为一个理论或者智力上的概念接受了，但是，当一个人活在概念之中，他就永远无法学习。概念会变得停滞不前。你也许会变换概念，但是从一个概念变换到另一个概念，这本身依然是静态的、僵死的。然而，感受到、敏感地看

never learns. The concepts become static. You may change them but the very transformation of one concept to another is still static, is still fixed. But to feel, to have the sensitivity of seeing that life is not a movement of two separate activities, the external and the inward, to see that it is one, to realize that the interrelationship is this movement, is this ebb and flow of sorrow and pleasure, joy and depression, loneliness and the escape, to perceive non—verbally this life as a whole, not fragmented, not broken up, is to learn. Learning about it is not a matter of time, thought, not a gradual process, for then time again becomes divisive. Time acts in the fragmentation of the whole. But to see the truth of it in an instant, then it is there, this action and reaction, endlessly—this light and dark, the beauty and ugliness.

That which is whole is free from the ebb and flow of life, of action and reaction. Beauty has no opposite. Hate is not the opposite of love.

到，生命这种运动并非内外两种各自独立的活动，看到它是一体的，认识到两者之间的关系就是这种运动，就是悲伤与快乐、喜悦与沮丧、孤独与逃避的这种起起落落，不着言语地洞察到生命是一个整体，而不是破碎的、分裂的，这就是学习。然而学习并不是一件关乎时间的事，不是一个渐进的过程，因为那样的话，时间又变成了分裂的元素。在整体的破碎之中，时间才会运转。但是瞬间看到了这个真相，一切就都显现了——这无尽的行动和反应、光明与黑暗、美丽与丑陋。

　　完整的事物摆脱了生命的起起落落，摆脱了行动和反应。美没有对立面，恨也不是爱的对立面。

Friday, March 30, 1984

Walking down the straight road on a lovely morning, it was spring, and the sky was extraordinarily blue; there wasn't a cloud in it, and the sun was just warm, not too hot. It felt nice. And the leaves were shining and a sparkle was in the air. It was really a most extraordinarily beautiful morning. The high mountain was there, impenetrable, and the hills below were green and lovely. And as you walked along quietly, without much thought, you saw a dead leaf, yellow and bright red, a leaf from the autumn. How beautiful that leaf was, so simple in its death, so lively, full of the beauty and vitality of the whole tree and the summer. Strange that it had not withered. Looking at it more closely, one saw all the veins and the stem and the shape of that leaf. That leaf was all the tree.

Why do human beings die so miserably, so unhappily, with a disease, old age, senility, the body shrunk, ugly? Why can't they die naturally and as beautifully as this leaf? What is wrong with us? In spite of all the doctors, medicines and hospitals, operations and all the agony of life, and the pleasures too, we don't seem able to die with dignity, simplicity, and with a smile.

Once, walking along a lane, one heard behind one a chant, melodious, rhythmic, with the ancient strength of Sanskrit. One stopped and looked round. An eldest son, naked to his waist, was carrying a terracotta pot with

1984 年 3 月 30 日，星期五

在春日的美丽清晨，沿着笔直的马路走下去，天空出奇地蓝，没有一片云彩，太阳暖洋洋的，还不太炙热。天气舒爽怡人。树叶熠熠发亮，有种光芒折射在空中。这真是一个美好得无与伦比的早晨。无法穿越的高山矗立远处，低处的丘陵则翠绿而迷人。当你静静地一路走来，不经意间，你瞥见一片落叶，色彩鲜艳，红黄相间，那是一片来自秋天的落叶。多么美的一片叶子，凋零得如此单纯，如此生动，充溢着那整棵树和整个夏日的美与生命力。奇特的是它并未枯萎。在更近距离的观察之下，你能看到那片叶子所有的叶脉、叶柄和轮廓。那片叶子就是那一整棵树。

为什么人类如此悲惨、如此不幸地死去，并且疾病缠身、身体委顿、老迈不堪、丑陋不堪？他们为什么不能自然而然地死去，就像这片落叶一样美丽？我们究竟出了什么问题？尽管有数不清的医生、药品和医院，还有手术以及生命中所有的痛苦和快乐，我们似乎还是无法带着尊严和微笑，简简单单地死去。

一次独自沿小径散步，你听到一曲吟诵，旋律优美，富有节奏，蕴含着梵文所特有的古老力量。你停下来环顾四周。有一位长子上

a fire burning in it. He was holding it in another vessel and behind him were two men carrying his dead father, covered with a white cloth, and they were all chanting.

One knew what that chant was, one almost joined in. They went past and one followed them. They were going down the road chanting, and the eldest son was in tears. They carried the father to the beach where they had already collected a great pile of wood and they laid the body on top of that heap of wood and set it on fire. It was all so natural, so extraordinarily simple: there were no flowers, there was no hearse, there were no black carriages with black horses. It was all very quiet and utterly dignified. And one looked at that leaf, and a thousand leaves of the tree. The winter brought that leaf from its mother on to that path and it would presently dry out completely and wither, be gone, carried away by the winds and lost.

As you teach children mathematics, writing, reading and all the business of acquiring knowledge, they should also be taught the great dignity of death, not as a morbid, unhappy thing that one has to face eventually, but as something of daily life—the daily life of looking at the blue sky and the grasshopper on a leaf. It is part of learning, as you grow teeth and have all the discomfort of childish illnesses. Children have extraordinary curiosity. If you see the nature of death, you don't explain that everything dies, dust to dust and so on, but without any fear you explain it to them gently and make them feel that the living and the dying are one—not at the end of one's life after fifty, sixty or ninety years, but that death is like that leaf.

Look at the old men and women, how decrepit, how lost, how unhappy and how ugly they look. Is it because they have not really understood either the living or the dying? They have used life, they

身赤裸，正提着一个燃有火苗的陶罐，他把这个陶罐装在另一个容器里。他身后有两个人抬着他白布覆盖的亡父，一行人都在吟唱。

你熟悉那首吟诵的内容，你几乎随声附和起来。他们从旁经过，你尾随其后。他们一边吟唱，一边沿路走下去，而那位长子泪流满面。他们把他父亲抬到河边，他们在那里早已堆起了一垛小山般的木头，然后把尸体放在木堆顶上，再把木堆点燃。这一切是如此自然，简单得不可思议：没有鲜花，没有灵柩，没有黑马拉的黑色马车。一切都非常安静，却又庄严万分。而你看到了那片落叶，也看到了树上的万千叶片。冬天把那片叶子带离它的母亲，它飘落小径，然后很快就会完全干枯，随风逝去，消失不见。

当你教给孩子数学、写作、阅读以及获取知识的那一套时，他们也应该同时被教授死亡的无比庄严。死亡并不是一个人最终不得不面对的一件病态的、不快的事情，而是要把它看作一件平常生活中的事——就像凝望蓝天和叶片上的蚱蜢这样平常的生活。这是学习的一部分，就像你长牙和患上各种不舒服的儿时小恙一样。孩子们有着惊人的好奇心。如果你看清了死亡的本质，你不会解释说，万物都有一死，尘归尘土归土之类，而是会毫无畏惧地向他们娓娓道来，让他们懂得生死实为一体——死亡并非是在五十、六十或九十年后的生命尽头才发生的事，而是就像那片落叶一般逝去。

看看那些年老的男人和女人们，他们看起来是多么衰弱，多么迷茫，多么忧愁，多么丑陋。是因为他们未曾真正懂得生与死的意义吗？他们用尽了生命，把自己的生命浪费在无休止的冲突之中，而这

waste away their life with incessant conflict which only exercises and gives strength to the self, the "me", the ego. We spend our days in such varieties of conflict and unhappiness, with some joy and pleasure, drinking, smoking, late nights and work, work, work. And at the end of one's life one faces that thing called death and is frightened of it. One thinks it can always be understood, felt deeply. The child with his curiosity can be helped to understand that death is not merely the wasting of the body through disease, old age and some unexpected accident, but that the ending of every day is also the ending of oneself every day.

There is no resurrection, that is superstition, a dogmatic belief. Everything on earth, on this beautiful earth, lives, dies, comes into being and withers away. To grasp this whole movement of life requires intelligence, not the intelligence of thought, or books, or knowledge, but the intelligence of love and compassion with its sensitivity. One is very certain that if the educator understands the significance of death and the dignity of it, the extraordinary simplicity of dying—understands it not intellectually but deeply—then he may be able to convey to the student, to the child, that dying, the ending, is not to be avoided, is not something to be frightened of, for it is part of one's whole life, so that as the student, the child, grows up he will never be frightened of the ending. If all the human beings who have lived before us, past generations upon generations, still lived on this earth how terrible it would be. The beginning is not the ending.

And one would like to help—no, that's the wrong word—one would like in education to bring death into some kind of reality, actuality, not of someone else dying but of each one of us, however old or young, having inevitably to face that thing. It is not a sad affair of tears, of loneliness, of separation. We kill so easily, not only the animals for one's food but the vast

些冲突只锻炼和增强了自我、"我"、自己。我们把日日夜夜耗费在了各种冲突和不快之中，偶尔有些许喜悦和欢愉，烟酒作乐，有灯红酒绿的夜晚，另外还有没完没了的工作、工作、工作。然后到了生命的尽头，我们面对着这件叫作"死亡"的事情，感到恐惧无比。我认为你一直有机会深刻地了解和感受死亡。我们可以帮助满怀好奇心的孩子去了解，死亡绝不仅仅是因为疾病、年迈和某些意外事故而损耗了身体，而是，每一天的结束同时也意味着一个人自己每天都死去。

并不存在什么复活重生，那是迷信，是教条式的信仰。地球，这个美丽的地球之上的一切，都在生生灭灭，诞生然后凋萎。把握这整个生命的运动需要智慧，并非思想、书本或知识的智慧，而是满载敏感性的爱与慈悲的智慧。有一点我很确定，如果教育者懂得了死亡的意义和庄严，以及它非同寻常的简单——不是从道理上明白，而是深刻地理解——那么他也许就能够向学生、向孩子传达：死亡、结束并非一件要去避免、要去害怕的事情，因为它就是整个生命的一部分，这样学生和孩子在长大成人的过程中，就永远不会惧怕死亡。如果我们之前的所有人类，一辈又一辈，还依然活在这个地球上，那将是多么可怕！那样就只有开始，没有结束了。

而我想帮助——不，这个词不对——我想在教育领域把死亡带入现实之中，不是别的什么人死去，而是我们每一个人，无论长幼，都不得不面对这件不可避免的事情。死亡并不是一件事关泪水、孤独和分离的事情。我们如此轻易地杀戮，不仅仅为了果腹而杀死动物，同时也为了取乐而大肆进行毫无必要的杀戮，还称之为"体育运

unnecessary killing for amusement, called sport—killing a deer because that is the season. Killing a deer is like killing your neighbour. You kill animals because you have lost touch with nature, with all the living things on this earth. You kill in wars for so many romantic, nationalistic, political, ideologies. In the name of God you have killed people. Violence and killing go together.

As one looked at that dead leaf with all its beauty and colour, maybe one would very deeply comprehend, be aware of, what one's own death must be, not at the very end but at the very beginning. Death isn't some horrific thing, something to be avoided, something to be postponed, but rather something to be with day in and day out. And out of that comes an extraordinary sense of Immensity.

动"——比如猎鹿，因为狩猎的季节到了。杀死一头鹿，就像杀死你的邻居一样。你杀死动物，因为你失去了与自然、与地球上所有生灵之间的连接。你为了如此之多罗曼蒂克、国家主义和政治上的理念，在战争中互相残杀。你因上帝之名而杀害人们，而暴力与杀戮是并肩而行的。

当你看着那片落叶，凝望它所有的美丽和色彩，也许你就会非常深刻地领会和懂得，你自己的死去必须就在一开始，而不是远在生命的尽头。死亡并不是什么可怕的事情，要去竭力避免和拖延的事情，而是日日夜夜、无时无刻不在的事情。而从这份领悟中，就会有一种非同寻常的"无限"不期而至。